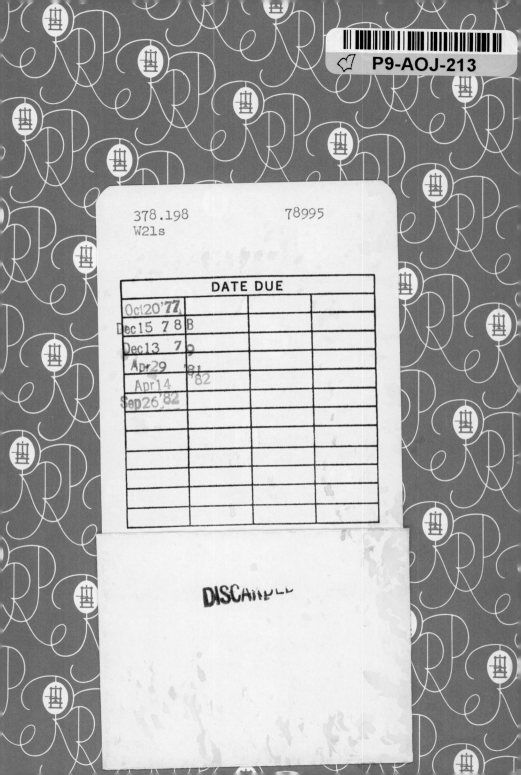

The Student Journalist
and
CREATIVE WRITING

THE STUDENT JOURNALIST AND

A NEW SOCIETY IS TAKING SHAPE BEFORE OUR EYES...METROPOLIS IS THE FORM OF THE NEW SOCIETY: IT IS THE POSSIBILITY OF UNIFIED HUMAN SOCIETY ARISING OUT OF THE CHAOS OF THE MASSIVE URBANIZED AREAS...WHERE CHILDREN MAY FIND A CLIMATE CONDUCIVE TO GROWTH WHERE MEN AND WOMEN HAVE THE OPPORTUNITY TO PARTICIPATE AS MEN AND RECEIVE THEIR REWARDS AND WHERE ADVANTAGES MAY BE DISTRIBUTED WITH EQUITY.

Gibson Winter

THE
STUDENT
JOURNALIST
GUIDE
SERIES

Creative Writing

by

WILLIAM G. WARD

with special chapters by

B. A. ALLEN

PUBLISHED BY

RICHARDS ROSEN

PRESS, INC.

NEW YORK

A recommended series of books to follow to continue your program of learning to report and write *all* the news. Besides this one, turn to these in the following order:

1. *The Student Journalist and Common Story Assignments* (how to report and write many kinds of stories from spot news to features about culture to light essays from the news).

2. *The Student Journalist and Writing Editorials; The Student Journalist and Thinking Editorials* (persuasive writing and reporting, from editorials to aphorisms).

3. *The Student Journalist and Depth Reporting* (investigative, interpretive, and analytical reporting and writing).

All are by the author of this book and published by Richards Rosen Press. *Common Story Assignments* is $5.79; the others, $3.99.

For a general guidebook to better school newspapers, see *Newspapering,* from N.S.P.A., 18 Journalism Bldg., University of Minnesota, Minneapolis. $2.50 per copy. Also by Bill Ward.

Standard Book Number: 8239-0246-3
Library of Congress Catalog Card Number: 79-158-564

Published in 1971 by Richards Rosen Press, Inc.
29 East 21st Street, New York City, N.Y. 10010

Manufactured in the United States of America

ABOUT THE AUTHORS

"I am not a theorist in journalism; I don't give advice about how to do something until I have done it myself." That is the philosophy put into "The Student Journalist and Creative Writing" by Bill Ward, a half-time teacher and half-time journalist. The book attempts to isolate, for the first time, three principal areas of creativity in journalism. First, there is the feature story (and Ward has been a feature writer). Then, there is the light essay (Ward has written essays for several professional publications). Finally, there is the review (Ward has reviewed books for newspapers and magazines).

His experience in journalism has been varied. He has been general assignment reporter, sports editor, columnist, photo editor, and copy editor for the Mankato, Minn., *Free Press,* the San Bernardino, Calif., *Sun-Telegram,* and the Minneapolis, Minn., *Tribune.* His articles have appeared in *The Nation, The Progressive, The National Observer, Saturday Review, Editor & Publisher, Journalism Quarterly, Camera 35* (illustrated with his own photographs), and *Scholastic Editor* and several other special magazines for student journalists. He has worked in public relations for two colleges.

In high schools, he has been at various times coach of basketball and football, and teacher of English, history, Spanish, and journalism in Grove City, Minn., Glendive, Mont., San Bernardino, Calif., and Rochester, Minn. Since 1963, he has been assistant professor of journalism at Syracuse University and at the University of Nevada.

For many years, Ward has been concerned primarily with what he calls literary journalism—the journalist as a writer of fiction, and the journalist as a creative force on the front page. His interest stems partly from a formal study of literature (a master's degree in English) and his own affection for creative writing. He is accustomed to battles with those who want to restrict the reporting and writing of journalists—especially student journalists—to formulas. Ward firmly believes the contemporary journalist must be more than a machine— he must be a fine writer and an ingenious reporter. Those two traits characterize the creative journalist, one who can translate the dy-

5

namic world of space travel and nuclear fission into a language meaningful and memorable to the citizen.

Professor Ward started as a sportswriter with newspapers when he was 16. In 1963, The Newspaper Fund named him one of the outstanding teachers of high school journalism in the nation. His students won many writing awards, including an unprecedented four national awards from American Newspaper Publishers Association-Columbia Scholastic Press Association. His students, in six years, published nine All-American newspapers. He, more recently, has been adviser to the *Daily Orange* (Syracuse University), an All-American college daily. He now is Director of Journalism at Southern Illinois University at Edwardsville.

He likes to think his combination of teaching, of professional journalism, and of studies in literature prepares him for writing *The Student Journalist and Creative Writing*.

Other writings—"Reporting and Writing Sports," a monograph published by the Columbia Scholastic Press Association. A textbook of journalism, especially written for high school journalists who do not have the benefit of formal instruction—published by the National Scholastic Press Association.

Some special chapters for "The Student Journalist and Creative Writing" were provided by B. A. Allen, whose combined background in literature and literary criticism and in radio-television is unusual—but a sign of the future. Allen surveys an area common to student literary magazines: poetry. Allen is a graduate of Syracuse University, with a degree in English. Critical work has appeared in *Television Quarterly*. Her professional experience includes script writing for the broadcast media. She has edited *Television Quarterly*, has taught speech at Syracuse University, and has a master's degree in radio-television.

This book is dedicated to teachers everywhere who pass on to the student a love of writing and a dedication to reporting, especially to four who shared their enthusiasm with the author: Mr. Edward J. Haley, Mr. John Barczewski, Dr. Robert C. Wright, and Professor Edmund C. Arnold.

INTRODUCTION

Although some people think it out-of-place to use the word "creative" with journalism (they prefer to think of journalism as a world of strict formulas and automatic systems and this vague attitude called cold objectivity), others see in journalism the breadth, if not the depth, of literature and innumerable opportunities to write creatively, with flair and originality. To them, the journalist is restricted by one necessity—that of truth. The journalist can use most devices known to the fiction writer and the essayist, as long as he confines himself to what is verified and validified.

Too many creative writers have been linked with journalism to allow it to develop as a formulated world: Hemingway as a young man, Stephen Crane most of his short life, Dreiser at the outset, Franklin, too, the poet William Cullen Bryant who was, for a half-century, an editor, even Sandburg, Twain, Freneau. Today, many journalists double in fiction (Allen Drury, Fletcher Knebel, Charles Bailey, John Gunther, Robert Ruark, to name a few), and the fictionalist in turn is asked to write for journalism (Mailer, Hersey, Steinbeck). Today, literature and journalism exist arm-and-arm to the degree that a novel can be predicated on the art of reporting (Truman Capote's *In Cold Blood,* for one).

Yet, an argument is there—whether journalism should be an outlet for creativity. Perhaps, it is matter of semantics—just what creativity entails. In this book, creativity means the freedom to report and write in any manner necessary to inspire readership, as long as facts are correct, mood is true, tone is honest, and theme is representative of the situation.

Mostly, creativity means the reporter can approach his story from any direction necessary to get a good story; it means the writer can draw from the styles and structures of all literature in an attempt to get the news across to the reader accurately and interestingly. It means the reporter/writer does not have to limit his work to that prescribed by reporting and writing formulas (i.e., 5-W's leads, and news stories organized according to descending importance of facts).

9

Call it freedom; call it ingenuity; call it imagination; call it inspiration; this book prefers to use the term creativity.

The reporter is being creative when, like Kitty Hanson, she joins girls' street gangs in New York City in order to write about them from a position of authority. Or when a sportswriter, tired of routine basketball summaries, roams the stands and the players' benches during a game in an attempt to get a fresh view of what happens. Or when a reporter, as columnist Russell Baker of the *New York Times* phrases it, "rubs two natural enemies together" in an effort to get at the facts.

The news writer is being creative when he uses narrative style to tell about an event as it happened. Or when he ditches the cumbersome 5-W's lead for a dramatic lead in an attempt to increase readership—as well as accuracy in the mood of the story. Or when he turns to an I-account, when he has been caught up directly by the swift wind of events.

(Strange how many people advocate a noncreative type of journalism while at the same time glorifying the journalistic heritage of such creative powers as Stephen Crane, Mark Twain, John Hersey, Richard Harding Davis, Damon Runyon, and Ring Lardner.)

This book, then, tries to focus on the three most creative aspects of journalism: writing features, reviewing the popular arts, and writing light essays. All three types can be found, every day, in most newspapers and magazines. In *The New York Times,* for instance, features are scattered throughout the paper; there is at least one review a day (and an entire section devoted to books on Sunday); and several essayists are placed regularly on the editorial page.

Other areas commonly regarded as creative, to a degree, are columns, editorials, page makeup, headlines, and photography and cartooning.

The problem is—how to stimulate a more creative journalist? As one solution, this book provides an antidote to those many textbooks which demand that a student first learn to handle fact, style, and structure according to unrelenting formula. Master those fundamentals, quoth the texts, and then you may advance to features. This procedure, however, requires back-tracking on the part of the student. He comes to scholastic journalism with a background of several years in English—writing essays, studying fiction and poetry, and in general stoking his creative powers. Is it then the job of the journalism teacher to retrain him? To reduce his style? Hopefully not! His experience needs refining much more than retraining. Simultaneously with learning to handle the straight news story in a somewhat formulated procedure of reporting and writing (something new to him), he can be encouraged to use his powers of originality—those developed, for instance, in English courses—to write the feature, essay, review, editorial, and column.

Students must be accepted by scholastic journalism as experienced writers . . . and observers of life.

Generally, the newcomer must be taught, not so much new patterns of writing, as (1) to be respectful to truth, (2) to interpose reporting between himself and writing, and (3) to discipline his style more than before. He must not be stripped of style; he must be taught to discipline it, to make it work for him. While being an individualist (like Runyon, Jimmy Breslin, Lardner, etc.), he must learn the strength of truth, in mood and tone as well as in fact.

So—this book is designed to serve as one of the basic textbooks for courses in journalism.

It is also designed for English courses which include a unit or two in reporting and writing for publications.

The book provides a refresher course, too, for students seeking to broaden their knowledge of reporting and writing. It provides advice and examples for those thousands who do not study journalism formally, but who must publish a newspaper or magazine.

How should this book be studied?—

(1) Slowly, chapter by chapter. By first reading the advice and then trying to apply it. The book is not designed for casual reading.

(2) As a ready reference for those setting out on special assignments or who need a checklist to apply against something written.

(3) Carefully, example by example. Most chapters begin with student work (to prove the exceptionally high level of accomplishment there), and conclude with professional work (for comparison's sake). Within chapters are included as many examples as deemed necessary to clarify points of advice. If examples are skimmed, much of the advice will seem superficial—even abstract.

For the many stories and photographs reprinted in this book, thanks go to a great many student and professional journalists. They are too many to acknowledge personally here, but names and backgrounds of authors are included with most articles. Their successes encourage other journalists—the greatest thanks of all.

(4) With attention to the use of typographic devices: starred (*) words are further defined in the glossary at the end of the book.

Features are discussed first, as the most common fare of journalists. Then come essays, and finally the most literary areas of reviews and poetry.

Lastly, it must be affirmed that the advice given here is practical; it is based on professional experience. Advice about reviewing comes from experience writing reviews; the same goes for the other areas.

The chapters about journalism were written by Bill Ward, a former journalist now a teacher (formerly in high schools in Minnesota, Montana, and California; then at Syracuse University and now at the University of Nevada, Reno). The three chapters about the more demanding areas of literature—poetry, figurative language, and the short short story—were written by B. A. Allen who has specialized in these fields.

The theme of the book is direct: journalism is both a challenge and a reward. Student journalists can find encouraging outlets for expression if they are, in fact, "creative journalists."

WILLIAM G. WARD

ABOUT THE PHOTOGRAPHS IN THIS BOOK

Just as the creative reporter can tell a better story, the creative news photographer can *show* a better story. A photographer needs the same qualities as a reporter—imagination, a desire to try unusual ideas, a strong sense of what is newsworthy, a determination to get into the middle of events (to be on-the-spot).

The news photographer heightens his work by bringing into pictures elements of mood, emotion, human interest, strong composition, unusual and surprising angles and viewpoints, silhouettes, framing, action, etc.

To photograph an event indiscriminately, flatly, is to be a snapshooter; the picture records the event but lacks appeal to the viewer. The creative photographer incorporates elements into his pictures to make them of special interest.

Like the reporter, the photographer must look for new ways to retell old stories.

In this book are included a dozen examples of news-feature photographs, most of them taken on the spot. A few were planned—just as some feature stories are planned. Some are the work of excellent student photographers: Sean Callahan, Robert Demetry, Russell Mur, and Eric Meola, all of Syracuse University. They have given permission to reprint their work. The rest are by Bill Ward.

The photographs are scattered throughout the book—rather than combined in one section—to constantly remind the reader that the creative journalist uses both words and pictures.

Contents

15

The Student Journalist
and
CREATIVE WRITING

NEWSPAPERS AS CENTERS OF LEARNING

Bernard Kilgore defined and at the same time sounded the challenge to the 21st-century newspaper in an address to the national Sigma Delta Chi convention in the late 1960's. He urged newspapers to consider themselves elements of education, especially of continuing education for those who had left school forever.

In part, Mr. Kilgore's remarks:

"I want to suggest that the newspaper of the future must become an instrument of intellectual leadership, an institution of intellectual development—a center of learning. One of its main functions will be to continue the education of an educated community. In short, and to translate this into terms more familiar perhaps to newspapermen of today—the newspaper of tomorrow will go highbrow. The newspaper editor of tomorrow will be an egghead. I really mean it!

". . . when I suggest that newspaper editors could and should rank with, say, true statesmen or college presidents or bishops, as responsible men in positions of intellectual leadership, it is not an entirely new idea. Just how this is to come about, I cannot predict in any detail, of course. I just feel sure it will happen because it must happen—because the opportunity is open, and the newspapermen of tomorrow will seize upon it."

Mr. Kilgore was the person most instrumental in elevating *The Wall Street Journal* to the position of one of the world's finest newspapers, and a leader in reporting and writing.

Creative Journalism

Chapter I

THE CREATIVE WRITER AND REPORTER

People will always remember where they were, and exactly what they were doing, on that day of November 22, 1963, when the president was assassinated. The moment stands illuminated, as though under a solitary globe of light down that shadowy street of memory. For older citizens, there is also the moment when President Roosevelt was announced dead; a radio crackled and the nation felt the emptiness of bereavement. And Pearl Harbor—it, too, is singular. All are moments heightened by emotion; perceptions made indelible in the mind. To the poet, the composer, the artist, and the writer, the moments demand expression.

Andrea St. George was a sophomore worrying about a geometry test the day President Kennedy died. The announcement of death came unexpectedly, brought by an indefinite voice over the school's public address system, while a geometry test lay untouched in front of her. The daughter of a journalist, a writer by nature herself, Andrea had to put into words what she felt and saw.

Tragedy in Dallas Stuns Student Body

By ANDREA ST. GEORGE

We heard "Somebody shot at the President," and we scoffed. We heard "The President has been wounded," and we doubted.

We listened to the familiar voice on the PA, telling us: "The President of the United States has been shot and wounded but it is not known how seriously. We will relay to you any further information we receive."

And we looked around at each other, stunned. But our minds wandered into other channels, and the bell rang, and we went to our sixth hour classes.

We joked about the announcement on the way and made bets about the validity. We laughed and listened to the rumors and scorned those who suggested there might be something to what we had heard. We knew that Presidents are not assassinated in 1963.

The bell rang. We began our sixth hour classes. Then the familiar voice came over the PA again, and we heard the static that precedes a radio relay. Things were beginning to take on the aspect of a missile launching.

There were signs of tension as we turned expectantly and waited for the static to clear. A pencil tapped but was quickly silenced. We waited.

An unfamiliar voice rasped, "This is NBC News reporting . . ." and paused, and all that we could hear was our own quickened breathing. We looked at each other, wide-eyed.

The announcement went on. ". . . critically wounded . . . last rites . . . stunned . . . unconscious . . . emergency room." All broke against uncomprehending ears like the breakers of an angry sea.

We stared at each other and a sob seemed to rise out of nowhere and everywhere. We were worried and scared and we wondered how long it would be before he was well. We knew that presidents do not die of bullet wounds in 1963.

The voices droned on. The first page of our geometry test lay unheeded in front of us. We heard Dallas, New York and Washington reporters tell us what they knew. Conflicting reports crowded the air. Rumors ran wild.

Then it came—the announcement we had known would not come. President Kennedy was dead of bullet wounds inflicted by a cowardly assassin.

Some broke into sobs and no one ridiculed them. Some turned their heads and stared out the windows at the gray hills, with tears that refused to come stinging in their eyes. Some simply stared into space, unseeing and unhearing.

Then the familiar voice that had first told us of the assassination attempt broke in and told us the scheduled pepfest was canceled, and that the sixth and seventh hour classes would continue as usual. Then the voice broke and said what we all would like to have said, that "We are as sorry as it is possible to be." And again the voice broke; then he announced that the flag outside the school would be flown at half-mast.

Then the voices and the static with the reports from Dallas and New York and Washington resumed, and went on and on. No one in our room spoke. The hour dragged on.

When the bell rang, we filed silently out of geometry. In the hall, two thousand pairs of feet moved almost silently to seventh hour. No one spoke. It was like a building inhabited by deaf-mutes. And as we moved through the building, we knew that an era had ended.

Our President had been murdered.

It is an essay fit to open this book about creative journalism. It is the work of a sixteen-year-old girl who already had felt the need to be life's recorder, which is the obligation of a journalist.

MOOD—Assigned ahead of time to do a photograph characteristic of fall, the photographer planned his production, much like a reporter does a planned feature. By combining symbols of fall—bleak trees, setting sun, and flight of geese—he was able to represent the mood of fall. The symbols did not come together accidentally. The photographer picked the stand of trees, waited for the sun to set, and waited for the geese which every evening made the flight from their feeding grounds, past the trees, to their fall residence at a game refuge.

There was the moment of disbelief when death was certified:

Some broke into sobs and no one ridiculed them. Some turned their heads and stared out the windows at the gray hills, with tears that refused to come stinging in the eyes. Some simply stared into space, unseeing and unhearing.

There was the return to reality—of pepfests and of seventh-hour classes and of flags at half-mast. And finally there was the summation, as all men and events—even death—must subject themselves to:

. . . And as we moved through the building, we knew that an era had ended. Our President had been murdered.

Andrea, in her hometown of Mayo Clinic and IBM offices, Rochester, Minnesota, wasn't alone in her grief. Student writers everywhere felt the need to summarize. In school papers in every state, inspired by grief genuinely felt, the creative journalists wrote their epitaphs, made their entries into the records:

President Kennedy believed in freedom; let us fight for it. President Kennedy wished for peace; let us work for it. President Kennedy dreamed of the end of poverty, disease, and ignorance; let us strive to make this dream come through (Cortland, N.Y.).

We can only be thankful that John Kennedy had the opportunity to stamp his character on the American scene. It would have been a lesser place without him (Jamestown, N.Y.).

And above all, John Fitzgerald Kennedy was the symbol of Peace, the brother of all men, and the Hope of the world. He will be remembered forever.

As never before, the student journalists were graceful in their words.

Today, more than ever before, journalism needs the gracefulness of the creative writer and reporter. In a world of nuclear fission, of exploration of space, of supersonic speeds, thermodynamics, population increase, and of explosion of knowledge, the journalist must be more than efficient, more than a technician. He must be inspired.

As never before, the journalist must translate the world grown fantastic into a language having meaning to the mass of readers. As never before, the writer must be able to compete with pictures and sounds now projected into every living-room in the nation.

As never before, the journalist must be a person of talent.

The call for talent has been sounded many times in recent years. For one, Paul Swensson, executive director of The Newspaper Fund, has called forth the creative journalist. In a speech, often quoted, about The Reporters of Tomorrow, Mr. Swensson, himself a long-time journalist, said:

> First of all, I believe tomorrow's journalists will return to the art of writing. Second, they will operate on a much broader base of knowledge. Third, they will find more opportunities not only as news generalists but also as news specialists. Fourth, they will do something about the heritage from my generation—that dream and goal of an informed citizenry.
>
> . . . They will bring a different attitude toward knowledge. They will bear the imprint of a new culture and citizenry, not purely American, not limited to this world, but of Space and Time, the Universe. The change has been perceptible, but not definable since mid-century. It is found in microcosm where sensitive editors are molding young staffs. The embryo can be seen at some colleges and universities where men of fine mind are pointing to a healthy and vigorous 1984, quite different from the Orwell forecast.
>
> The first imperative, of course, is the ability to write well. My generation will not be remembered as an era of great writers. Hopefully, it may leave a record of great reporting. The last great cluster of fine writers flowered in the Thirties. Tomorrow's newsrooms must and shall be crowded with young men and women who share . . . a reverence and ambition for words.

A writer! The modern journalist cannot be mere technician, a person of formulas only and of boundaries and of scientism in his writing. He must be a writer by nature and by inclination, one whose regard for words invites the reader into communion and one whose mastery of phrases invites the reader into understanding. The modern journalist can no more fit all his words into an inflexible framework of inverted pyramids and 5-W leads and Flesch formulas than an artist can be content with casting plaster animals from one monotonous mold.

There is the greater challenge to be met. The formula that suffices for traffic accidents and council meetings and court cases and football games is not sufficient for the challenges and opportunities of the 1970's and 1980's. The journalist must have the variety of words and frames to encompass all of man's achievements—and disasters.

That is where creativity emerges—having the resources to cope with the variety of life's stuff. Today is no time for incoherence, for inarticulate writers; it is no time for the mute.

Words must not break down—as they failed the nation's finest journalists during a spring afternoon in 1952. The journalists had assembled on a hillside in Nevada's desert to watch the detonation of an atomic bomb, a 20 KT bomb, the one which fell on Hiroshima. There they sat, men of words written and spoken, men of pictures. The best. Their chatter, human and mechanical, made a hive of the hill. All were confident of their ability to describe the explosion; they had, after all, seen death and destruction before. They had witnessed the greatest of man's events—war, murder trial, Rose Bowl game. Words had usually risen to the occasion—and whenever a stammer threatened the word-man, he could lapse into the mock heroic style of the 1920's and 1930's. Clichés in a pinch.

But the bomb silenced for a long time the word-men on the hill that afternoon. First, the fireball and the mushroom cloud flaming above them. Then the line of concussion rushing across the desert floor to shake the hill. Then the awful thought of unrelenting deaths. For many seconds and, for some, minutes—an eternity to the men of quick words—the hill watched in awe under the cloud. The reporter of wars, trials, and games was mute. All of his established patterns of words were indeed trite. His past was hackneyed. He was incapable of new demands. When the hill finally regained the use of language that afternoon, it was an awed, humble journalist the world heard and read. And the hill learned that afternoon that a new age of journalism had been born . . . and the need for modern journalists had been declared.

What words and what forms will be used to describe the landing of the first man on another planet, or galaxy? What words will be used to tell man at long last that he is not alone in the universe? What can be used to describe the further miracles of science, to explain too to mankind their significance? What words, after decades of recurring war, famine, and poverty, can be found to convince man of the necessity for brotherhood, for compassion, and for peace? The words, at first, must come from the journalist—undoubtedly those same student journalists who sought the words to tell of the death of their president. Later, the words can come from the poet and the philosopher and the historian.

That demand for a more creative journalist, for a much more intellectual journalist has been detailed by Mr. Bernard Kilgore of *The Wall Street Journal*. Writing in *Nieman Reports* (March, 1966), Mr. Kilgore said in part, "I want to suggest that the newspaper of the future must become an instrument of intellectual leadership, an institution of intellectual developments—a center of learning. One of its main functions will be to continue the education of an educated community. In short, and to translate this into terms more familiar perhaps to the newspapermen of today—the newspaper of tomorrow will go highbrow. The newspaper editor of tomorrow will be an egghead. I really mean it!"

Note the hint of defensiveness in his remark, "I really mean it." Maybe he heard the scoffing of the journalist-by-formula; or the doubt of the old world journalist of sass and sex and sensation; or the man of few words who hides in the routine of hackneyed journalism.

Maybe, Mr. Kilgore fears the repercussions if the student journalist of today fails to prepare for the challenges of tomorrow.

Creative journalist—it is an arbitrary term which here needs definition, not defense. It means, in one sense, a journalist who knows fully the art of fine writing in all its dimensions (fiction, poetry, drama). It means, too, a journalist who not only can report facts, but can transmit the mood and tone of an event, who can impress upon the reader the significance of what happens. Facts for authority; mood and tone for empathy; interpretation for lucidity. Those are the responsibilities of the creative journalist.

Newspapers, magazines, books, radio and television, cinema—today all need the creative journalist.

In 1931, Lincoln Steffens in his autobiography spoke of the creative journalist. He recalled that when he edited a newspaper in the 1890's, he looked for reporters "whose professors of English believed they were going to be able to write and who themselves wanted to be writers."

Steffens said he had room for those who hoped to be poets, novelists, and essayists. He also declared he would fire reporters who no longer saw red at fires: "We preferred the fresh staring eyes to the informed mind and the blunted pencil."

Most of the chapters in this book are concerned with writing. But here—at the outset—is a plea for reporting. Most students come to scholastic journalism with the luster of writing about them. They already are romancing words and ideas. But they are strangers to reporting. They must learn that reporting comes first, then the writing. They must learn to share love, that reporting must be undertaken with the same ardor as that given writing.

Reporting commits the journalist, first of all, to be on the scene of news. He must select a special viewpoint from which to witness the event, and learn all there is to know about the subject—a journalist is, at the same time, an expert about many topics. When the journalist turns to his typewriter he must have seen and felt, so that he can lead the reader to seeing and sensing. The journalist, too, must have a distinctive way of telling the story; after all, he is the descendant of a long line of story tellers. The journalist, finally, must be able to

EXPRESSIONS—The mood of news events is told by facial expressions, as in this instance of a happy cheerleader. A news photographer should be conscious of smiles, tears, sneers, squints—any expressions which convey moods and are consistent with the news story. Such photography requires split-second responses. (Photo by Robert Demetry)

transmit enough information about the topic to instill in the reader the sense of confidence which goes with knowledge.

The president of Yale, Mr. Kingman Brewster, Jr., in a speech in 1964 at the 20th anniversary dinner of the *Hartford Courant,* stressed the significance of the journalist.

The paper, then unlike any other daily news medium, has the chance to absorb the reader, to create the mood with the power of the word, without distraction. This takes *writing,* not just the headlining of releases. It takes live reporting, not the rearrangement of words from a teletype.

Maybe the reason why so many of the best journalists came from sportswriting is because there is no known way of releasing the story of a game before it is played!

While a newscaster may relay news of the event before a paper can reach the streets; the feeling, the meaning of the event, will depend on the word of the live reporter.

Mr. Brewster advised teachers and editors to encourage the creative journalists. Let Mr. Brewster have the final words to the chapter: "Indulge the *creativity* of your young reporters."

Chapter II

THE MODERN JOURNALIST AND THE ART OF REPORTING

THE NON-FICTION NOVEL

The phrase seems ambiguous, mixing as it does the concepts of two general areas of writing, that of true-lifeness (nonfiction) and that of imagination, whether in part or in whole (fiction). True, the novelist long has dealt with true-life situations, but he has been free to distort, to twist and turn, to exaggerate his material—in short, to insert his imagination between reality and his work.

Novels have always combined fact and fiction. Some novels are true to history and to historical characters (for instance, those by Zoe Oldenbourg, John dos Passos, Irving Stone), but plot and characterization are sometimes supplemented by imagination. The author reserves the right to tweak history, if need be, to create a better novel. This historical novel, a blend of fact and a little fiction, usually entertains the reader but sometimes confounds the historian.

Then, there is the autobiographical novel in which the author uses his own experiences as material, but recasts it in the mold of his imagination. Herman Melville did that in his early seafaring novels (*Typee, Omoo*), and to a lesser degree in *Moby Dick*. Ernest Hemingway has been an autobiographical novelist. So have Thomas Wolfe and Mark Twain. But again each has felt free to modify reality to the needs of the novel.

And the documentary novel—it long has been the device of the fiction writer who researches reality, supplements the research with imagination, and presents a true-to-life—but not true-life—picture of a social problem. One such novelist, Upton Sinclair, a half-century ago studied, on the scene, the tragic lives of immigrant laborers in Chicago's meatpacking district. Sinclair then wrote a chronicle of a typical family and its disintegration amid poverty and indignity, reporting what he saw, heard, and felt in Packingtown. The novel, *The Jungle,* caused an uproar in the nation, and many critics attacked Sinclair for being melodramatic, for exaggerating the situation. But Sinclair, in defense, declared, "I went out there and lived among the people for seven weeks. I would sit in their homes at night, and talk with them, and then in the daytime they would lay off their work, and take me around, and show me whatever I wished to see. I studied every detail of their lives. . . . *The Jungle* is as authoritative as if it were a statistical compilation." That novel, too, was true-to-life, but in a representative way. John Steinbeck defended himself in somewhat the same manner when his documentary novel, *The Grapes of Wrath,* a portrayal of the migratory worker in California, was severely attacked as inaccurate.

But now, in the 1970's, the nonfiction novel is suggested by some writers as the next art form in literature. It may already be here. In 1966, novelist Truman Capote, with nine books behind him, declared that his new book *In Cold Blood* heralded the new art form—that of reporting.

If *In Cold Blood* truly is predictive, then the nonfiction novel could be defined something like this—a true-life situation reported with such depth, thoroughness, and accuracy that it can be narrated in the fashion of a novel. It represents the work of an expert reporter; yet, in its scope and its structure and style, it is the work of a novelist.

Capote set out *In Cold Blood* to be reporter-novelist. By using first-hand observations and countless interviews, he reported the episode of a multiple murder in Kansas. He was so thorough in details, he dared to reconstruct conversations, to recount action in the fine details of gestures and movements, to delineate characters and their motivations—and even to daring to report what people thought. As a writer, Capote used all of the novelist's devices of suspense, of revealing character through actions and words, of casting subplots, of building to a climax (the revelation of the murder scene) and following with the denouement.

Capote, for the first time in American literature, told a true story in all its scrupulous accuracy, subordinating the imagination of the novelist while elevating the style and the structure of a novel.

The book was successful: in sales, 140,000 copies in print at the date of publication; in dollars, an estimated two million in the first year. In critical success—well, it was attended to by such popular magazines as *Life, Newsweek,* and the *Saturday Review.* From the start, it headed the best-seller lists—the nonfiction list because Capote billed the book as a nonfiction novel.

More nonfiction novels are sure to follow. In the world of publishing, success generates imitation.

And reporting, the art of the journalist, becomes significant to the art of literature. Journalism and creative writing meet in the square, on center-ground, and they walk on arm-in-arm.

In literature, the 1960's could be called the Decade of Journalism —when a vocation becomes a profession, when a craft becomes an art form—and accordingly greater demands are made of the journalist as, at the same time, greater hopes are his.

One journalist who has accepted the challenge and reaped the rewards is Cornelius Ryan, who started as a newspaper reporter in England during World War II, and who by the 1960's had turned to books of nonfiction successfully. At the same time that *In Cold Blood* was leading the list of best-sellers, Ryan's *The Last Battle* was closing from behind. And like *In Cold Blood,* Ryan's book was immense in its reporting. To compile the precise record of the fall of Berlin and of the end of the Nazi empire, Ryan devoted five years of time and $60,000 to research. He plumbed every source of information, including interviews with Soviet marshals who closed from the West the ring around Berlin. It was literally a fantastic piece of historical compilation; yet, Ryan when interviewed by a writer from *Saturday Review,* said, "There is nothing new in what I'm doing. It's only old-fashioned reporting."

Again, the modern journalist finds himself not so much a slave of newsprint as a professional writer and researcher who is at ease with book-length projects. The journalist like Ryan is not just contributing to the literature of his day, he is directing the trend of literature—more and more nonfiction and more and more journalism involved. Look at the lists of best-sellers of all kinds during the 1960's:

Allen Drury, a Washington correspondent, combined a reporter's inside view of Washington politics with the techniques of a novelist to produce *Advise and Consent,* which led best-seller lists. Some other journalist-novelists of the 1960's: Fletcher Knebel and Charles Bailey (*Seven Days in May*); John Hersey (*A Bell for Adano, The Wall, A Single Pebble, The Child Buyer, Too Far to Walk*), whose report about *Hiroshima* may antedate Capote's *In Cold Blood* as *the* non-fiction novel; columnist Robert Ruark (*The Honey Badger,* other novels); John Gunther (*The Lost City*); Richard Powell (*Daily and Sunday, The Philadelphian*); A. B. Guthrie (*The Big Sky, The Way West*).

A great many journalists turn their travels into books of observation and opinion. For instance, Lisa Hobbs after a visit to Red China reported her experiences in the essayistic *I Saw Red China.*

Other journalists, having become experts in such areas as science, education, and business, write technical accounts for the layman. Walter Sullivan, science editor of *The New York Times,* is one: his *We Are Not Alone,* a study of the possibility of life in space, was nominated for a National Book Award. For the elections of 1960, 1964, 1968, T. H. White wrote definitive accounts in his *The Making of the President* books.

Still other journalists, not so much experts in technical areas as experts in the art of general reporting and investigation, produced

TIGHT COMPOSITION—For the purpose of impact, only the essentials of cheerleading are included: pom pons, school monogram, megaphone, and the shout. The creative photographer used a low angle to add dramatic effect and moved close to his subject to eliminate unimportant details. When printing the picture, he burned in the corners to cut down the distracting white space above the cheerleader. The cheerleader is Dee De Deluca of Syracuse University. Student photographer is Robert Demetry, also of Syracuse.

authoritative accounts of events and situations, as did William Bradford Huie whose *Three Who Died in Mississippi* was the authoritative account of the death of three Civil Rights workers in Mississippi in the summer of 1964. A New York reporter, Dale Wright, posed several months as a migrant laborer before writing *They Harvest Despair,* a collection of essays. Michael Dorman chronicled the integration of the South in *We Shall Overcome.* Gay Talese, of *The New York Times,* wrote a brilliant account of the people and progress of the Verrazanno bridge in *The Bridge.* Ted Szulc of the *Times* reported the Dominican revolution of 1965. Several reporters did the same for the Castro-led revolution in Cuba. Reporters David Halberstram and Malcolm Browne documented the first years of the war in Viet Nam (in *The Making of a Quagmire* and *The New Face of War.*)

Many become biographers. Every booklist includes the work of the journalist.

Some publish works of review and criticism. Walter Kerr is one. Stanley Kauffmann is another.

Still others collect their essays—ranging the spectrum of human emotions and moods—into volumes. There are humor essayists such as Art Buchwald and Russell Baker; columnists such as Jimmy Breslin, Red Smith, Janet Flanner (winner of a National Book Award), and Jim Murray; feature writers such as Gay Talese and Tom Wolfe; commentators such as Walter Lippmann and Eric Sevareid.

And others, journalists close to life, essay in special books about life. H. Allen Smith is one. So was the late James Thurber. Harry Golden is another.

Some journalists have turned, too, to the short story (Paul Gallico). A very few have written plays (Ben Hecht). Almost none writes poetry (Carl Sandburg is one).

Above all, the modern journalist is versatile. As reporter and writer, the world of literature and of books is open to him, especially in this decade of preference for nonfiction (*Publishers' Weekly* reported that in 1965 nonfiction outsold fiction 2 to 1). Fantasy has been replaced by a consuming interest in space travel and the atomic age, fantastic enough in their reality. Escape through adventure needs no fictionalizing, either—man's own adventures seem unbelievable enough. The chronicle of man past and present, when systematically explored by the reporter, defies imagination. Social problems no longer depend on the novelist for exposure, the investigative reporter does it. Tragedy is real enough; humor is omnipresent within a massing society. In all instances, the reporter and his precise reality prove as successful in literature as the fiction writer and his augmented reality.

POINT-OF-VIEW JOURNALISM

And there are those reporters, part-time and full-time, who seek in their journalism a distinctive point of view from which to tell the story. Generally, the point of view is firsthand experience and personal involvement. Norman Mailer, Tom Wolfe, Nicholas von Hoffman, John Hersey (as in *The Algiers Motel Incident*) in 1970 were some of the principal point-of-view journalists. They represent the 20th-century blend of journalist-historian-novelist-essayist-social scientist-biographer. Their predecessors include such distinguished persons as Victor Hugo (novelist-journalist), Dr. Samuel Johnson (essayist-journalist), Charles Dickens (novelist/documentarian-journalist). The list is extensive.

Such hybridization of forms of writing and commentary has provoked constant discussion—and confusion—among those persons who always want to classify and categorize styles of writing and types of reporting. Here the journalist—over there the novelist. Here the reporter—over there the social scientist.

Mailer found himself the center of controversy in 1968 when he subtitled his 120,000-word book *The Armies of the Night* this way:

History as a Novel
The Novel as History

Then to complete a triumvirate of forms he claimed his book was the product of a journalist. (It was an intensive on-the-scene report about a march on the Pentagon in 1967 by antiwar groups, all told through his deep, personal involvement in the event and with his personal opinions and reactions included liberally.)

Mailer had started with the novel form soon after the end of World War II with *The Naked and the Dead*. He moved on to social criticism and to filmmaking. It seemed inevitable that he would move on to reporting contemporary events. Mailer showed up at the national political conventions in Miami and Chicago in 1968 and wrote, book-length, about what happened there. He claimed he was revealing the history-making aspects of those events by using the instruments of the reporter.

He reported the poet Robert Lowell as telling him, "You know, Norman, Elizabeth and I really think you're the finest journalist in America." That accord Mailer never really accepted with enthusiasm, nor did he discard it with alacrity.

What Mailer was trying to do, when reporting like a journalist and writing like a novelist, has been explained by Gay Talese (author of the best-selling biography *The Kingdom and the Power*) this way:

> The new journalism, though often reading like fiction, is not fiction. It is, or should be, as reliable as the most reliable reportage although it seeks a larger truth than is possible through the mere compilation of verifiable facts, the use of direct quotations, and adherence to the rigid organizational style of the older form. The new journalism allows, demands in fact, a more imaginative approach to reporting, and it permits the writer to inject himself into the narrative if he wishes, as many writers do, or to assume the role of a detached observer, as other writers do, including myself. . . . I attempt to absorb the whole scene, the dialogue and mood, the tension, drama, conflict, and then I try to write it all from the point of view of the persons I am writing about.

In not-so-subtle terms, Mailer in *The Armies of the Night* referred to his presence in the report as EGO.

Nicholas von Hoffman of the *Washington Post* became another controversial journalist when he began to use imaginative styles and structures and points of view to report, in depth, complex social and cultural movements—such as the drug culture (see *We are the people our parents warned us against*). Von Hoffman has proved himself a meticulous, sensitive, and intelligent reporter. He has explored the breadth and depth of styles to get across a "sense" of what he is reporting, not just the "facts."

Well, the Mailers and Herseys and von Hoffmans and Taleses show us the horizons of reporting and writing in journalism, just as in the past Stephen Crane and Mark Twain and Walt Whitman did.

They help certify to all of us that the modern journalist, increasingly so, is the writer, artist, commentator, critic, social scientist, biographer of the 1970's and 1980's.

The Feature Story

Chapter III

THE NEWS FEATURE

The senator-to-be came to town to deliver a campaign speech, and there besides the local party members and the voters-soon-to-be and the kids of curiosity were the reporters. A dozen reporters, some professionals and a great many students, turned and twisted the event into a thousand shapes, each seeking a distinct product.

One student reporter, John Sistarenik of Schenectady, N.Y., reported the speech in a factual, straightforward fashion. He started his story with this lead:

Robert F. Kennedy is running for the United States Senate on a voting record—that of his opponent. In a speech at Manley Field House last night, the Democratic candidate said that Senator Kenneth Keating's record in Congress has not been satisfactory.

And Mr. Sistarenik, a lean, sandy-haired, intense student of journalism, chose the direct path to reporting the story. The style was lean, impersonal, and direct. He relied on facts, quotes, and other highly-objective information to tell the story of Kennedy's speech at Syracuse, New York. The information was meticulously gathered; the reader after finishing the story felt he knew everything that had been said.

It is a good example of what is called *the straight news story*.*

But another student, Linda Heffner, of Coatesville, Pa., saw the event differently. She arrived on the scene early, and left late, and the excitement of the crowd caught her up. The sights and sounds of campaigning were just as significant as the words spoken, she decided. So she told the story in a much different manner. Her lead started with a sense of mystery, with a touch of drama, like the opening of a short story:

They started arriving at Manley Field House about 3 p.m. The day was wet and overcast, but that didn't matter to them. They were here to see him, and little else mattered.

They were mostly girls, either Syracuse University students or residents of Syracuse and neighboring districts. They carried pictures of him; they wore all kinds of buttons with his name and picture on them. Michele Morgan and Kay Altman, both 16, from Syracuse, came as soon as classes in their high school were over. Michele carried a cardboard placard which read, "We Love You."

And Linda was well on her way to what is called a *news feature.**

All reporting requires a degree of creativity—to get to the story, to ask questions which will bring out newsworthy answers, to sense the mood * and tone* of an event, and to find an angle (a theme) which will interest the mass of readers. But the news feature much more than the straight news story depends upon creativity. For that reason, not all reporters are capable of reporting and writing features.

As for John and Linda, they can handle both kinds of stories. In this instance, John followed up his lead with hard, factual comments such as the following:

Kennedy told the capacity crowd of 2,500 that Keating has consistently voted against such bills as education, housing, and unemployment.

Linda pursued her narrative account:

As the cars stopped, his car was mobbed. He stepped out and it was mass confusion as hundreds of feminine hands reached out to touch him. He didn't seem to mind though. In fact, he looked as if he enjoyed every minute of it. One girl broke through the crowd and handed him a sweater. He held it up for everyone to see. They laughed and cheered. The sweater was pale blue and tiny; it was a baby sweater.

Even the closing paragraphs had different values. In the straight news account, John tagged on a final item, something which is not especially important and which could be cut without troubling the story at all. John's last paragraph:

After this university speech, the visibly-tired Kennedy left in a motorcade for another speaking engagement at the Randolph House. Several students attempted to shake the hand of the candidate as he left, but only a few succeeded as the motorcade sped from the building.

Kennedy speeds from the scene into the gathering night. End of story. In this paragraph, John allowed himself some observations, but they were so unmistakably true-to-the-happening as to be coldly factual.

In Linda's news feature, the final paragraph was vital. To cut it would have been to render the story nonsense. In fact, she built to a

MOTION—Movement can be heightened in several ways: by showing an oblique line of action, by moving in close to the action, and as in this photograph by blurring the action. A slow shutter speed (about 1/25 for most activity) will do it. Here a motorcycle drill team passes by as its captain (parked) double-checks their formation. Again, a photographer may be in trouble if he becomes too arty in his recording of news events. Many readers will look at this photograph as being blurred—and therefore poor photography.

paragraph which finally told the reader who "he" is. Suspense ended with this concluding one-sentence (for impact) paragraph:

After a few minutes a slightly nasal voice pierced through the cheers, giggles, screams, and squeals. "I'm running for the Senate," said Robert F. Kennedy.

The speech began two hours late, and Linda's story ended where John's started.
Here are the two stories. Read them carefully.

The straight report of Robert Kennedy's speech,

By JOHN SISTARENIK

Robert F. Kennedy is running for the United States Senate on a voting record—that of his opponent.

In a speech at Manley Field House last night, the Democratic candidate said that Senator Kenneth Keating's record in Congress has not been satisfactory.

Kennedy told the capacity crowd of 2500 that Keating has consistently voted against such bills as education, housing, and unemployment.

The 38-year-old former Attorney-General stressed the need for federal aid to education. He explained that in California 93 out of every 100 high school graduates attend college. Only 54 out of each 100 attend in New York. In spite of New York's basic need for federal assistance in this area, Kennedy said that Keating voted against federal aid to schools.

Turning to the unemployment issue, Kennedy said that his opponent was opposed to the creation of a Youth Conservation Corps. The corps was a part of the war on poverty and would have enabled youths to obtain jobs.

In reference to the housing situation, the candidate explained that he had a 15-point program to alleviate the shortage of adequate dwellings in the state. He did not elaborate on this plan but mentioned that the Republican incumbent had been on the Senate floor fighting against housing measures.

In the case of the test ban treaty, Kennedy said that Keating did not give his support to the pact until the day it came up for a vote of approval in the Senate.

Citing the challenge of the changing world, Kennedy commented, "I stand with the future and the party of hope." The huge audience, consisting mostly of Syracuse University students, applauded loudly when he added that the sneers of the cynics and the despair of the weak-hearted are not needed today.

He compared his opponent to the man who said that he must find out where his people are going so he could lead them.

Answering questions from the audience, Kennedy said that he believed the busing of school children over long distances was unconstitutional.

When asked if he was using New York State as a stepping stone to the presidency, he replied, "I want to be a good United States Senator from New York." Kennedy denied the carpetbagging charges against him by saying he had spent much time in the state and knew all of its problems. The Kennedy family has had a home here since 1925, and the Democratic hopeful was born in the state.

The question of Keating's part in the Cuban missile crisis brought a moment of hesitation from the speaker because of the complexity of the missile situation. Kennedy finally said that there had not been any missiles in Cuba in August of 1962 as Keating had reported. They were first erected in the middle of September.

Kennedy contended that Keating's allegation the following February that missiles still existed on the island forced the Secretary of Defense to reveal photographs to prove otherwise. Keating's information, according to Kennedy, was against national security.

After his university speech, the visibly-tired Kennedy left in a motorcade for another speaking engagement at the Randolph House. Several students attempted to shake the hand of the candidate as he left, but only a few succeeded as the motorcade sped from the building.

The news feature about Robert Kennedy's speech,

By LINDA HEFFNER

They started arriving at Manley Field House about 3 p.m. The day was wet and overcast, but that didn't matter to them. They were here to see him and little else mattered.

They were mostly girls, either Syracuse University students or residents of Syracuse and neighboring districts. They carried pictures of him; they wore all kinds of buttons with his name and picture on them. Michele Morgan and Kay Altman, both 16, and from Syracuse, came as soon as classes in their high school were over. Michele carried a cardboard placard which read, "We Love You."

A stage had been hastily constructed to the right of the main entrance to the fieldhouse. It was gaily decorated in crepe paper and two men in dark green coveralls were setting up a microphone.

They finished their work and the stage was set.

Inside the fieldhouse a small army of policemen waited. Syracuse University Security Police as well as special details of the Syracuse Police Force were on hand for his arrival.

At 6 p.m. the crowd outside had grown considerably; it was now about 1700 (according to a Syracuse police officer), but it was still girls, girls, girls. It was an enthusiastic crowd, but a cold crowd. They huddled in doorways to keep warm and they seemed to think that by talking and singing they could keep warm. So they talked and sang the Syracuse Alma Mater. Some walked among the crowd and distributed more placards and booklets about him.

Inside the fieldhouse, six nuns from Saint Patrick's convent in Syracuse sat in the last row of the center section. Sister Patrick Denise wore a button with his picture on it. She wore it on the sleeve of her habit and when she rested her arm in her lap the button clanged against the beads of her Rosary. Sisters Rose Campion and Mary Benedicta also wore buttons with his picture on them.

By 6:45 most of the seats in the fieldhouse were filled and the doors were closed. Policemen stood at every entrance. Every time a door was opened to admit someone with a pass, a crowd would try to squeeze in also. One girl in a Dartmouth sweatshirt pleaded with a policeman to let her in. She said she had been waiting three hours. "Send a letter to your Senator," the policeman said softly as he closed the door in her face.

At 9 p.m. he had still not arrived; he was almost two hours late. The crowds inside and outside were getting restless. Inside they were hot, outside they were cold, but few complained.

Every time a car turned into the circle in front of the fieldhouse, the crowd, now numbering about 3,000 and still mostly girls, would cheer, but it was a night filled with false alarms.

Then he arrived.

Girls screamed and pushed toward the cars that were coming up the driveway, while some pushed closer to the makeshift stage. Placards covered with his picture dotted the crowd as did homemade signs, two reading, "Welcome to Syracuse" and "SU Loves U."

As the cars stopped, his car was mobbed. He stepped out and it was mass confusion as hundreds of feminine hands reached out to touch him. He didn't seem to mind, though. In fact, he looked as if he enjoyed every minute of it. One girl broke through the crowd and handed him a sweater. He held it up for everyone to see. They all laughed and cheered. The sweater was pale blue and tiny; it was a baby sweater.

He made his way to the stage, all the while holding out his hands for people to grab.

Inside the people were still listening to screams and shouts. Then someone shouted into the microphone, "Let's show him we love him." The crowd answered with loud screams and cheers.

After a few minutes a slightly nasal voice pierced through the cheers, giggles, screams, and squeals. "I'm running for the Senate," said Robert F. Kennedy.

Both stories are legitimate. Both are newsworthy. Both are basically factual. What Linda reports happened—just as surely as John's words were spoken. Both stories are informative and rewarding to the reader.

But, they are rewarding in different ways. From John's story, the reader knows all about Kennedy's speech, but not about the circumstances which surrounded it. From Linda's story, the reader knows all about the circumstances, but nothing about the speech. In an imaginative newspaper, the two stories would be used side-by-side, a straight news story complemented by a sidebar.* Then the reader would know all.

Chances are, however, that Linda's story would be much more fun to read—and possibly would get better readership. Campaign speeches are routine; but the circumstances never are.

As far as we are concerned in this book, the question is—how could two trained reporters come up with such different stories? The answer is attitude partly—and partly intent. Writing preference might be included. And certainly, so is creativity.

Let's presume to imagine the thinking and the actions of the two reporters. First, John:

He has been told by his editor (and remember that reporters work for editors) to report Kennedy's speech. The editor is specific, "I want about 600 words for the morning edition. Kennedy and Keating have been swapping charges. That looks like a story. Pay careful attention to the speech." Already, John's story is being determined. At the Fieldhouse on time, John notes the crowd, the kids, the enthusiasm, the color. He is interested and he watches closely what happens. But all this to John is color, the frosting on the cake, or the baubles to the garment, or the halftime show at the football game. The reader should be concerned about the candidate's words, which decide the vote—or should—not the antics of the crowd. During the speech, John carefully notes the words, sizes up the crowd's response, and gives his readers a fact-packed, sensible account of sensible and significant material.

He gets an A for his product.

Linda, on the other hand, has greater leeway in instructions from her editor. He says, "Come back with a good story about Kennedy's speech. And let's get some readership. All of these campaign speeches are getting dull. Old-hat stuff." While watching the crowd, Linda is amazed by its youthfulness and enthusiasm. That, in itself, is a portent. This time the real story is in the crowd's attitude, which is more significant in its response to the candidate than are the candidate's words to the crowd. Other candidates have not received the same kind of reception. Here is what is truly different—and newsworthy. Linda writes it as it happens, an on-the-scene, narrative account. She borrows all the devices of fiction—description, action, sounds and dialogue, suspense and style. The candidate's words may be an echo of previous speeches, but her story is fresh.

She merits an A for her product.

Chances are that Linda is by nature a more informal and creative writer. She has been brought up with a yearn to do fiction. She likes words and the mind-pictures they make. She responds, too, to human interest. She is impressed by people and what they do, as well as say.

She is a natural-born feature writer.

But, being a good writer, she can do the straight story, too, when necessary. After all, a good writer is one who can vary his styles and structures to fit the need and who can draw upon a wide range of personal responses to provide material. Linda immerses herself in events—and is a feature writer.

Some editors distrust the feature story. When they see a technique of fiction, such as narrative writing, they see fictional content. When they see a human interest story, they see personal involvement in the news—subjectivity.* To them quotes (dialogue) must have in part been made up. Description is too easily exaggerated to be trusted. Feature writing gets fat—and lazy—and takes up too much precious space. Nonfacts cannot be taken at face value and must be suspected.

Editors, sometimes, are right to distrust the feature story. That is, if they don't trust the reporter. But editors should realize that a proper feature writer understands he must be as precise as the straight-news writer to ensure accuracy and honesty, that he must constantly guard against exaggeration or fictionalization of the news, and that he must be the most disciplined writer of all. A person who easily adds weight must always watch his diet.

The reward for discipline is the knowledge that news features are the most read and the most remembered stories of all.

Chances are likely that Linda's account of the day Robert Kennedy visited town will be remembered long after the speech story has been confused with a hundred other such stories.

Perhaps it is time to define and to classify the news feature so that in the Audubon book of newspaper stories it can be properly identified. Definition is improbable, if not impossible. First of all, a news feature is developed from an on-the-spot news event. It rarely is pre-plotted; at most it is loosely expected. By attending the event, the reporter makes observations and undertakes interviews which demand feature treatment—which in turn demands a style and attitude different from that of straight news.

If the blackbird is standard style, then put a splash of red on his wing and you have a red-winged blackbird. If a straightforward, objective-as-possible story is the standard style, then put a splash of color into it and you begin to have a news feature.

Therefore, if the news feature proceeds from the event, then the reporter must have an eye for the different, the spontaneous. He must have imagination as well as alertness. He must be creative, not only as a writer, but as a reporter. What better reason for encouraging student journalists to do the news feature! It brings into play the full range of writing; it reveals the spectrum of the reporting talents. Feature writing concerns life in all its moods; events in all their uncertainty; people in all their attitudes. A feature writer is in a league, therefore, with the novelist, the short story writer, and the essayist.

Nothing will become routine because the journalist constantly can explore, as a feature demands, the unique. Reporters often complain that after one year on a newspaper, routine sets in. "I feel like I am going over the same ground again," he says. "The same elections, the same annual budgets, the same anniversaries and seasons." But, they are never the same; it is only the reporter who tries to force them into the same pattern he used the year before.

News features are worthwhile because they soften timeliness. Weekly and monthly publications are too often stale with coverage stories. Yesterday's event is better forgotten, unless something new is said about it. Take for instance, a basketball game—two weeks old by the time the paper comes out—other games have intervened—fans looking ahead to the next game—two weeks of talk have followed the game—plus the fact that the newspaper in the community has covered it. News value: zero, unless something different can be said about the game. Well, it so happens that when East Side defeated Grant 61-55 two weeks ago, the East coach beat his alma mater; in fact, he defeated his high school coach. Fans didn't realize that fact; the local daily, doing a straight news account the morning of the game, mentioned it in one line. But the student sportswriter talked to both coaches, got several anecdotes, got an exchange of friendly jokes, found out that the young coach used the old coach's system of play. The sportswriter also put into the news feature the score of the game, the high scorers, the significance of the game—for record purposes—but he built the piece around a new, fresh angle. The reader said, "I'll be darned. I didn't know that. Hmmm, it's interesting." And he read on.

One of the few methods of updating a story is through the news feature. The student election is over; everyone knows the results. But the readers don't know that the new student president is the third brother in the family to hold that office. A news feature takes over—and the spot event is timely, again.

The school play was seen by most of the students. They don't know, however, that it was the most profitable play in history because of a promotion crew which tried several new sales techniques. The news feature tells that story—and the play is of interest again.

All students heard the convocation speaker. But few knew of the difficulties he had getting to the assembly—and of finishing his talk.

Ad infinitum. One thing the feature writer senses is the certainty of events to be different. He knows that somewhere in every situation there lies a news feature. Timely. Readable. Interesting. Flexible. He must be alert to get it.

Nondaily papers should rely on the news feature as standard for coverage stories.

And, not only does the news feature provide the finest training in writing, not only does it soften timeliness, and not only does it increase reader interest, but it makes journalism much more fun. The reporter feels he can make full use of his talents as reporter and writer.

The editor says, "The state Republican leaders are meeting at

"But Really—A 21-page feature about your first date?"

BY J. DANIEL WINTERMANTEL OF ARCHBISHOP WALSH HIGH SCHOOL, OLEAN, NEW YORK.

Apple Valley this week end to talk about what went wrong in the past campaign. Go out there for the week end and send back a story each day about what has happened. Keep it straight; we have tight papers over the weekend."

The tight, straight news stories come in for the week end. But several unstraight things happen within the reporter's eyesight and hearing. The sergeant-at-arms is back for his 30th consecutive annual meeting. The state chairwoman is disturbed that the men didn't listen more attentively to the women during the campaign. As the reporter talks to people, watches what goes on, gets to the scene of all activity, he sees that there is more than fact to the convention. There is color, and life, and emotion and the unusual (that red-winged blackbird, again) which demand to be reported. There is body and life to the political meeting. On the day after the conference, he confidently— and happily—plays his news feature.

How the Professional Does It

Football and Nautical Figures of Speech Punctuate GOP Parley

A hundred Republican victims of the November election results wandered into sunny-crisp, friendly Apple Valley over the week end to regroup forces.

Someone likened them to a beaten football team.

But the gloom wasn't an after-game, locker-room variety. It was more the Monday-after type . . . a memory of aches and knocks, uncertainty as to who called the wrong signals.

But a gradually-returning tingle toward the next game.

Such metaphors were common. They seemed to fit in when other explanations of the November loss failed. Almost everyone at the convention had his favorite.

Gov. Goodwin J. Knight turned a neat nautical figure of speech. The party was caught on the shoals, he telegraphed to this meeting of the California Republican Assembly Board of Directors. The rebuilding "must not be a salvage operation. We cannot go far with a patched hull."

Still-in-office Senator Wallace F. Bennett flew in from Utah with a collection of football images. He dotted a Saturday night speech with them—when he wasn't interrupted by a Jazz combo next door jumping Gershwin tunes. The Salt Lake City paint and glass manufacturer compared the unsuccessful 1958 Republican Party to a football team always wanting first down and goal to go from the one.

He asked for more "sacrificing" during year-round campaigning.

So did Mrs. Cecil B. Kenyon, state women's president, and Vice President "Dick" Nixon, as he signed his name to a special telegram.

Nixon felt that greater sacrifices are necessary if the party is to regain state control.

Mrs. Kenyon, an energetic grandmother who loves her political job, added, "We must educate Republicans first that they've got to be willing to spend time and money 365 days a year to support the government they want."

Senator Bennett sacrificed on the spot—forced into the incongruous position of talking political philosophy before 125 banqueters while the nearby jazz combo played "The Lady Is a Tramp" and the Saturday night dancers stomped and sang.

But the senator had quips to meet the situation.

A heavy, swarthy, mustached conga-specialist threw open the banquet doors and tried to lead his serpentine line into the Republican Assembly.

Bennett said, "They must be some Democrats." A thin voice in the audience commented, "That must be true. They have something to dance about."

Sgt. Frank A. Freeman, veteran of every CRA meeting since 1933, stopped the conga.

But the jazz combo continued. The senator cut short his tightly-organized speech. "I guess I am interfering with the life, liberty, and pursuit of happiness of the people."

Outside of music and metaphors, the conference was hard-thinking, not too sure of answers. Only twice did delegates applaud Bennett. But they talked Sunday morning about his ideas for strengthening the party.

They were shocked once. CRA President John H. Phillips introduced the eight-year-veteran of the Senate as "one of only four remaining Republican senators west of the Mississippi."

Someone made the correction: "One of four west of the Rockies." And the convention breathed again.

One such senator, Barry Goldwater of Arizona, was a magic word. His name—a winner amidst chaos—raised enthusiasm whenever mentioned. Letters went out asking him for statewide personal appearances.

• A great many ingredients went into that news feature—and many more could have. In general, a news feature makes use of the following elements:

Facts
Quotes and dialogue
Sights and sounds and description
Human interest
Anecdote and incident
Reporter involvement; I-accounts
Imaginative leads
Basic narrative style
Unusual story styles and structures

In succeeding chapters, we'll take those elements one at a time— all challenging to the creative journalist, whether handling the news feature, the planned feature, or any other type of story.

Chapter IV

THE I-ACCOUNT

How the Student Does It

Police Beam Help into Chicago Darkness

By TERRY BREJLA

"One night may be very quiet, but others you can practically feel the trouble brewing. In fact one good thing about my job is that I can never tell what's going to happen next."

That's the way things are in the eleventh district, according to a Chicago policeman on the night shift. My ride was arranged by Chaplain Robert Holderby and Director of Public Information Mel Mawrence of the police force.

In the first few minutes of our ride, Sergeant Mike Meeks (he told me to call him Mike) and I got to know each other quite well. Still under 30, he has been a Chicago policeman for more than seven years, a sergeant for more than two.

"One of the secrets of being a good policeman is to be systematically unsystematic," commented Mike. "We've got to keep changing our routes or people will know when to expect us at a certain place. This method is most effective, for our mission is to prevent crime, not necessarily to catch it in progress."

Our first stops were false alarms. We checked on what looked like a car theft, (the owner and another man were pushing a stalled car out of an alley), and answered a theft call which took us into a seedy looking tavern.

We followed another call to a miserable-looking boarding house where we were met by four other squads, including two task force cars. After talking to the manager, an elderly lady who had difficulty understanding us, we concluded that the trouble was on the fourth floor.

After making our way up a back staircase, the police keeping me in the center for safety, we found an hysterical woman. She was attractive

48

and in her mid-twenties. She told us that an armed man, who had been beating her, had locked himself in a room at the end of the hall.

When she recovered from a second fit of hysteria, the woman asked to be lifted up to look through the transom. Then she opened the door, revealing an empty room.

"This theater is a real dive," Mike said as we made our next stop. The manager smiled faintly and nodded as the sergeant asked if everything was all right. Mike took my arm and led me to the refreshment stand.

"Want some popcorn? I put a lot of salt on it. Sometimes I think I buy it just for the salt."

Later, after threading our way through a jungle of drying clothes, we squeezed into a tiny apartment overflowing with half-naked children. We found a young man sitting with his head in his hands.

The man's ear had been gashed when a friend pulled a knife on him during an argument about the friend's wife. Sgt. Meeks examined the ear and decided it needed a stitch or two.

As we left the building, the man told us the address of a gambling game that his "friend" was running.

He repeated over and over, "I ain't lyin' to you, officer, I was goin' to the game myself."

On our way to the game, the sergeant radioed for some other cars and a squadrol ("paddy wagon") to meet us there. I was instructed to stay in the car. A few minutes later, the officers emerged from the building with 10 handcuffed men.

"This is probably the most common type of call we get," Mike told me while we were on our way to a reported domestic disturbance. "Usually a husband and wife are quarreling, and the wife wants us to remove the old man from the premises."

The call had come from a tearful young girl who said her parents were fighting and hitting each other. As we approached their room, we heard screaming but things got peaceful as soon as they saw us.

Before returning to the station at 11:30, we had arrested two prostitutes and taken care of an old man who had been robbed and beaten.

Sgt. Meeks is in charge of eight cars. The semi-supervisory nature of his job meant that we had probably been less active than other cars.

Before going home, I glanced at the reports and statistics in the station. District 11 leads Chicago in most types of crime, but police there, as everywhere, continue to work—to help people.

#

We have been studying the news feature, that journalistic piece which arises, unpredetermined, from a spot-news event. We soon will look at the planned feature, which is more architectural in that it is preplanned, plotted, and then executed by reporters.

We can say that the news feature springs from inspiration; the planned feature, from aspiration.

Terry Brejla's feature, which opens this chapter, is some aspiration and much more inspiration. The situation is contrived and common—a student reporter takes a night ride in a cruise car. But once on patrol, inspiration assumes command. All that transpires is spontaneous, and the reporter must be ready to cope with it. What happens to the police happens to the reporter. He is involved in the news situation, and that is why reporter Brejla is wise to use a first-person account, an I-account.*

Brejla serves as a stand-in for the readers at Lyons Township High in La Grange, Illinois. As public spirited as the Chicago police may be, they cannot take every citizen who seeks excitement or senses curiosity on night patrol. In place of first-hand experience, the citizen/reader can undergo vicarious experience, riding along with the reporter. Brejla sees and senses, hears and feels for the reader.

The I-approach is used by every type of writer to attract attention —and to hold it.

The broadcast journalist uses it consistently. Here is Edward R. Murrow, broadcasting during World War II, from London, about a bombing flight he had made: "I began to breathe—and to reflect again—that all men would be brave if only they would leave their stomachs at home."

Novelists write in the first person: Such as Herman Melville in the opening paragraph of *Moby Dick:*

Call me Ishmael. Some years ago—never mind how long precisely— having little or no money in my purse, and nothing particular to interest me on shore, I thought I would sail about a little and see the watery part of the world. It is a way I have of driving off the spleen, and regulating the circulation. Whenever I find myself growing grim about the mouth; whenever it is a damp, drizzly November in my soul . . . then, I account it high time to get to sea as soon as I can. This is my substitute for pistol and ball.

In that first-person manner starts one of the great narratives of American literature.

In poetry, Walt Whitman, at one time a reporter, voiced in *The Solitary Singer:* "I celebrate myself, and sing myself/And what I assume you shall assume. . . ."

The greatest war correspondent of them all, Ernie Pyle, put himself at the war front with the soldiers and then wrote of "We."

Magazines specialize in first-person stories bylined this way: "By Henry Smythe, as told to Tom Magerkurth."

Even motion pictures occasionally are narrated in first person.

And one of the most popular television series of all-time was entitled "You Are There" and attempted to put the reader on the scene.

In literature of all kinds, "I" provides a strong narrative voice. It does for the creative journalist, too, who seeks fine literature in his own field. But the journalist must work under restrictions:

(1) He must directly experience the event. He cannot be a spectator or an attentive observer. He must be involved—yes, immersed in the event.

(2) The event must have exceptional news value.

(3) The "I" must be so controlled that the story is devoid of

TEXTURES AND PATTERNS—Blurred snowflakes tell the story—the first snowfall of the year, a strong mood photograph. The "first" is always newsworthy, a time when readers are sympathetic to winter. The feature photographer selected a streetcorner, shot at a slow speed (1/30) to blur the snowfall, and let texture strengthen his news photograph.

egotism. "I" unfortunately is used to boast and to overbear. It is therefore a term to be heard and read with suspicion. The writer must be sure that the reader doesn't become, in a sense, I-sore.

(4) The reporter must be especially careful not to editorialize or overcomment about the news. He must realize it is but a careless short step from the liberty to report to the license to editorialize.

In writing about his night ride with police, Terry Brejla keeps himself under control. He doesn't overuse the ego-ridden "I." He prefers "We," referring to the police and himself: "We followed another call to a miserable-looking boarding house. . . ."

He doesn't embellish his narrative, but rather lets the events happen simply and directly: "Later, after threading our way through a jungle of drying clothes, we squeezed into a tiny apartment overflowing with half-naked children. We found a young man sitting with his head in his hands. . . ."

He brings himself to the forefront "I"—in just six situations. First, when he arranges his ride (paragraph 2), then when he meets Sgt. Meeks (paragraph 3), when he is convoyed up a stairway by the police (paragraph 7), when his friend patrolman offers him popcorn (paragraph 9), when he is told to stay in the patrol car (paragraph 15), and when he glances at the police blotter (last paragraph). In each instance, the resorting to first-person serves a purpose. Reporter Brejla is not intent on being Superman—nor the Omniscient Observer —nor the Wit—nor the Ham Actor upstaging everyone else.

His personal reward is a byline, "by Terry Brejla." Every I-account must be bylined. And it doesn't hurt to run a picture of the reporter on the scene, or at least a mug shot* of him (keep the mug shot to a half column).

But, be careful! The first-person narrative can be addicting. Suddenly, the reporters get I-weary. *I Was at the Winter Carnival. I Took a Trip with the Football Team. I Was on Stage in the Spring Musical. I Went Spelunking. I Ran for Council President.*

Result: I-strain.

Only significant experiences merit an I-account. *I Spent the Day with the Beatles. I Survived the Tornado. I Went on the Washington Peace March. I Was Trapped by the Blizzard of '66. I Had a Date with Brigitte Bardot. I Had a Rendezvous with an Atomic Bomb.* The reader is the key: if he would be eager to undergo the experience, then a story is worth reporter experience.

That same view is held professionally, for instance, by UPI (United Press-International), the international news and photography association. In June, 1965, officials of UPI carefully examined the I-account as a method for telling the news and decided they should encourage it. *The UPI Reporter,* a mimeographed bulletin from the office of Roger Tatarian, vice-president and editor of UPI, told about the decision:

There was a time when the pronoun *I* figured more prominently in daily journalism than it now does. It hasn't disappeared completely, of course; we all carry eyewitnesses' accounts of major events from time to time and occasional our-reporter-was-there pieces. But the *I's* have been scarce nevertheless.

At one of our staff conferences the question was raised whether more stories would not be more readable if the reporter told them in the first person. One of the most impressive arguments was another question: What is more interesting to read—a general dissertation about London or a letter from London in which some individual tells you what *I* did or saw or what happened to *me?*

The consensus was that the *I's* had it and that we should use them more frequently. As a result a new slug line—"PERSONAL REPORT"— has been appearing on the wires in recent weeks.

A memo to the staff included these admonitions:

"We want to personalize many stories that traditionally have been presented in an impersonal way by the reporter.

"The use of *I* can be effective only if it is not overdone, and if it is done logically and naturally. There should be enough of it to give the flavor of a letter to the folks at home, but not so much as to make the writer hog the center of the stage.

"The *I* is by no means the only essential ingredient of the PERSONAL REPORTS. There must also be a central theme; a simple collection of impressions or scattershot notes is not enough."

The I-account is nothing new. When the author of this book wrote in 1951 and 1952 for an Army Public Information section, we had an office rule that a reporter must first *do,* and then *write.* In the course of a few months, this writer (1) inhaled vomiting gas while trying to write about defenses against gas warfare; (2) fell off a 14-foot fence while writing about how to capture a typical, walled-in Korean village; (3) while writing about amphibious assault training, saw a neighboring boat blown skyhigh; (4) got entangled in barbed wire while writing about the infiltration course; (5) got captured by the invaders while writing about night maneuvers.

But the sacrifices were worthwhile. The I-approach is a great way to get a story, a great way to write a story—and a great way to do first-hand research about the latest first-aid techniques. I-ronically.

Historically, the reporter has had illustrious company. The first-person narrative was used by Victor Hugo in describing a revolt in Paris: ". . . I have seen this crime. I have seen this tragedy, this butchery. . . . It is for this reason that I can sign this book as an EYE-WITNESS."

Horace Greeley used it in an epic interview (1859) with Brigham Young: ". . . I stated that I had come in quest of fuller knowledge respecting the doctrines and polity of the Mormon Church and would like to ask some questions bearing directly on these, if there were no objection."

It was used when reporter Henry Stanley finally located Dr. Livingstone in Africa (1872): ". . . as I come nearer I see the white face of an old man among them. . . . I am shaking hands with him. We raise our hats, and I say: 'Dr. Livingstone, I presume?' And he says, 'Yes.' "

It was used by Richard Harding Davis at the fall of Brussels (1914): "At seven this morning I was awakened by the tramp of men and bands playing jauntily. Whether they (the Germans) marched all night or not I do not know; but now for twenty-six hours the gray army has rumbled by with the mystery of fog and the pertinacity of a steam-roller."

It was used by announcer George Hicks at the Normandy invasion of France: "We can hear the thud of shells or bombs landing on the French coastline, perhaps eight or ten miles before us, and the steel bridge on which we stand vibrates from the concussion. . . ."

It was used by William Laurence at the atomic bombing of Nagasaki: ". . . We removed our glasses after the first flash, but the light still lingered on, a bluish-green light that illuminated the entire sky around."

Thus, the first-person narrative can be used when the reporter is an integral part of the event; and when he seeks an emotional effect, basically of humor or of horror; and when the reporter, after personal investigation, is making an exposé.

Such was the situation in April, 1952, when a professional reporter was sent to Camp Desert Rock, Nevada, to witness the first public detonation of a 20 KT atomic bomb, the size that obliterated Hiroshima.

Here is his account, on-the-spot and first-person narrative:

How the Professional Does It—The I-Account

The day was perfect. Desert air, crisp. Morning, spring bright. Sun, a rich glow. We scrambled into the rear of a 2½-ton truck, mess kits and canteens jangling like the "Toy Symphony."

"All set?" the driver hollered from the cab.

"Let'er go," Sgt. Riley answered.

The truck lurched forward. We were on our way to a rendezvous with an atomic bomb.

One of our instructors had said, "You're going to sit on the rim of hell." We didn't believe him. It was too much a God-lit morning. Even a 20-KT bomb, the one that had smashed Hiroshima and was destined for us, couldn't dull our delight.

It was April, 1952, in the Nevada desert. We rambled out of Camp Desert Rock, a tent outpost, and rumbled into the spring-blooming desert, bound for Frenchman Flats. There, the army planned to explode an atomic bomb in front of a few hundred soldiers.

The purpose?—to demonstrate that troops can survive The Bomb.

Our truck stopped at a checkpoint. Crazy rhythms of barbed wire surrounded a solitary hut. A handful of MP's there guarded a company of Yucca trees and a battalion of primordial rocks. Then our truck again soared across the floor of the desert, bound for Ground Zero.

For the previous week, we had listened to lectures about The Bomb. We had seen pictures of Hiroshima—before and after. We had been gorged with physics, statistics, tactics, and cold, tent-outpost beans. One lecturer had warned us, "When you troops return to your camps, you'll be called on to tell other units what you've seen and heard here."

Another had said, "Don't worry. All reasonable precautions have been taken to insure your safety here."

Another was less reassuring. "I can let you in on some classified information. You'll be about 10 miles away from ground zero. That'll be the closest any American troops have been to the bomb. We think you'll be all right."

So, surrounded by April glory, our truck rounded a rock pile. There was the stadium—white, desert flats for a playing field and a gently rising hill at one end as our bleachers.

The blast was scheduled for 10 a.m. We had nothing to do for a while but to eat sandwiches and apples. We had time to lie back, to stare into the sky, and to warm to our grandeur.

The plot for the day's performance was simple. A B-50 was to drone over the Flats—so high we wouldn't be able to see it. A bombardier was to sight Ground Zero, push a lever, and a few seconds later. . . .

The public address announcer finally interrupted our reverie. He had been chattering aimlessly to us for an hour.

"Plane overhead. Everyone take position," he announced.

Our position: sitting on a hillside.

We couldn't hear the plane. The world turned to mute. Desert winds hushed. Men exhaled—and that was that.

"Bomb Away."

A flash of light! It was so brilliant it darted between clenched eyelids.

"Oh, God," someone on the hill said.

We opened our eyes and looked up.

"My God," someone said. That was all.

A magnificent cloud arose from the desert floor that April morning. No artist had ever held its palette of colors. No magician had ever mastered its surprises. We weren't on the rim of hell; we were in its pit, spellbound by the beauty of iniquity. We sat there for an hour and saw shapes and colors few men had seen. For an hour we pondered what few men had been asked to confront. We wondered about the world at Ground Zero . . . and at Zero Hour.

Later that afternoon, we again piled into our grousing truck and, well-chastened, were jolted along the desert road back to camp. The picnic mood was gone. We were, for one afternoon, men who had looked full into hell.

One of us rephrased a passage from Stephen Crane: "We had been to touch the Great Death, and we had found it to be . . . the Great Death."

Chapter V

THE SIGHTS AND SOUNDS FEATURE

How the Student Does It

By JAMES JACOBS

4 p.m., Thursday, May 6, 1965:

Light from the hot afternoon sun reflected off the façade of the Niagara Mohawk Power Building in Syracuse, New York, causing many of the onlookers to shield their eyes. The polished black granite wall mirrored the demonstrators who were picketing the company. Everything was silent except for the freedom chants emanating from the inner circle of parading demonstrators.

Police were deployed on the corner of S. Franklin St. and Erie Boulevard West, directing the rush hour traffic, yelling at lingering drivers to move on. Most of the onlookers were just coming from work. Others were students, inactive sympathizers, or the press.

"Are these the people from Selma?" a guy in the spectator crowd was asked. Stan Coloski, a white teacher at all-Negro Madison junior high, answered: "About half of them are from Selma and the others are from the city."

"How has it been going so far?"

"There haven't been many hecklers," said Coloski, "except for those loudmouths over there."

A 1957 white sedan drove by on S. Franklin Street with a Confederate flag tied to the side. Shaking fists jerked in and out of the windows. As they went by, the demonstrators stopped their song and shouted back angrily: "Stop and talk to us!"

The car stopped three blocks from the demonstration, in a deserted gas station.

"What's the flag for?" the three in the front seat were asked.

The driver did most of the talking.

"We don't think the niggers should be picketing here, that's all," he said. "This is too nice of a town. Niagara Mohawk hasn't done anything wrong."

"What do you fellows plan to do?"

"Hell, we're going to come back with our friends and picket some against them," he answered again. He adjusted his sunglasses and drove off.

"That's just what is so frustrating," said Reverend Harvey Bates, co-chaplain, United Campus Christian Fellowship of Syracuse University. "These few uninformed repeat time-worn slogans and spread untruths about our purposes here. We do not want Niagara Mohawk to lower its employment standards, we would just like to see some flexibility for a while, to act as a stimulant to Negro high school kids who lack motivation for employment here."

Dr. Byron Fox, professor of sociology at Syracuse University and a member of CORE, said, "Unfortunately, there is a lack of communication between responsible people. The half-truths and vague generalities about the problem of raising the Negro to full citizenship confuse the issues and bewilder not only the racists and purveyors of hate, the pseudo-believers, but the well-meaning humanitarians as well."

Another man stepped over to voice an opinion. "Well, I'll say one thing, man," Calvin Johnson spoke as he joined the swelling group, "it takes a lot of guts to picket."

Five o'clock.

By now the civil rights demonstrators were gathering for a policy discussion.

"There will be a march by the demonstrators to the Public Safety Building," announced Scott B. Smith, Selma freedom rider. "We shall march through the downtown area and anybody who wishes to join us, may."

The 38 demonstrators formed a line and departed from the front of the building. They passed a sign in the window which read: "Meet the Warmest-Hearted Guys in Town at Niagara Mohawk."

One of the lingering spectators watched as the group marched past him and down the street.

"Yeah, I work here and it took me a long time to get the job," said Henry Blank, white, of the bookkeeping department.

"What do you feel about these protests by CORE regarding alleged racial discrimination?"

"I'll tell you, man; I got my life to think about, not them."

He rejoined his friends and walked towards a waiting car.

The protest group marched in snake-like fashion, singing their freedom themes as loud as possible. Cops led all the way on motorcycle and on foot, making sure that the Public Safety Building would be reached with maximum speed.

By 5:15 p.m. the group had formed a circle around the flower beds in front of the building's plaza. The warmth of the sun had begun to fade.

"Will you all join hands please," said the Reverend Emory Proctor, pastor of A.M.E. Zion Church, "while we sing one verse of 'We Shall Overcome.' Then hum one verse and pray in silence for strength and guidance."

The traffic on S. State Street had come to a standstill. It was still warm enough for the car windows to be open. The passengers sat looking straight ahead. Once in a while, a few glanced at the group in prayer: heads down, weaving in rhythm to the hymn, eyes closed, some in tears.

Albert Cady, a student from LeMoyne College, moved from the spectator crowd. A spectator all day, he walked towards the circle, separated clasped hands and joined with them.

Nobody was really looking at the demonstrators, they were sort of glancing around, questioning themselves, talking quietly to each other. No one jeered.

Suddenly, a boy rose quickly from the circle of praying demonstrators and dropped to his knees. He clasped his hands in prayer, wringing them as he raised his head, demanding an answer. "Why can't we be free, O Lord?" he asked. "Why must we always beseech you to help us?"

The demonstrators kept their heads down, weaving and chanting as before. The spectators stood frozen. Only the CBS camera crew reacted, running over to the boy, focusing what would be national attention on the praying youth.

He finished his brief prayer and returned to join the circle. The press quickly gathered around the boy.

"What's your name?" began the onslaught of questions.

"I'm Reverend Thomas Masters," replied the 12-year-old boy. "I come from Pasadena, Calif., and I'm traveling around the country with my mother wherever I am needed. I was an evangelical preacher at the age of 3 and I was ordained in Detroit when I was 11 at the Church of the Living God. I go to T. Aaron Levy School now, but I will leave for the South when the school year is over."

The cameras stopped whirring. Satisfied, the press officials walked away. There was one guy left with the boy.

"What paper are you from?" asked the young minister, hopefully.

"Sorry, but I'm just . . ."

The boy shrugged, looked amazed and returned to the circle with his compatriots.

"Jim Crow must go!" he yelled triumphantly.

#

In the book *Walden,* there is a chapter entitled simply, "Sounds." In it, Henry David Thoreau enumerates the sounds—some music, some clatter, some noise—which reach his solitary hut at Walden Pond. As he wisps away the day, he hears, as he describes it, "the noise of some traveller's wagon on the distant highway." Then comes the rattle of railroad cars and the whistle of the locomotive. And bells: "Sometimes, on Sundays, I heard the bells, the Lincoln, Acton, Bedford, or Concord bell, when the wind was favorable, a faint, sweet, and, as it were, natural melody, worth importing into the wilderness." There is the "distant lowing of some cow . . . and the whip-poor-wills, chanting their vespers for half an hour."

He learned to hear them all. "The distant rumbling of wagons over bridges, the baying of dogs, the thrump of bullfrogs . . . the screech owls take up the strain, like mourning women their ancient u-lu-lu."

Thoreau, the pragmatic transcendentalist, was a gifted reporter of sounds.

The American novelist Stephen Crane, too, was an author sensitive to sound—and a reporter of sight. In *The Red Badge of Courage,* he sees precisely and in color.

[A description of a battlefield during the War Between the States]

The guns squatted in a row like savage chiefs. They argued with abrupt violence. It was a grim pow-wow. Their busy servants ran hither and thither.

A small procession of wounded men were going drearily toward the rear. It was a flow of blood from the torn body of the brigade.

Once he saw a tiny battery go dashing along the line of the horizon. The tiny riders were beating the tiny horses. . . .

As he gazed around him, the youth felt a flash of astonishment at the blue, pure sky and the sun-gleamings on the trees and fields. It was surprising that Nature had gone tranquilly on with her golden process in the midst of so much devilment.

Sights and sounds. The journalist cannot escape reporting them. Sights and sounds are as much a part of events as are people and places. And, just as a reporter is neither blind nor deaf, he cannot be expected—by an editor—to be blind and deaf.

That is why the feature opening this chapter is eminently readable. The reporter, a college student at the time, confident of his objectivity of observations, writes in pictures and sounds. He sees the event: "The traffic on South State St. had come to a standstill. It was still warm enough for the car windows to be open. The passengers sat looking straight ahead. Once in a while, a few glanced at the group in prayer: heads down, weaving in rhythm to the hymn, eyes closed, some in tears."

And the reporter hears it, not just the words spoken, but the shouts, the whirr of cameras, the rush of noon traffic. He pieces together sights, sounds, quotes, settings, and actions into a spot-news feature that lifts the reader out of his after-dinner chair and drops him onto South Franklin Street, into the demonstration. Here is the most objective piece of reporting and writing possible, the story that is told in its entirety, not a skeleton of a story, nor a skeleton fleshed, but a story fully garbed. Mood * and tone* are as essential as facts and quotes.

The reporter, Jim Jacobs, a college student from Syracuse, N.Y., to get his story had to be on the scene for a long time. A husky ex-marine and an ex-defensive end, Jim says of the story, "The demonstrations lasted three days. This reporter was on the scene for three days—interviewing marchers, leaders of demonstrations, watching the national press workers closely to see how they handled themselves, following the marchers about, chasing down automobiles containing counterdemonstrators, interviewing them, listening to comments of spectators and passers-by and talking to employees of Niagara Mohawk (a power company) as they left the building."

Jacobs, an English major, loves literature and brings literature into his journalism. Of reporting, he says, "The closest thing to writing fiction is doing a sights and sound piece because the little things are important in both types of writing—scenes, time, how people look and react, movement. You are writing a short story, only you are reporting. . . ."

Jacobs realizes that a reporter is much more than an automaton who asks questions and scribbles down quotes. Jacobs has said, "Each action means something and you must listen and watch carefully for every little detail that will accentuate or add personality to the story."

After seeing and hearing Jim's story, the reader will truly understand what went on downtown during the Selma March-in at Syracuse in May, 1965.

The sights-and-sounds feature and the I-account are related, of course. Both make heavy use of on-the-scene observations. Both are narrative in style. Both must produce mind-pictures. But they vary in two ways: (1) in point-of-view, the reporter keeps himself out of the sights-and-sounds story and as a result, there is no personal opinion involved; (2) in technique, in the sights-and-sounds story, the reporter interviews people for their quotes and facts; everything he puts into the story is as objective and impersonal as a trained reporter and observer can be. In the I-account, the reporter can afford to be a personality.

In the sights-and-sounds story, the reporter is a story-teller who keeps himself and his ideas out of the picture. In Jacob's article, we sense the reporter only in the existence of the passive verb, "was asked." We know the reporter is at work, but unobtrusively.

Unfortunately, many editors distrust the sights-and-sounds story —as they do much in the realm of feature writing. Those editors are distrusting their reporters; they will not give them credit for being trained observers—perhaps, even the most impartial of all observers. If a person by vocation is trained to see and hear as objectively as humanly possible, he can be considered reliable.

An editor, unfortunately, is bound to his desk. The reporter must serve as his eyes and ears. If the editor permits only the straight news story, his paper will be dull, stereotyped, and even inaccurate. His reporters will be stultified by routine, by sameness.

In return for confidence, the reporter, however, must discipline himself to honesty and accuracy. He cannot become personally involved to the point of extreme subjectivity. Take, for instance, the student protests in 1965 and 1966 against the war in Viet Nam. Marching and picketing arose on campuses across the nation. A great many reporters were unfair in their coverage, because, in sights-and-sounds stories, they selected details to prove preconceived viewpoints —for instance, that protesters are beatniks and beatniks wear beards and are sockless. Therefore, the reporters duly noted and reported the bearded and the bare-soled. The clean-shaven and well-dressed were ignored.

Result: One side of the story was told giving the reader a distorted picture. This sentence is taken from a story in a New York newspaper: "Men were bearded with hair down to their collars; college girls were barefooted and wore baggy sweatshirts." The true report should have been: "Some of the men were bearded; others were clean-shaven and dressed in suit and tie."

Aye, there is the danger to the sights-and-sounds story—the reporter presents a distorted view of the event by presenting selected details, and then conveniently ignoring the countering details.

The difference between the disciplined reporter and the dishonest reporter is one of professional status. Editor and reader can trust the professional; they must discard the unprofessional.

One such professionally-inclined reporter was a high school student, Wes Toepke, who several years ago was asked to do a sights-and-sounds story of Elvis Presley's first movie. When it reached the Rose Theater at his hometown at Glendive, Montana, Wes got permission to sneak into the girls-only preview. Once there, he looked and listened, and reported to his school paper; it won a Montana state writing award that year:

Cheers, groans, sobs, and jeers greeted Elvis Presley in his Glendive debut in "Love Me Tender" at a "girls-only" matinee at the Rose theater Dec. 5 at 4 p.m.

Fans and the curious lined up for a windy block to see their ideal in action. And for two hours, the Rose resembled a Roman colosseum on gladiator day.

The girls began clapping and yelling, "We want Elvis," even before the show began.

They seemed disinterested during the first part of the show, but laughed and screamed when they saw Elvis for the first time in a field behind a plow. That scene triggered the attitude for the rest of the show.

For instance, the gals resented manly Elvis's crying on actor Richard Egan's shoulder and yelled, "Don't cry." He apparently didn't hear.

Screaming and clapping during Elvis's first song, the gals also laughed when he started his second song. Remarks were made with great abundance—and imagination.

Comments during the singing included: "I wish he would stand still; he acts like he's got ants in his pants."

"It is sickening."

"Gee, he is good."

After his song "Poor Boy," the girls kept yelling "poor boy." Some no longer could restrain themselves and roamed the aisle, yelling "poor boy."

As Elvis was riding away with his brother's friends, some girls yelled, "Go back to mama."

But some girls were moved to great emotion when Elvis was dying. One or two sobbed unashamedly. Some were still crying when the show ended. Others laughed at the death scene.

In this feature, the reporter has been only an observer. He hasn't asked anyone why she wants to see the movie, or what she thinks of Elvis, and what she thinks of the film. The reporter hasn't described much—other than the basic actions of the crowd. He came, he sat, he reported.

In this case he doesn't need the interview comments nor the extensive description. The feature is lean, quick-to-read, and leaves a clear impression of what happened.

At the Rose, Wes stresses two points of description: the scene looked like that at the Roman Colosseum during festive days (combination simile and allusion). The girls lined up for a *windy* block; and they cried *unashamedly* (modifiers). Both are effective points of description, and because they are so isolated in the feature they have added power.

Otherwise, Wes describes by using the standard devices of narrating action—nouns and verbs, substantives in movement—girls yelling, clapping, laughing, crying.

An occasional figure of speech, action verbs, modifiers (words and phrases)—not much else is necessary to description.

Figures of speech—It is enough here to caution against overusing figures. The right figure in exactly the right place—that's the rule.

Modifiers—Somehow, the modifier has become a villain in today's prose. Poet Carl Sandburg once summed up the feeling when he said, "I am still studying verbs and the mystery of how they connect nouns. I am more suspicious of adjectives than at any time in all my born days. . . ." Ernest Hemingway used to preach stripping language clean, "to lay it bare to the bone." Of course, modifiers got stripped, like so many leaves on a stalk of celery; the leaves are pretty, but not especially part of the diet.

Adjectives, too, can be pretty to look at, but not especially significant. Adjectives can be flat, colorless, insipid:

He had a *solid* build. It was a *great* game.

Adjectives can be overused until they lose freshness, become hackneyed:

The road winds across the *shimmering* coastal plain down to the *blue* sea (too many things shimmer; seas are blue unless otherwise described).

Innocent victims—*grim* prospects.

Once, a writer seeing the sunset told Jack London, " 'Tis a Cyclopean blacksmith striking frenzied sparks from the anvil of the horizon." London looked to the horizon and disagreed, "Hell, I say this sunset has guts."

Adjectives can be redundant, unnecessary because the verb or noun already includes the meaning:

shouting mob of students . . .

She *silently* nodded her head. (Unless something is loose in the works, of course.)

He *quickly leaped* from the chair. (We hear the Olympics is adding a class for slow-motion leapers.)

A *muffled* whisper . . .

Adjectives can exaggerate what happened and reporters cannot afford to use hyperbole. For instance, rarely does an athlete play a "fantastic" game—but the adjective is used commonly.

Some adjectives are ambiguous:

The paper was *almost totally* devoid of news.

Adjectives, if stacked, can be confusing (the stacked adjective results from an attempt to create adjectives by placing nouns before nouns):

Syracuse University Athletic Director Jim Decker's office. (Normal syntax for *all* writers: The office of Syracuse's athletic director, Jim Decker. . . .)

Adverbs can repeat the inherent meaning of the verb. Verbs make adverbs obsolete. In most cases, a verb and an adverb (held firmly) can be replaced by a verb (gripped).

Adjectives editorialize needlessly:

Trustees will meet tomorrow to name a successor to *beloved* Dean Richard Poole.

To a journalist, it is a rare modifier which fits perfectly. It is a gem which when found is added to the luster of the story. Otherwise, modifiers are ignored.

Action verbs—The most powerful description of all is contained in the action verbs. If they are selected for precision in meaning and power and movement, verbs quicken the pulse of writing. One popularly repeated bit of advice by a journalist goes like this: "There is strength and force in short words—words that blast and boom, throb and thump, clank and chime, hiss and buzz and zoom . . . words that work hard at their jobs, that pry and push, that slash and hack, that cut and clip, that chip and saw."

Of course, those quick words are verbs—"active, vigorous, vivid verbs."

Choose verbs wisely. When rewriting, pause with each verb long enough to test its muscle.

Note the verbs used in this vignette by a sports columnist:

Coach Murray Warmath *slumped* in his chair in the gloom of his office

TELLING A STORY—Just as the best cartoon is one which does not need a gag-line, the best photograph is one which, without accompanying words, tells the story. Here, the worried look on the coach's face, and one player, adjusting helmet, coming into the game while another is being helped off tells of an unhappy Saturday. The photographer—like the news feature reporter—saw the ingredients come together for a split second, which was just long enough to catch the photograph.

on a gloomy Monday morning. Rain *spilled* gloomily down the two windows of the room which is located in the northwest corner of Cooke Hall.

It was 1959. His Minnesota Gophers *slumped* in last place in the Big 10 conference.

Gloom.

The reporter said, "Coach, a wire service wants to know what you credit Minnesota's outstanding defensive record to."

Warmath *shuffled* through the papers in a desk drawer. He *rattled* an ink stand. He *grumbled* to himself. The only other sound—the rain.

"Coaching," Warmath finally said. He *pivoted* in the swivel chair and *rattled* the drawers on the other side of the desk.

The reporter was dumbfounded by the frankness.

"Coaching. I guess that's the main reason," Warmath said.

He *dismissed* the reporter with a gloomy Monday morning nod.

Comparison—Another method of description is to reduce an unfamiliar object to a familiar one; for instance, as to length, width, or size, most readers can't visualize the liner Queen Mary as being 1,031 feet long. But they can visualize her as a little longer than three football fields.

Using a familiar object to describe an unfamiliar situation is exemplified by the following anecdote, again involving football coach Warmath:

Murray Warmath pushed away the salad bowl and the soup spoon, picked up a cracker, and carefully placed it on the table cloth in front of him.

"This is Minnesota," he told a Detroit sportswriter.

"Up here is Canada. They raise hockey players there, not football players."

He pointed west of the cracker. "Out here, there's nothing but jackrabbits."

"Down here is Iowa territory and over here is Wisconsin, Illinois, Indiana, Michigan, and most of the Big Ten.

"We won't get any players in those states."

Warmath patted the cracker. "Either we get our players here or . . ."

He jumped his hand to the edge of the tablecloth . . .

"We have to jump way out here to the coasts."

That is why he had recruited Sandy Stephens and Judge Dickson from Pennsylvania, Tom Hall and John Mulvena from Delaware, and a host of other out-of-staters for his 1959 team.

Minnesota could provide linemen, he said. But not backs.

"Figure it out. Just how many great backs has Minnesota had. Bruce Smith? Sonny Frank?—he was from Iowa. Pug Lund? Paul Giel? That's not very many for 30 years."

He waggled a finger at the reporter. "Minnesota has produced a great many fine linemen. But the backs?—We've got to find them somewhere or be losers."

He flicked away the cracker.

And during the next two years, the Gophers won a national championship and a Rose Bowl game.

Salient point—If it is impossible to describe systematically from top to bottom, or left to right, or front to back, then description is better handled by a point of prominence. In describing Iwo Jima, a writer can start with Mount Suribachi which dominates the scene and then ignore or quickly pass by the rest of the island. In describing Jimmy Durante, a writer can concentrate on the nose; the rest is insignificant. In describing a crowd of demonstrators, he sees the waving signs; they are symbolic and the rest is minor.

Descriptions are better if succinct and memorable in wording. Masters of words have produced many immortal passages of description, such as these which appeared originally in *The New Republic*:

About Evangelist Billy Sunday: "He was a recruiting sergeant, not a drill master." (Francis Hackett)

Woodrow Wilson as he departed for the Paris Treaty Conference after World War I: "He went into the jungle with a map of the world but without a compass." (Walter E. Weyl)

Henry Ford: "He is the sum of a great number of contradictory things which by their nature cannot be added up." (Robert Littell)

Harry S. Truman: "He is a typical American whose strength is his averageness." (Michael Straight)

And some final points about description in the sights and sounds story:

Rather than isolate the description in one paragraph or two, blend it into the narrative, a bit here and a piece there. Thus the picture is put together gradually and systematically in the mind of the reader. He grasps it gradually, just as he sees a jigsaw puzzle emerging.

Be careful that description doesn't turn into needless insult. To write that a competitive swimmer *splashed* his way to victory, in an attempt to be descriptive, is to insult a graceful, carefully trained, and nonsplashing athlete. To say that a heavy-set man "heaved into sight like a battleship coming over the horizon" (Churchill was once described that way) is colorful and picturesque, but perhaps unduly insulting. To characterize a big nose as "an Eiffel tower standing on an arid plain" is sarcasm without purpose. Mark Twain once described a person's nose as "rambling on aggressively before him with all the strength and determination of a cow-catcher; a red mustache seemed not unlike the unfortunate cow."

A reporter isn't concerned with being caustic or sarcastic—or even satirical. That is the privilege of the editorialist, the essayist, and the columnist. The reporter is concerned with an honest and accurate account of an event, as it happened.

And most of all, in being descriptive, don't be trite. Even the professionals are unduly trite at times, such as in these opening paragraphs of a story filed out of Viet Nam:

The road to Qui Nhon is long, hot and dusty.
It snakes down from the hills and across the shimmering coastal plain of Vietnam to the blue sea.
Along the road these days flows the flotsam of war, borne on a river of anguish. . . .

If journalism is "literature in a hurry," as one 19th century English critic said, then much of it is unworthy of emulation. It, hurried, becomes patchwork. But, hurried as it is, some of the literature of journalism is powerful in its effect.

Such as our closing piece ("As the Professional Does It"), an on-the-spot, sights-and-sounds story by one of the finest feature writers in American journalism, Gay Talese, formerly of *The New York Times*. When rookie patrolmen get their first assignments—to the subways—he goes along. He sees ("Patrolman Edwards showed the rookies how they should stand, feet apart, so as not to be shoved in front of an onrushing train by 'some nut' "). He hears (mostly dialogue). He gleans facts (105 rookies board at 50th street). He describes ("Their nightsticks are new, their whistles unbitten, and when they walk their beat—the shiftiest in the city—they sometimes sway and lose their balance"). He keeps himself out of the story (no references to "I").

And Mr. Talese sets a professional example for the learning journalist.

Rookie Policemen Tour the Subway

*Veterans of Transit Force
Give Newcomers Some
Pointers on Life Below*

Pickpockets Spotted

*Men Try Out Subway Legs and Learn
How to Stand on Platform Safely*

By GAY TALESE

Their nightsticks are new, their whistles unbitten, and when they walk their beat—the shiftiest in the city—they sometimes sway and lose their balance.

They are among the 105 rookies just added to the subway police force, and it may take days before they learn to walk determinedly through the unsteady aisles of moving trains and get used to patrolling a world where there is neither sunshine nor rain.

But yesterday, escorted by some veterans among the Transit Authority's 1,077-man police force, the rookies were given a tour of the lower level of New York—an underground city that, because of a number of recent crimes, has gained a reputation for being almost worse than the world above.

"Okay, fellas, my name's Edwards," said a 6-foot 4-inch Transit Authority officer to three young rookies who stood, a bit self-consciously, in their new uniforms along the platform. "And I want you to realize that down here you're working among some of the trickiest crooks in New York, and among the best pickpockets in the entire world."

The rookies seemed impressed. Patrolman Silas Edwards continued: "Down here, they'll take your money when you're cold sober, and when these pickpockets get too old, or lose their nerve, they'll work on the lushes."

Within 15 minutes, while passengers along the platform watched—and a few wondered aloud, "Why all the cops?"—Patrolman Edwards showed the rookies how they should stand, feet apart, so as not to be shoved in front of an onrushing train by "some nut"; and how, by looking under telephone coin boxes and spotting unconnected wires, they could quickly report it and make life less prosperous for coinbox riflers.

Within an hour, he had taken the rookies to three subway stations, shown them the locations of police telephones (clamped on the sides of change booths), and urged that they check each night to be sure that commercial establishments' doors are locked.

Finally he told them that the Transit Authority police—sometimes called "cops in the hold"—are as fine as New York's finest in the fresh air; both forces earn the same money, he said, and have the same pension and other benefits.

The only difference, he said, is that the subway police have to talk louder, think faster and move faster.

After boarding a southbound IND local at 50th Street, Patrolman Edwards led his rookies through the swaying corridors of cars, stopping them a few moments after they had passed two standees who wore dark glasses and leaned close to other riders in the car. He asked:

"Did you notice those two?"

"Yep," said a rookie.

"Notice how they shifted when they saw us coming?"

"Yep."

"Pickpockets," he said.

The rookies nodded knowingly, and half-smiled a moment later when the train stopped and the two men in dark glasses left in a hurry.

Chapter VI

THE PLANNED FEATURE

Ted Shove Plays Friend During Typical Day

Postion of Security Officer Requires Versatile Man

By MARION HENNING and JOHN LOWE

Following Ted Shove, Pacific's security officer, about campus during a typical day is like trying to keep up with Dick Tracy on one of his famous escapades.

Things can appear to be going along at a smooth pace until suddenly they pick up and move swiftly for Shove.

Last Tuesday two Hi Tide reporters served as Ted's shadows for a full day. They observed that he is friendly and easy-going; yet, he is right there, "Johnny on the spot," the instant he is needed.

"That's my job," he explains simply.

For Pacific students Shove is part "cop," and part friend. One boy said, though, "He's mostly just our buddy. Even the kids who get in trouble like him."

"The thing that amazes me," said a girl, "is the number of students he knows . . . what kind of a car they drive, how they behave and who they go with. For instance, he'll see a girl and say, 'Hey, try and keep your boyfriend in class.' "

The typical day is as varied as Heinz soups.

During first period, Shove simply observed and in his words "just kinda watched them." He shooed a few stray fellows back into the quad with a friendly "Better get back where you belong."

Toward the end of the period, a boy came up to Shove and confessed to throwing a coarse note in Ted's car not long ago. Shove seemed to take particular pleasure in this confession since he had known the culprit for nearly two weeks, and he had been waiting for the boy to admit it.

72

During the second period Shove closed some of the entrances to the parking lot. Then he took his own car and checked streets adjacent to Pacific for cars that should have been parked in the PHS parking lot. Violators were tagged, and Shove put them down on a list.

Third period wasn't so bad and Shove had time to take a coffee break. "First lunch is the period that I really get around." And this particular lunch period proved that. A girl taking money in the hot lunch line took a quarter from a boy and realized that it didn't seem authentic. She reported it and swiftly identified the culprit. The boy quickly admitted it. Later on several other counterfeit coins were found.

Shove came to Pacific in September. Since that time, he has eased the duties of other faculty members.

He has taken full charge of the parking lot. He is responsible for the enforcement of Pacific's basic regulations. He spends Friday and Saturday nights either officiating at a game or at a dance.

During his "spare" time, he attends "Criminal Procedure with Juveniles," a course at Valley College. When no dance is scheduled for Saturday night, he becomes a deputy sheriff and checks to see if doors of stores and businesses are locked.

He is in charge of an area extending from Rialto through Highland.

His two free nights are spent at home with his wife and five children ranging from two to eleven years.

Each morning he arrives early to help park some 400 cars. "Whoa," he exclaims, as a driver nearly rams the bumper of another car.

One ring of the telephone in the custodian's office is likely to change Shove's entire day.

"Can you open the outside gate on the football field?" or "Could you drive to the bank now to deposit some money?" asks a voice from the other end of the line.

And his day adds another task.

The two reporters found the job of security officer challenging. The officer must be a psychologist. He needs to know what makes teenagers tick and what it is that occasionally makes them do wrong. He must be understanding, yet strong enough in his convictions to keep kids on the right track.

Although Ted has not worked in other high schools, he judges Pacific as being very good discipline wise and above average in behavior.

Shove says that his job at Pacific is just what his title implies: "To keep this school as secure as possible."

"Oh, yes," said one reporter as Ted was getting ready for the 3:15 traffic jam, "Why did you decide to take this job anyway?"

"I like kids—that's all."

#

Each fall brings to the campus new teachers and new students, but the fall semester brought to one California high school something startling new—for the first time a campus security officer, known too as the Campus Cop. The officer was a congenial, patient, and dedicated man who brought comfort to some, concern to others. He was there, in a mass school of 2,500 students, to help maintain order. Yet, many students and teachers felt uncomfortable—Have times come to this, they wondered. Do we need police protection on our campus?

The editors of the school newspaper watched the new officer's activities for a couple of months, noted the degrees of comfort and concern felt by members of the community, and then decided to do a special story about him. But a problem arose—how to really tell *his* story and not sensationalize it. The solution—let's assign reporters to be with him through one full day of his work to see what it is like to be a campus patrolman.

Two reporters, John Lowe and Marion Henning, did just that. Their feature story, A Day in the Life of a Campus Patrolman, was used to introduce this chapter. It won an award in the state of California for best feature of the year.

When readers put down the paper that November of 1958, they knew for the first time not just who the new patrolman was but what he was there for and how very well he was succeeding.

Part of the feature was planned: the idea, in particular. Much of the background material about the officer was prepared beforehand. The point of view—two reporters and their observations of a situation—was planned.

But the rest was not.

Planned features are a staple in the diet of newspapers. The idea originates *before* the event, whereas, in the news feature the idea develops *during* the event. The planned feature exists in the mind of editors, and maybe reporters, before the event occurs; the news feature springs into the reporter's mind while he covers an event. Both features put stress on the reporter, but the planned feature also puts stress on the editor, who exists as a creator of ideas.

For instance, an editor wonders what the present American citizen knows about the Declaration of Independence. In contemporary movements toward freedom African countries are constantly referring to the Declaration. Yet, Americans seem to distrust such revolutionary spirit. So, the editor has the Declaration typed in the form of petitions and sends his reporters into the streets to see how many citizens will sign. The results form the feature story (many citizens do not identify the Declaration and refuse to sign the petition). Up to the point of execution, the feature was carefully planned, and its findings anticipated.

Thus, the planned feature has at least three characteristics, as follows:

(1) It is anticipated—possibly to the style of writing, the mood of the story, the point of view, and perhaps the conclusions.
(2) It requires depth reportage* and research to verify or to disprove what is anticipated.
(3) It must be carefully written, in a timeless manner, so that it has strong readership.*

But there must be limitations to the planned feature. For instance, a poor idea must be quickly discarded. The editor suspects the honesty of most people so he plants a wallet on the sidewalk, hides a reporter behind a nearby doorway, and sees what happens. The idea is weak because (1) it has little news value, and certainly no tie-in with the times; (2) it is inflexibly pre-conceived, what with the editor expecting proof that people are dishonest; (3) it is a worn-out idea, overdone by feature editors and writers.

Every planned feature, therefore, must be put 1-2-3 to the test and if it fails any of them it must be discarded. To repeat, the planned feature

(1) must be newsworthy and have some time value to it.
(2) cannot be forced to prove a preconception.
(3) cannot be worn-out or silly and must be in good taste.

Planned features generally start with editors and move down to reporters. Sometimes reporters will suggest the idea to editors who then will approve or disapprove it. For example, a high school editor wondered how to lend excitement to the coverage of a cave-exploring club (spelunkers). He decided to send a reporter underground with the spelunkers. The reporter, Gordon Sorensen, came back with a graphic, sights and sounds feature:

Sunday, May 16, was a snowy, desolate day. And there I was—pinned into a space too small for a snake, much less me. Trapped in a cave 16 miles out of Chatfield, I was somewhat panicked. If you like being jammed into a Volkswagen with 30 or 40 other people, I would say you are a born speleologist and should have been in my place.

It all started when I was assigned to write a story about the JM speleology club. First, I thought the only way to find out about cave-exploring was to accompany club members into a cave. My second thought occurred just 10 seconds after I had entered my first cave. . . . "Perhaps I hadn't lived a really good life and now wouldn't get a chance to correct my mistakes." . . .

Gordon went to do and came back to tell. That type of feature is based upon *participation*.

‣ Another kind of planned feature is based upon *visitation*. The reporter goes to see and comes back to report. For instance, when a small town got into the state amateur baseball tournament, a reporter was dispatched to see what fame had done to the town, to see how it was responding to the excitement and the attention. His feature story, based upon preplanning by an editor, started like this:

Outwardly, Arlington seemed to be going about its usual business Thursday. The only indications of something unusual were signs painted on store windows along Main Street.

Hebeisen's Food Store announced in bold, white wax letters: "Closed at 4:30 p.m. Friday. Come on you Black Sox."

On a window of the Pinske Building was painted a peppery baseball character wearing a blue warmup jacket and pointing a sharp finger down Main Street. The sign gave evidence that Arlington—population 1,700—is in the semifinals of the Minnesota state amateur baseball tournament. . . .

Through interviews and through observations, the planned feature was carried out by the reporter.

Other planned features are taken from the calendar and the almanac. They concern birthdays and anniversaries and holidays and special events and annual festivals, like fairs, and homecomings and historical dates. For each occasion of the calendar, editors and reporters pool their ideas for planned features. What do we do this Christmas?—we send a reporter toy shopping . . . we send a reporter to be Santa Claus for the annual Crippled Children's party.

How do we handle homecoming in some distinctive manner this year? How about the special issue for the first day of school?

What about Ground Hog's Day, the editor asks. Let's forget it, says the reporter.

♦ All such planned features are based upon _expectation_—expectation that, sure as the calendar, the day will come about. So certain is the expectation, and so early is the planning that special sections are written, edited, illustrated, and printed far in advance of the holiday.

Other planned features are based upon *contrivance*. In every paper, *The New York Times* publishes a biographical feature called "Man in the News." Each feature tells about some person who has been instrumental in making the day's news. On the day before Christmas, 1965, the Times chose as "Man in the News" Santa Claus. The story started as follows:

> The personage in whose name millions of benefactions, mostly for the pleasure of children, will be strewn tomorrow morning under decorated trees, stuffed into stockings or piled on mantelpieces throughout most of the Western World is sometimes regarded as mythic.

The Santa Claus piece is a contrivance—a variation upon the customary column. It is based upon *experimentation*. Photographing the world from a child's height would be contrivance—and perhaps a proper way of telling pictorially the story of kindergarten's opening. Faking an interview with prize-winning cows, as one reporter did at a state fair, is contrivance.

But contrivance must be handled carefully—it must be factually correct, and in its gadgeted manner it must tell the story without distorting or otherwise falsifying the news.

Then, there are planned features based upon research. For instance, a reporter becomes disgusted with parking meters and their omnipresence. Started as devices for controlling parking in crowded shopping areas of the city, the meters became sources of revenue. They soon extended into sections where parking was not a problem. The reporter notices that some cities are eliminating meters; he writes to find out why. He notices that many cities are burdened with repairing meters and protecting them from looting; he keeps the clippings and begins an investigation of how much it costs to maintain meters. As time goes by, his *tickler file** fills with clippings, articles, notes, observations, and anecdotes until he has enough material for

SILHOUETTE—Photographing the subject *against* the light sources produces silhouette and adds excitement to a photograph. Student photographer Eric Meola (of Syracuse University) made this picture of Dave Brubeck by moving backstage during a concert and centering Brubeck against the spotlights. To even the most unsophisticated viewer, silhouette is meaningful.

his planned feature, "It's. Time to Get Rid of Parking Meters." Such planned features are dependent to a degree upon *accumulation*.

Other features, preplanned, are set in motion and allowed to run day after day. These would include man-on-the-street polls, all kinds of letters and contests, and requests for contributions from readers.

These recurring features can get out of hand. One of the nation's most unconventional newspapers, the New York Graphic (1929-1932), depended so heavily upon contests and reader contributions that the contest editor had 16 assistants.

The recurring feature, of course, is based upon *continuation*.

• There, you have it. Planned features are largely dependent upon the principles of participation, visitation, expectation, experimentation, accumulation, and continuation. They all are dependent upon an idea man. He may be the editor-in-chief. He may have the special title of Features Editor. His forte is ideas. He is able to see the news in new forms. From his periods of creative thinking, he is able to conceive of routine, recurring news being covered in new ways. He assumes responsibility for covering a topic, he fashions a feature method for it, he passes along his anticipations and expectations to reporters who, in turn, execute them.

Other planned features result from conferences of editors. "Okay, how do we handle homecoming two months from now," the editor-in-chief asks. The other editors present ideas, most rejected and some accepted. Then the editors decide which reporters can best execute the ideas—and out go the assignments.

The reporter faces the most difficult of all assignments. While meeting the expectations of editors who develop the ideas, he must bring to the story honesty, accuracy, and simplicity—the key words to reporting and writing. At the same time he follows orders, he himself must be self-reliant, a difficult duality for any reporter. That is why many reporters cannot handle features successfully.

In the news feature, which we discussed in a previous chapter, of course, the pressure is not as intense. The editor is not necessarily expecting a feature story; the reporter is free to develop it at the scene of the news.

In the following chapters, we will discuss further the styles and methods for writing and reporting feature stories, whether planned or news.

Chapter VII

UNUSUAL STYLES AND STRUCTURES

How the Student Does It

JM Student Waited, Feared

Swaying, Great Noise; Then Earthquake

By DON SAUER

"Earthquakes are so terrible. They give you a strange swaying feeling as you are thrown to the floor—to wait for something else to happen."

(That is how Hernon Perez, an exchange student from Chile now studying at John Marshall, started to describe the earthquakes that turned his native country into an international disaster area this summer.)

". . . On the morning of May 21 at 6 a.m., I was asleep in bed, when suddenly a swaying feeling and a great noise awoke me. I reached for the light, still half asleep, to turn it on. It kept swaying out of my reach," Hernon recalled.

"By the time the first earthquake was over, everything loose in our house was broken," he described. "The windows were gone, and the walls had split apart. Throughout my town there was still great noise."

(Most of the people in Chile live in the southern part of the country. Here is a plateau between the sea coast and the Andes mountains. Here on a narrow strip of land lives most of Chile's population. Here is where Hernon lived when the earthquakes struck.)

"I ran to my parents' room when it was all over. No one said anything, but we were all concerned about getting out of the house. We wasted no time gathering up belongings, but ran down the stairs from the second story of the large house.

"The earthquake had done much damage to the town . . . the most noticeable result was that the nearby river was now dry.

"The worst effect was that it cut off the food and water supplies. The city water system had been broken, and the people were afraid to go into buildings to get food."

80

(The American newspapers reported that one village, Queilen, lost 630 of 800 people.)

"We stayed at the home of friends for the day," Hernon continued his narrative. "They happened to have many chickens, so we ate chicken, chicken, chicken. All day we looked to the sky for help to come by plane.

"None came because, we learned later, everyone thought that the tidal wave which usually accompanies an earthquake had flooded the city.

"That night, Saturday, sleeping was very hard because the swaying of the earth kept us awake."

(One authority estimated the Chilean quake was as strong as the one that wiped out San Francisco in 1906.)

"Sunday dawned bright and clear. No one expected another earthquake. Then at 3 p.m. came the second one.

"This time our city was practically leveled. We lost our house, and most of the rest of the buildings were destroyed.

"This time the sea and its tidal wave did threaten our town. Just as it looked as though we were to be drowned, the wall of water went into the course of the dry river. The sea soon had a column of water extending 3½ miles up the river," Hernon recounted.

"Now the town really was in trouble. Then the next day the expected plane arrived—an American plane.

"Supplies rushed from the United States fed and relieved all the victims. In a few days our family was taken away from the ruins on another American relief plane."

(The final count: at least 5,000 dead, the newspaper tolled.)

A student reporter, Don Sauer, was perplexed by his notes. He had interviewed a foreign exchange student from Chile, and he had what appeared to be two stories. One was the story of a Chilean earthquake, told expertly from first-hand experience by the interviewee; the other was based on the factual news details of the earthquake. Don wanted to use quotes for most of the story; the problem was —what to do with the nonquote factual material so that it wouldn't interrupt the monologue.

Eventually, Don decided to break in with nonquote material at convenient pauses in the student's narrative. But that brought about problems of writing effective transitions back and forth—more wasted words and awkward pauses. Finally, Don decided to alternate the monologue with the nonquote material—and to show the alternation visually so he wouldn't have to spend time on these transitions. He chose to print the narrative part of the story in ordinary body type, and the other material within parentheses, in bold-faced type.

Thus, for his feature story, Don chose a most unusual structure. As a feature writer, he might have chosen an unusual style; feature writers are prone to doing strange things.

His story, incidentally, was effective enough to win first-place in the state contest for interview stories that year.

Don's choice of structure can be challenged. Is it understandable? Or is it too unusual for the reader to follow easily? Is it gimmickry which, because it is different, detracts from the content of the story? If the aims of journalistic writing are simplicity, clarity, and accuracy, does gadgetry undermine those principles?

Before deciding upon his approach, Don had to ask himself those questions, and once deciding he wouldn't be hurting the story, he went ahead. Only the reader could really tell him whether the story succeeded.

• Feature writers are constantly faced with such situations. Because of their determination to be imaginative, they want to experiment with the styles of writing and the structuring of stories. For instance, a feature writer sent out to cover a university football rally wrote in mock term-paper style with its formal vocabulary, its foot-notes, and its complex sentence structure—all violations of journalistic style. Did he succeed in communicating with the reader? Or did he merely satisfy his desire to be different?

Another reporter, sent to cover an anti-Viet Nam rally, came back with an open letter to the boss:

Memo to: City Editor
From　　: Reporter John Douglas

Elevenish, taxied Walnut Park there to observe the March to End the War in Viet Nam. March not there. Total population of park, boy sparrows observing girl sparrows and boys from Syracuse observing girls from Syracuse. . . .
There followed delay of one hour. Toes got cold. . . .
Approx. 12:40 p.m., marchers arrived, a baker's dozen in all . . . [and so on].

In this case, the writer's problem was not one of being readable, but whether in his strange format he might not give the improper mood to the story, one of levity where seriousness was the atmosphere.

Another reporter was asked at Christmas time to rewrite "A Christmas Carol" as a traffic safety message. He did it, too, with Scrooge in the dream sequence visiting the sites of traffic accidents. That writer's problem was one of literary sacrilege—in a way, that of taste—that of offending the reader.

Thus, every time a feature writer departs from the usual styles and structures of journalism, he is gambling with high stakes. He is taking a chance at distorting the news, at alienating his audience, at becoming complicated and confused rather than enlightening.

But a feature writer, being imaginative, plunges ahead with his libertarian philosophy of writing. He bends and twists forms. He

COMPOSITION (The Art Photograph)—There's not much news value to this photograph of a high school wrestling match, but it does have eye-appeal because of the composition. It doesn't tell a story, but the design does please the reader. Occasionally, a newspaper can use such photographs. Yearbooks and literary magazines can use them consistently. To get this picture, the photographer selected a viewpoint from the balcony, and waited until the action below him reached the right point in his pre-conceived plan of composition. The print was made on high-contrast paper to wash out the grays and leave a black-and-white design. (Photo by Bill Ward)

slashes and yanks at style. He masters the traditional forms only so he can construct irregular ones. And much of the time, he gets away with it. He is reassured by one fact—that the unexpected is eminently noticed.

And he doesn't gamble recklessly. He knows enough about writing to be sure, for instance, that the "you" viewpoint to a story is dramatic:

You look at Johnny Unitas, the Baltimore quarterback, and you wonder how any guy so small can be so big on the football field. You want to ask him some questions about that bigness, but you don't want to disturb him as he sits there, after the game, shirtless and sockless, on the locker room bench. You decide just to stand there and study the greatest miracle-maker professional football knows.

The feature writer also knows that the climactic order of a story —which saves the major point of news for the very end, the reverse of the usual order—is suspenseful:

No Use for Gifts Now—

Neighbor Hears Girl Shout for Help, Kills Assailant

(AP)—A neighbor, fearing for the safety of a young bride-to-be, shot and killed a man he saw smashing the girl's bathroom door Sunday, police reported.

Lynn Ann Donatoni, 19, had returned from a day of wedding-gift shopping and an evening bridal shower. She was preparing for bed, police said, when Amelio V. Castorena III, 25, appeared at the door.

"He was terribly mad about something," the girl told police later. She said she ran to the bathroom and locked herself in. She said Castorena began battering the bathroom door.

Lynn Ann said she opened a window and screamed for help. A neighbor, Gerald Scott, 63, awakened. He grabbed a .22-caliber pistol and ran to a driveway between the two houses.

He said he saw Castorena scuffle with the screaming girl.

Scott fired once. The bullet struck Castorena in the chest, killing him instantly. The girl told police she had no idea why Castorena would attack her. Police questioned Scott, then released him.

But Lynn Ann will have no use for the gifts she bought earlier in the day.

Castorena was her fiancé and they were to marry soon.

And the feature writer knows that most variations on style and structure are, by mood, humorous, and he uses them when he wants the reader to be amused by what is written. The feature writer, therefore, lives in a type of journalistic no-man's land, fraught with disaster, but because he knows all the rules of survival he is able to exist successfully—and even happily. He does so by asking himself several questions each time he wants to expose himself to danger:

1. Does the mood created by style or structure fit the mood of the event being reported?

2. Is the article readable—and easily so—by the most unsophisticated person in the audience? Or has it become too complicated to be followed easily?

3. Is the article informative, with news accurately and specifically presented—with the same honesty as in a straight news story?

4. Will it quickly catch reader interest, and then hold it to the end?

5. Is it compatible with the style and structure of the newspaper, in words and in makeup?

Any "no" answer will flunk the idea on the spot.

And the feature writer must be thoroughly familiar with established styles and structures before he can depart from them. For instance, he must understand the *inverted pattern* of most stories—you know, the story is summarized in the lead and then the least important material is placed at the end. Then he can savor and use the climactic order.

As for structures, he knows many have been tested and proved true. For instance, these structures:

Writing an open-letter to the reader or the boss or the interviewee (such as the feature which ends this chapter). Variations include the memorandum.

Alternating paragraphs, such as in an article which contrasts what the U.S. Surgeon General says about smoking (in regular body type) with what cigarette advertisements claim (in italics, in every other paragraph).

Doing tricks with type faces and with letters and numbers. In a story about a boy who caught his head in a picket fence, the reporter used the special characters on his typewriter to tell the story.

There was a boy's head.   0
There was a fence.   1111

Then the boy put his head 0 into the fence 1111 and was stuck 11011. To remove the head, the firemen had to bend the fence 1(0)1.

Repeating a phrase or a sentence to create what in poetry is called a refrain.

[From a news report by A. T. Steele about the fall of Nanking, 1937.]
I saw Chinese troops needlessly applying the torch to whole blocks of homes and shops.
I saw a terrific two-day bombardment of Nanking's defenses, which finally softened and shattered Chinese resistance.
I heard the din of cannonading and machine-gunning accompanying the final Japanese assault on the strongly held south gate.
Later I saw a scene of butchery outside that gate. . . .
These things I saw too:
[then follows a listing of sights of war].

As for styles, again, several have been proved reliable, such as these:
Addressing the reader directly, using "you" as the dramatic point of view.
Writing in dialect, maybe ethnic in nature, maybe semi-literate in nature. Damon Runyon, one of the most famous Broadway reporters and columnists of all time, consistently turned to dialect and semi-literate characters:

When I started to play a card she ses oop oop oop. So I played a different card and after awhile I won the game. That put me five games ahead of Bill and then the next hand when I started to play a card Ethel says oop oop oop again.
Bill Kelly put down his cards and ses look Ethel what is this oopoop-ooping stuff?

Writing in a colloquial, conversational, even exclamatory style, Damon Runyon reported Charles A. Lindbergh's return from Paris:

A bashful looking long-legged gangling boy with cheeks of pink and with a cowlick in his hair that won't let the blond locks stay slicked down, came back to his home folks today one of the biggest men in all this world.
LINDY
My heart, how young he seemed!

Using fragments of sentences, strung in elliptical fashion, to create a mood:

Many mysteries lie along the canoe trails in Canada's Quetico Park. Splashes in the middle of the night. Beaver? Didn't see any dams coming in. Otter? Probably. Bear? Glad we've got the food pack strung up in the tree.
Sound of human voices singing around the bend of the river. The wind? Must be. Haven't seen humans for days. Around the bend. No humans in sight. Pine trees sing, too.

And poetry—at times it can be used in part for humor.
Where do the ideas for style and structure come from? From the reporter's imagination! The variations are limited only by his imagination.
A professional journalist and a master of style was Mr. Franklin A. Rogers, editor-in-chief of the Mankato, Minn., Free Press. As a columnist, he brought to the reader a freshness of style, a twist of viewpoint, a strength of opinion that encouraged avid readership.
One of his favorite devices was the open letter. "Dear Boss," he started many of his columns, and then followed with a semi-humorous, often satirical account of some event, one which he was covering personally. For instance: the national political conventions. In 1964, from the Democratic convention at Atlantic City, N.J., at a moment when no one knew whom President Johnson was going to select as his vice presidential running mate, columnist Rogers filed this report from the "unofficial headquarters" of vice presidential hopeful Hubert Humphrey (he did get the nomination).

It Isn't—But Is—Isn't It?

Atlantic City, N.J.—

DEAR BOSS:

I hope you are not looking for me, because I write to you today from a place that does not exist. I am in the headquarters of Hubert Humphrey for vice president, which is a fictional area on the tenth floor of the Shelburne hotel.
I know these headquarters do not exist, because Senator Humphrey

says so. I was taken to them by a phantom of a man who, before he officially ceased to exist, wanted Senator Humphrey to be president. In his currently ethereal state, he wants the senator to be vice president.

*   *   *

It all came about when I chanced to see this spirit that used to be a man floating along noiselessly in the Shelburne lobby. I tell him that I am looking for a place where I can place my typewriter while pecking at it, and he says he has lots of rooms where Humphrey's campaign headquarters would be, if there was such a thing. The only trouble, he says, is that the rooms are pretty well filled by people who would be Humphrey workers except that there aren't any.

But come along, anyway, he says, and we'll see what we can do.

*   *   *

We subsequently arrive at the tenth floor, where the uniform of a policeman, unfilled no doubt, is guarding the premises. This man, says my spirit of a friend, is okay and you can let him in. All right, replies the policeman's uniform, which, things being what they are, speaks rather plainly.

We look into one room and it is jammed with desks and chairs which, if I didn't know different, I would swear were filled with people. This room will not do, says the spirit, because it is too crowded.

We look into another room and it is the same thing, and into a third and a fourth. If we had a headquarters, it would hold a heck of a lot of people, don't you think inquires my spritely companion. I say I think so and, if I didn't know better, I would swear there were a lot of people there already. That, he replies, is what your imagination can do to you.

Anyway, he says, I guess you can sit at this desk where one of our people would be sitting, if we had any. So I sit down and I write this letter to you.

*   *   *

It is a little lonesome with nobody on the premises which don't exist, anyway. But I really don't mind. Right now I am feeling pretty good because I find it possible to imagine I am doing my work while sitting on the lap of a pretty secretary.

Hoping you are the same, F.R.

Chapter VIII

THE ANECDOTE

During a 0-0 baseball game this season, pitcher Henry Smythe kept begging his team-mates to get him some runs. His pleas were to no avail, and the innings went by 0-0. Finally, in the first half of the 9th inning, Smythe himself hit a homerun, and as he crossed homeplate for a 1-0 lead he was greeted by his centerfielder who growled, "There. You've finally got your run. Now, go on out there and hold 'em."

That, my friend, is an *anecdote*.* It is an incident, a thin slice of life, a dimesworth of action. The word usually is misspelled, variously emerging as antidote, anetdote, and (perhaps, more true than error) anticdote. It is an antic, one which has a point to it, ranging all the way from amusement to amazement to moral.

Anecdotes are eagerly sought after by writers of all kinds. Good anecdotes are hard to find. Magazine writers keep clip files of anecdotes. Newspaper reporters try to extract them from interviews. When someone discovers a worthy anecdote, it is sure to make the rounds of several columns, a Sunday magazine piece or three, and any number of after-dinner speeches. Especially, if the anecdote is a true one.

The writer, in particular, has many uses for anecdotes—for leads, for instance. Let us repeat the anecdote which opened this chapter— and add one more line to the end of it.

During a 0-0 baseball game this season, pitcher Henry Smythe kept begging his team-mates to get him some runs. His pleas were to no avail, and the innings went by 0-0. Finally, in the first half of the 9th inning, Smythe himself hit a homerun, and as he crossed homeplate for a 1-0 lead he was greeted by his centerfielder who growled, "There, you've finally got your run. Now, go on out there and hold 'em."
That is just one example of how pitcher-hitter Smythe, almost alone, has kept the Boston Blue Jackets out of last place in the National League.

You see, that anecdote makes a splendid, *extended lead.** It is interesting to read; it provides a quick reward to the reader (a laugh?); it brings in the 5 W's (Who: Smythe; What: keeps the team going; When: this season, of course; Where: in the National League; How: by hitting and pitching; Why: who really knows?—or cares about the Blue Jackets?). It also sets the theme (more to follow about Smythe, the one-man team). It is immeasurably better than a 5W & H lead because an anecdote, at least, is bright and alive.

No wonder writers seek anecdotes as though they were holy grails.

Anecdotes are versatile, too. They can be used over and over for a

SPACE AND BACKGROUND—No doubt what is happening here. The defense has goofed, and someone has gotten loose to score on a pass—with no one near him. This embarrassing moment is told by submerging number 45 (Jerry Hill of the Baltimore Colts) in space: the filled stadium in the background and the expanse of the end-zone (note the oblique stripe) in the foreground. Cropping down to the player would destroy the story-telling properties; a creative photographer must have a strong sense of news values.

variety of stories. Let's take the Smythe anecdote again, add these final lines, and see how many different themes it can form:

In anger, Smythe stomped off the field and went on a sit-down strike which he has refused to give up for six weeks now.

Which isn't so unusual these days—what with National League pitchers having their greatest hitting year in history. Team-mates have gotten to expect pitchers to carry the whole load.

Which just goes to show how tactless major league centerfielders have gotten this season.

Same anecdote; three endings and three widely different stories.

☞ Anecdotes are like relief pitchers in a way. If they don't start the story, they can be brought in at any point of trouble to try to save the day. An axiom of writing advises that whenever a story sags, or begins to get dull, then bring in an anecdote. It will reawaken the reader and, reinvigorated, send him plunging on.

If a long biographical feature about Smythe bogs down, a quick *transition** will bring the anecdote to the rescue; like this:

Yet, Smythe isn't one of those pitchers who, off the mound, is useless to the team. Far from it. Like the time earlier this season when during a 0-0 game . . . [and back we go to the anecdote]. . . . And he did, too. But Smythe doesn't talk much about the hitting; mostly it's pitching he's interested in . . . [and back to the story].

Artificial device? Maybe. It is like giving an athlete a whiff of oxygen. But it helps pep up the reader.

Anecdotes also make successful conclusions to feature stories, like this one:

All of which goes to prove that Smythe is the most valuable player in the league. Just how much he is depended on is illustrated by a game earlier this season when Smythe, caught in a 0-0 pitching duel, kept begging. . . . [And there it is—the anecdote again.]

In other ways, anecdotes can be used to illustrate a point of opinion, a situation, or a fact. (Opinion: pitchers are the most important members of a team. Situation: Smythe works best under pressure. Fact: Smythe is the leading pitcher in the league in hitting).

Anecdotes can be used to exemplify a moral. In that sense they are like quoting Scriptures or Poor Richard's Almanack or the law to win an argument. (Moral: a man must be self-reliant. Moral: Man must expect not from others what he can do for himself.)

Anecdotes can do everything; they are the handymen of writing. They can dramatize that critical episode in a person's life when a decision is made, a step is taken, or Fate is overtaken and life changes significantly. Suppose Smythe in anger punched the center-fielder, quit baseball, and invested his money in custard stands. Now, he has a string of them and is one of the newest millionaires in the nation, and *Fortune* magazine does a story about him. If the 0-0 episode hadn't happened, he might be nothing more than a minor league manager today—or a salesman of athletic equipment. Yes, that decisive moment (our anecdote) must be told in full.

So you see: anecdotes are so lively that they truly can be called anticdotes.

Think what can be done with this anecdote, picked out of a promotional story from the National Broadcasting Company:

Astronauts Shepard and Grissom were caught speeding in Daytona, north of Cape Canaveral. The policeman asked for Grissom's driver's license. When the officer saw the name, he jokingly asked if he was Grissom the astronaut. When Grissom nodded, the cop said, "Oh, yeah, and I'm Alan Shepard."

"No," Shepard spoke up from the front seat. "I'm Alan Shepard."

There, see how refreshed you are—and now are ready to plunge on to the end of this chapter.

Yet, anecdotes are not omnipotent. They are marred by flaws. If overused, for instance, they can become clichés. Writers of journalism textbooks, for instance, are fanatic about this anecdote, a *cliché* among clichés:

A green reporter was sent out of town by his editor to cover the Johnstown flood. The kid was so overwhelmed by the disaster that he wired back to his editor a story that began, "God sits on the hills and looks down sadly on Johnstown tonight. . . ." His hard-boiled editor cut off the story on the spot and wired back immediately: "Forget flood; interview God." ✸

That anecdote has been used so often, it promotes only mental groans. It has had too many possibilities for its—and the readers'—own good. Thus, anecdotes must be selected—like vegetables—for freshness and firmness.

And, anecdotes must be brief. As in the case of a joke, the punchline must come swiftly.

A pastor delivered a powerful sermon describing the tragedy of being poor and urging the rich to share their wealth.

After the service, a friend asked how the sermon went. Said the minister, "Well, it was partly successful. I convinced the poor."

Anecdotes should be written in narrative style, like an episode in a story, with some action, a little dialogue, a touch of description if possible, and a strong final line.

In a small Kentucky town, the deputy sheriff was touring the courthouse lawn to round up a jury panel. One man volunteered his services immediately.

When the judge entered the courtroom, he spotted the man seated in the jury box. "What's he doing there?" asked the judge.

"He volunteered to serve," answered the deputy.

"Get him out of there," the judge roared. "He's the man on trial."

Anecdotes shouldn't be forced or stretched to fit a theme. They aren't especially elastic.

The policeman who had stopped a woman driver for erratic driving was deeply puzzled when she said, "I was just making an S turn."

He had never heard of an S turn.

"Well, I had started to make a U turn," she explained, "and halfway through I changed my mind."

[Then follows an article about traffic safety, but anecdote and story don't match.]

And, anecdotes must have some muscle to them; no place in writing for the before-type who gets sand kicked into his face.

As for finding anecdotes, the writer must be constantly alert. He can get them from interviews. Whenever the interviewee mentions a likely episode, he can be asked to recall as fully as possibly what happened, who said what, and when. The anecdote, through questions and answers, is pieced together.

Anecdotes pop up during conversations. "That reminds me of the time that . . ." and the talker is introducing an anecdote. That is why sportswriters spend so much time in talk sessions with coaches and players. Good managers and publicity men are always dredging up anecdotes; they get space in the newspapers. For instance, after an especially close game, a sportswriter asked baseball manager Al Lopez what he was thinking about during the critical sixth inning. Lopez rubbed his jaw and answered, "I guess I was thinking up something to tell you writers."

Free-lance feature writers who may suddenly be asked to cover any kind of topic clip likely anecdotes out of newspapers, especially the little one or two paragraph fillers which space out pages. In they go, into the files under neat categories.

Out they come when needed.

SIGNS—Watch for posters, graffiti, and other signs that tell a story, make a whimsical point, provide a powerful background. Here: a makeshift parking lot obviously reserved for . . . Bohanon.

Chapter IX

LEADS

Edgar Allan Poe, as a writer, was a master in many ways—a master of suspense, a master of ratiocination (the hero solves a problem by piecing together clues), and a master of several styles.

And, he was a master in quick-starts to stories. A journalist would say that Poe was a master at leads. Take, for instance, Poe's "The Cask of Amontillado." It starts as follows:

> The thousand injuries of Fortunato I had borne as I best could; but when he ventured upon insult, I vowed revenge. You, who so well know the nature of my soul, will not suppose, however, that I gave utterance to a threat. *At length,* I would be avenged; this was a point definitely settled—but the very definitiveness with which it was revolved, precluded the idea of risk. I must not only punish, but punish with impunity . . .

In one opening paragraph, Poe establishes the mood; he gives the reader a clue as to what is going to happen; and he introduces the characters (Fortunato and "I"). He even says several things about the two characters, some revealing things.

In the second paragraph, Poe suggests the method of death to be used for Fortunato—immolation. In the third paragraph, Poe reveals the method by which the murdered is to be tricked—a trip to a wine cellar. By the fourth paragraph, Poe is past the introduction and into the narrative itself.

In a matter of four paragraphs, Poe introduces his characters, suggests the theme of the story, establishes a style of writing, and snares the reader's interest. In Journalism, those are the qualities of *leads.** In the first few paragraphs, a journalist wants to introduce his topic in a manner designed to interest the reader.

Basically, when the news is straight-forward and factual, and has built-in interest, a straightforward statement is sufficient for the lead. An example:

President Johnson announced Tuesday he will enter Bethesda Naval Hospital Thursday night for removal of a poorly functioning gall bladder. (AP story).

Who, what, when, where and why—all wrapped up neatly and succinctly. It is a straight news lead—a factual lead to be followed by a factual story.

But a feature story exudes a different mood, which must be established in the lead. Remember Poe's short stories? He sets loose the wisps of mood right from the outset.

Here is the first paragraph of Poe's "The Masque of Red Death":

The Red Death had long devastated the country. No pestilence had ever been so fatal, or so hideous. Blood was its Avatar and its seal—the redness and the horror of blood. There were sharp pains, and sudden dizziness, and then profuse bleeding at the pores, with dissolution. The scarlet stains upon the body and especially upon the face of the victim, were the pest ban which shut him out from the aid of and the sympathy of his fellow-men. . . .

Mood closes in from the sixth word "devastated" and continues with "fatal . . . pestilence . . . horror . . . pest," etc.

Likewise, a proper feature story, which draws heavily upon mood and emotion, cannot start seriously and end humorously. Nor can it start tragically and end hilariously. It must present a unified mood, beginning with the lead; for instance, this lead which started a review of the movie, "Pffft!"

"Pffft!" Phooey!

No question about attitude, tone, or mood to come.

And how about these leads, all by student journalists:

A young boa constrictor has arrived by banana boat from South America to fill a four-year vacancy in JM's biology department.

The basketball brother act of Glasrud and Glasrud was disbanded this year after a successful run of three years.

Neither wind nor rain could stop the Rochester track team as it whipped up three records and splashed to their seventh straight district title here May 19.

David Swenson, a JM junior, needed dense smoke in a hurry for his Science Fair project, so he quickly telephoned the Pentagon in Washington.

Each lead has a flair; yet, each presents the elements of the story. Those leads weren't easy to do. Writing a lead is tense business. Because it must be exactly right, it may have to be worked and re-worked. One student journalist, Joel Barker of Rochester, Minn., searched for several hours for a lead to a sports story. On the sixth try, he came close to what he wanted. On the seventh, he found it, as follows:

Although John Marshall High doesn't have to worry about Indians,

Spot Feature—Like the reporter, a photographer can find feature ideas to photograph at most events. At a high school track meet, a photographer saw a youngster, in the infield, pacing himself with the distance runners. The photographer set himself and when the race reached his spot, he snapped the news-feature photograph. No caption is needed; the photograph in itself tells the story. Most spot features involve humor: many, human interest; a few, tragedy.

it still has a scout . . . in the person of 10th grade English teacher George Parkinson. For the last 10 years, Parkinson has been scouting other football teams so that the Rochester Rockets can be better prepared to meet their opponents.

According to Joel, once the lead was written, the rest of the story fell into place. Every journalist can testify to similar experiences. If the lead establishes theme, mood, and structure, the rest of the story will follow on it naturally.

(Incidentally, Joel's story was named the best sport story written by a high school journalist in the nation in 1962. The selection was made jointly by the American Newspaper Publishers Association and the Columbia Scholastic Press Association.)

Walk into a newspaper office—note the reporter poised, hands alert, over the typewriter. Nothing happens. Five minutes later, he is still poised. And nothing happens. Chances are 10-1 he is caught on a lead.

Walk into the den of a magazine writer. He is slumped onto his desk, snowballs of paper littering the floor around him. Chances are 20-1 he is trapped by a lead.

Writers of headache commercials have missed a sure bet!

The importance of leads was stressed by Mr. Earl J. Johnson, former editor of United Press International, who wrote this in 1964 in *The U. P. I. Reporter:*

Lead sentences in news stories deserve as much attention as lead sentences in other good writing. The best lead is usually the one that makes one simple, declarative statement. If a writer can capture the essence of his story in a short sentence and not louse it up with more than a single thought he is off to a good start. He has caught his reader's attention.

Edward Gibbon was quoted as saying that once he got the first sentence of "The History of the Decline and Fall of the Roman Empire" the rest followed. This was his first sentence:

"In the second century of the Christian era, the empire of Rome comprehended the fairest part of the earth, and the most civilized portion of mankind."

Contrary to popular belief Gibbon's "Decline and Fall" is not difficult to read. It's a long story but not as involved as many dispatches we see on front pages. People who think Gibbon is difficult probably have old copies set in fine print.

The first seven sentences of "Decline and Fall" average slightly more than 18 words each. The author's paragraphs are too fat for the narrow columns of a newspaper but inside the paragraphs he knew how to use periods.

This reference to Gibbon was cited recently in our own ceaseless campaign for shorter sentences.

A fully experienced teacher and writer has described the challenge of leads this way: "The lead is always hell in any magazine piece because you have to break the psychic ice. You sit down with a dreadful piece of blank paper, and your notes stacked beside you, and then awful frustration of mind and matter begins. This is the worst moment in writing."

Especially, in writing leads to feature stories and magazine articles which should be original and most creative.

They do fall into certain categories. The *dramatic lead*, for instance:

Fred Cox stood in the shadows of Metropolitan Stadium late Sunday, poised for a field goal which would upset the World Champions, the Green Bay Packers. The kicking expert for the Minnesota Vikings stood slightly to the right of the goal posts, just 13 yards away. The attempt appeared to be routine, no more difficult than kicking an extra point.

But Cox didn't make it!

From that point, the story is easy to tell. Why didn't he make it? What events led up to this dramatic situation? What did Cox say later about the kick? And his coaches and the opposition? After a transition, the writer brings in other aspects of the game, and a football feature-summary is finished.

The dramatic lead serves well its several purposes. Mainly, it forms a picture in the reader's mind, puts him on the spot, and encourages him to read on. At the same time, it establishes the 5 W's of the story.

Look at this lead from a student story about Student Council elections:

Tom Mahler, a JM junior, leaned against the gray, block wall outside room 3-101. He shuffled his feet and waited for the recount of ballots which would decide whether he was the new JM Student Council president.

Inside the room, 14 students sorted the ballots for the second time. . . .

Well, you can see the story looming. A pattern of narration is established which can be maintained throughout most of the newsfeature.

Here is a dramatic lead from *The New York Times:*

Saigon—The four silver United States Air Force Thunderchiefs were over Muygia Pass, 75 miles north of the 17th parallel on the remote North Vietnamese-Laotian frontier.

It was 2:30 p.m. last Wednesday, and the F-105 pilots had almost completed their bombing mission—bombing the road that leads through the pass and strafing the trucks that were carrying war materiel along it.

Ground fire was intense, but the pilots were dodging the 57-mm. antiaircraft shells with considerable success. Suddenly, one orange burst tore at the tail of the third Thunderchief in the formation.

"It was a shot in a million," said the pilot of the plane. . . .

And thus the story of a pilot shot down and perilously rescued is started. In this lead, study the precision of details. They are specific —and exact, proof that the creative journalist respects reality.

The dramatic lead can do many things. It can narrate action (such as the pilot being shot down) or it can be mostly descriptive:

The sun, sitting low on its haunches, leans back against the horizon and glares across the practice field of the Minnesota Gophers. It is 3:40 p.m. during a sultry, September late-afternoon. At the far end of the field, a handful of coaches and managers cast long shadows as they play touch football. . . . [The beginning of a feature story about a typical college football practice.]

The dramatic lead can consist mostly of dialogue.

San Francisco (AP)—"Todd doesn't smile much," said the nurse, "but he's been waiting for you."

The lanky young man looked at the skinny little boy and picked him up.

"He's heavy with those braces on his legs," the nurse said.

"Not for me, he's not," said Gary Barnes, an end from Clemson.

Forty-eight of the finest football players in the game . . . visited the Shrine Hospital for Crippled Children Thursday . . .

Yes, the dramatic lead is versatile, but so are the other kinds of popular feature leads.

For instance, there is the *surprise lead*. In pointing out something unusual, it tries to draw the reader into a trap. The lead starts him thinking in a normal pattern, and then when he is comfortably underway, shocks him . . . or at least surprises him.

The sultry-looking brunette sat on the diving board, dripping with water. She picked up a gadget, turned on the juice, and she was dry.

A 29-year-old mother gave birth to a son on a moving subway train during the rush hour yesterday morning. It was the fifth birth for Mrs. James Marston, but the subway system's first.

The leading building material in New York City is not steel, cement or glass. It is graft.

Another popular feature lead—*the punch lead*—belts the reader on the chin. It wastes no time. Like a Joe Louis left, it comes in intent on a first-round knockout.

"Shoot me, if you dare."
And a Colton youth shook his long, blond tresses in anger, turned his back to two drawn police guns, and walked away.

"Earthquakes are so terrible. They give you a strange swaying feeling as you are thrown to the floor—to wait for something else to happen." That is how Hernon Perez, an exchange student from Chile, started to explain. . . .

(Lead to a feature about a deer hunter) "He just came thumping along and I drilled him."

Just three seniors have survived what school officials call "the toughest course in the curriculum."

In Nashville, they tell about the country musician who was asked if he could read music. "Sure," he replied, "but not enough to hurt my playing. [From *The National Observer*]

• And then there is the *lead of allusion,* the one which makes reference to history and to literature—and to contemporary events:

A State Fair blue ribbon for student artist John Dilley is as certain as death, taxes, and Yankee pennants.

Flags are blooming today—like the poppies row on row. [Feature for Flag Day.]

The bread that local residents cast on the Saugutuck River has come back to haunt them.

And *the gadget lead* which is more inventive than creative:

CLOVIS, N.M. Dec. 30—A man dressed in western hat and boots drove a late model auto to a used car lot here and took a newer one out for a road test. When he didn't come back, police discovered the car he left had been stolen from a lot in Amarillo, Texas. Amarillo officers found that the car left there had been stolen from a lot at Lubbock, Texas. Police at Lubbock determined that a car the man left there was taken off a lot at Hobbs, N.M. Hobbs police were trying to find out where the car left there came from.

A stupendous, sensational, colossal feat that defied the imagination was performed here yesterday by the International Hippodrome Circus. It opened.

The lead can draw on the power of *a figure of speech;* generally simile or metaphor:

On the theory that two—and maybe more—can live cheaper than one, the nation's rail lines have been aflutter in recent years with earnest proposals of corporate marriage. (From *The National Observer*)

A tremendous bill for surgery for the face and figure of Alaska was in prospect today.

Like Joshua at the battle of Jericho, John F. Kennedy Friday night marched around and around blowing a mighty trumpet. But it was questionable whether the walls would readily come tumbling down.

* Or it can be *direct address,* a statement to the reader:

Something lacking in your lettuce or heavy atoms in your hash may be getting you down, a panel of scientists suggested yesterday.

And there is the good, old, simple statement which in itself introduces the feature element; however, in this case, no mood exists in the lead:

Most students have never heard of Brazzaville; yet, senior Tony Harris must become an expert about its current foreign policy. [Feature about preparations for a model UN assembly.]

Well, feature leads are as prolific as the imagination is powerful. But most of them, unfortunately, should be colored yellow—for Caution. Remember the earlier advice that a feature writer, being free from restraint, must exercise greater discipline? It applies to leads, too.

A feature writer must be sure that what he calls a lead does not *mislead.* How? Let us count the ways they can mislead:

By bringing in editorial comment—or, in nonjournalistic language, bringing in personal opinion. One of the most controversial leads was written by Damon Runyon about the execution of Sacco and Vanzetti: "They're frying Sacco and Vanzetti in the morning." It wasn't used.

By concentrating upon a minor point in the story because it, in itself, is sensational and the main story isn't.

By setting up a premise which usually doesn't exist: The lead usually starts with an "If" or a "Suppose that" or a "—doesn't really exist, but."

By being sarcastic or silly or nonsensical when the subject matter doesn't warrant such extreme treatment.

By using a figure of speech, unfamiliar to the reader.

Hyperbole (exaggerating for purpose) is especially dangerous, mainly because most readers interpret it literally. It requires sophistication for a reader to interpret figuratively.

By not really introducing the principal topic of the feature.

By being fictionalized in part or in entirety just to be readable.

The road to good feature leads is mined, booby-trapped, tortuous to boot and threatened by predatory animals. That is why many trips are started over it, before one is completed.

But lead, a feature writer must. And when he writes a readable one, he feels the little tug of a medal on his tunic. Such as in the case of this one:

A new spy mystery of the U-2 variety flew out of Turkey yesterday but crashed into a wall of official silence in Washington.

(David Wise in the *New York Herald Tribune*)

CONTRASTS—Not only white building and black car contrast, but idea of church contrasts with modern sports car. Look for white and black in the same picture; also contrasts in themes and subjects. Note reflections in the car hood.

Chapter X

USING QUOTES

Canadian Geese Following Miss Kloos?
It's Due to Her New Chair and Horn

By TERRI MILLIKAN

Miss Phyllis Kloos, JM Spanish teacher, is back in a wheel chair—the second time in three years.

Two years ago she tripped one morning before school and spent the next five weeks teaching from a wheel chair.

The more recent accident occurred Feb. 4 in front of the Mayo clinic.

Here is the way Miss Kloos described her accident:

"I was in a cab on the way down to the Methodist hospital to get a lung x-ray to see if I was over pneumonia and to see how it would feel to get on my feet for a change (she had been sick in bed for over a week), but it didn't last long,'" she started her narrative.

"The cab I was in was third in a group of three cars. By the time the first car had taken off after the crash, we were in no shape to follow him. The girl behind him had stopped suddenly to avoid hitting him, and the cab driver couldn't stop and rammed into the rear of the girl's car.

"The cab driver informed me later that it cost $500 to repair the cab. Of course, most of this is merely hearsay. I didn't stick around taking notes afterwards.

"The impact of the crash had thrown me off the seat and my toe had gone under the back of the front seat, the ankle following. As there was actually no room for the ankle, it was really quite painful. I yanked it out with considerable effort, sobbed quietly for a few minutes while the policemen asked all their questions. Then I took another cab to the Methodist where I was told to come back for x-rays the following Tuesday.

"I returned on Tuesday to find that my foot was broken, and the doctors advised me to spend the next two weeks in bed. This was a poor idea as far as I was concerned so I convinced them to let me try bandages and a wheel chair for a week.

105

"Until I got my motorized wheel chair it was quite tiring. But now there is nothing to it. After a few driving lessons I learned how to stop before ramming into something. The fast speed isn't too bad."

One of her students recently brought her a bicycle horn to honk at any pedestrians who might get in her way.

"It sounds like a duck call," she said. "I'll probably have mallards or Canadian geese following me around."

Critic and author Kenneth Rexroth was telling about dictating a book. "I like the way it came out . . . there's this sense of talk . . . it makes nice disheveled reading."

We doubt that disheveled reading is automatically the result of talk in a story; we do know that readers like the way it comes out of the page. One sure way of giving impact to a story is to use dialogue. It lends a sense of it-really-happened-that-way. It appeals to the ear, which in most cases is more practiced and alert than the eye. It has the sound of authority: "If he's the expert and he said it that way, it must be so." It is vital to episodic writing.

Call it a quote—or conversation—or dialogue—it sits to the right hand of the feature writer.

Such is the case of the short feature opening this chapter. The student, a high school senior, was asked to interview a teacher who had been confined to a motorized wheel chair. The student, wisely deciding that the teacher narrated the story in a style which, in itself, was highly readable, served as stenographer and used mostly quotes in the story. The reporter let the person interviewed tell the story.

Journalists do the same thing with such colorful talkers as the famous pitcher Dizzy Dean. Who else but Diz himself could say about an injured Mickey Mantle sitting out the game, "You can hurt yourself easier by being hurt than by going out thar on the playin' field." So, Mr. Reporter, let him talk. Such as when Diz gets rattled while broadcasting a baseball game: "That loads the Brooklyn Dodgers fulla bases." Or when he describes the seventh inning stretch: "Well, the fans has all stood up and woosht the Yankees good luck."

Yes, Diz makes "nice, disheveled reading." And he is quoted verbatim because he tells a story better than his recording journalists can. If the one interviewed is a creative talker, then the reporter lets him have the floor.

Such as baseball manager Casey Stengel who, as a commentator during the World Series, criticized a batter who leaned over the plate: "He who bows his fanny doth not hit too much." Or when the Gemini 8 astronauts were interviewed after their near-disastrous flight in March, 1966, one of them said, "It's just utterly fantastic up there."

Here is another quote—memorable, arguable, or just talkable:

Russian novelist Mikhail Sholokho after winning a Nobel prize, talking about foreign critics of Russian writers: "I would like to address foreign advocates of the calumniators: Don't worry, dears, over the safety of criticism in our country. We support and develop criticism. But slander is not criticism and mud from a puddle not paint from the artists's palette." (As reported by Stuart H. Loory in the *New York Herald Tribune.*)

Quotes must be used with discrimination and with purpose. When they are colorful, as in the case of Stengel's, they demand to be used —fully.

Also, when the quotes express something controversial, they should be used: Here is Major Donald E. Keyhoe, United States Marine Corps retired, speaking at a press conference (as reported by Associated Press): "There is substantial evidence we are being observed by some sort of device which is far more advanced than anything we have and is controlled by a superior civilization."

What Keyhoe says should be quoted; it certainly will be requoted by readers in their daily conversations!

Quotes should also be used when they fit these categories:

When they express something not likely to be believed by the reader. Better let the words be the speaker's and the disbelief be turned toward him, not toward the reporter. Major Keyhoe again: "These things (unidentified flying objects) are real and under intelligent control."

When they express an opinion of the one interviewed.

When they express something momentous, highly significant to the news, such as a political figure announcing his candidacy.

When they express something technical and therefore difficult to simplify for the reader, such as a scientist discussing a potential cure for cancer.

When they express something which may be in error (again, better let the source of the possible misstatement take the blame).

Quotes also are used to sustain a pattern of dialogue in a story:

As in September, 1965, when reporter Stuart H. Loory was trying to track down in Moscow a rumor that Premier Khrushchev was in the hospital. Here is part of his story:

> The two newsmen were challenged by the doorkeeper at the apartment house yesterday morning. "There is no one there (Khrushchev's apartment); they are all at the dacha," she said.
>
> "When did you see Mr. Khrushchev last?" a reporter asked.
>
> She answered: "He's sick. He's in the hospital."
>
> "How long has he been in the hospital?"
>
> "For more than a month," she answered.
>
> Then she said Mrs. Khrushchev had last visited the fifth-floor apartment about a week ago.

In Loory's estimation, the dialogue is so important in helping the reader decide the credibility of the story, he reproduces it completely.

Otherwise, if a quote has no particular value, it should be discarded—most of them have to be. At the rate of 120 spoken words per minute, a short, 15-minute interview could produce 1,500 words. In transcription, that would equal two galleys of type—a story too long by newspaper standards.

The reporter must therefore evaluate quotes and use only those which have worth. Other information can be summarized in indirect quotes.

The whittling process begins on the spot with the interview. The reporter through experience develops a quickness of identification whereby he can size up the news value of a quote as it is being delivered. He tags it as important and writes it as extensively as possible in his notes. In some manner, he marks it as a direct quote— he may star it or underline it or surround it, as normal, with quote marks. Some put parentheses around direct quotes. Others place them far to the left margin of their notes, and other nonquote material is indented to the right.

Whatever the process, at the end of the interview, the reporter has in his notes several direct quotes, maybe never more than 100 words. These are the best and most important words the interviewee spoke.

The interviewee's other comments have been discarded as valueless, or have been grouped and summarized in the reporter's words at several points in the notes.

If the reporter has a practical ear for quotes, most of his noted, direct quotes will be used in the story. If not, he must further winnow them, from notes to final story.

At all costs, the reporter wants to use only readable quotes. To overuse them, or to use weak ones, would be to blunt one of his most reliable writing tools.

A blonde, pert, energetic high school senior was faced with that problem of whittling down quotes one spring day. She set out to interview a most quotable person, Jack Benny. At the hotel room, she and several professional newsmen were met at the door by Mr. Benny, who proceeded to hand out cigars. "Here, I guess you can use one, too," he said to Karen.

Space for that issue of the newspaper was limited, so Karen was asked to do a tight story. She reduced quotes to a minimum; included some indirect quotes; added description and color; and worked in the 5 W's of the story.

Here it is, given immediacy and life by quotes:

Violinist, 39, Is . . .

Lyrical About Music, Liarical about His Age

by KAREN MILLER

Strains of violin music came from under the door of the Skyline suite at the Kahler hotel in Rochester.

The scales and chords were gentle and full and came from a 200-year-old Stradivarius.

A few minutes later, the door was opened by a quiet man dressed in sports shirt and slacks and wearing black velvet slippers. The violin was lying on the bed.

Jack Benny was in town.

He was scheduled for a checkup at the Mayo clinic. "I feel about as good as I always do," he told reporters clustered in his room. "I never have a checkup when I feel bad. I won't want to know what's wrong with me. I don't want any worries."

He was more interested in talking about his violin.

He said he practices a little bit every day. "You even have to practice to be bad," he said. In reality, he is an accomplished violinist and has been invited to play with the Minneapolis Symphony Orchestra. "I have a ball doing my concerts."

Jack Benny didn't learn to play the violin in high school. He attended high school for only one year and is probably the only high school drop-out to have a high school named after him. In Waukegan, Ill., recently, a new high school was dedicated to him.

In speaking about teenagers, he told reporters, "My only message to high school students is to do better than I did. I want them to really learn something."

Then he talked of many things.

About his lack of mechanical dexterity: "If a light goes out in one of my rooms, I'm the kind of guy who wants to buy a new house."

About his age: He's not 39, but 68. "That's how you stay young . . . lie."

About sick humor: "There are only a couple sick comedians. I'm not even sure what sick humor is."

About Jack Paar: "Jack is one of the most versatile men in show business . . . no one else in show business could do the job Paar is doing."

Karen was careful to immortalize in print Mr. Benny's exact words. She knew that creativity in journalism does not mean to make up or rearrange quotes. A quote is an inviolable substance. It must remain pure in nature as long as it is identified with these marks: "   ". Any words falling between quotation marks must be exact to what the speaker said.

No, no changing of quotes to purify the speaker's public image. If you want to use a quote that is ungrammatical or that is certain to get the speaker in trouble, reread it to him and ask if he objects to your using it. Can you imagine changing the words of Cassius Clay or Harry Truman or Malcolm Muggeridge—or of Dizzy Dean to: "The fans all have stood and have wished the Yankees *'bien vida.*" It just ain't Diz. Or changing President Truman's words to: "If you can't tolerate the heat, then you'd better get the dickens out of the kitchen."

No, no changing of quotes to make them sound better, to give them added punch. The creativity of journalism lies not in fictionalizing quotes, but in recognizing them in their natural form and using them.

If, for any reason, you don't want to use a direct quote as spoken, then summarize it in indirect form: For example:

Direct quote: (Baseball manager Johnny Pesky about the hazards of managing) "The one thing you know when you're a manager is that someday you're going to be fired. It has to happen. Every man who ever managed was fired sooner or later, unless he owned part of the club."

Changed to indirect quote: According to Pesky, every manager can expect eventually to be fired. The only ones who escape are those who own part of the club, he said.

The indirect quote covers more ground in fewer words. It also gives the writer a chance to avoid using a direct quote if something is wrong with it.

There's enough trouble to quoting interviewees without revamping what they say. One of the migraines of the profession is the outcry of, "I was misquoted!" If the reporter took liberties with direct quotes, chances are the complainant was misrepresented. If the reporter listened carelessly, chances are the complainant was misunderstood. If the reporter didn't ask that confusing statements be explained, chances are the complainant was misinterpreted. If the interviewee was tricked into making irrational statements, chances are he was misled. If some minor point he made was enlarged by putting it into the lead of the story, chances are he was misjudged. If the interviewee talked too glibly, chances are he misspoke or was mistaken.

It all comes out, "I was misquoted!"

So quotes must be meticulously noted; they must be intelligently summarized; they must be constantly double-checked during or after the interview with the source; and *they must be used for purpose*.

In return for careful use, they form the lyrics of journalistic writing—unless they are badly fragmented, that is. Somewhere in the annals of bad advice to writers, someone suggested that quotes should be stripped down to phrases, to bits and pieces. A concentrated power should result, like a clenched fist. Don't believe it! Fragmentary quotes, taken out of context become distorted, and often are blown up out of proportion. They are hard to follow in a sentence pattern. Look at this series of shattered quotes:

(The police commissioner of New York is talking about review boards): He said "a board of second-guessers" would further undermine police morale and discipline, which already were poor because of "undeserved criticism."

Mr. Murphy declared that police across the country were "caught squarely in the middle" of the tension aroused by the Negro struggle for equal rights and were "deeply resentful" of the "campaign of vilification" that had been directed against them from both sides of the controversy.

Impossible to read accurately? Dishonest in use of quotes? For one thing, every time a " appears, the reader must turn a switch which takes him from nonquoted to quoted matter. Here the one interviewed talks; here he doesn't; here he is talking; here he isn't. It is impossible to adjust to so many fragmentations.

Secondly, the direct quotes and the reporter's words are interwoven to form a crazy pattern. The sentence either sounds all quote or all nonquote. What results is a third type of quote—the direct indirection. The reporter takes over, giving his source an occasional chance to break into the monologue. One managing editor calls it, "An elusive dodging in and out of quotes."

Quotes, therefore, are best used fully, and in context.

A couple other points about quotes:

Only once in a while do they make good leads. In most instances, they aren't tough enough or comprehensive enough to introduce a topic. If a quote is strong enough for the lead, it is strong enough to be memorable.

And quotes must be attributed to a source: Henry Smythe said.

Or, if the quote is taken from a formal statement: Henry Smythe stated.

Or, if added as an afterthought to another statement: Henry Smythe added.

Or, if expressing the speaker's final conclusion (not necessarily his final word): Henry Smythe concluded.

In most cases, simply, Henry Smythe said. Never Henry Smythe grinned; but, he said it with a grin. Never Henry Smythe chuckled (a strange way of talking), but Henry Smythe said and then chuckled.

Basically, Henry Smythe said . . . unless *true to the action and tone of voice* Henry Smythe shouted or repeated or exclaimed or emphasized by pointing his finger at the crowd.

Be cautious with verbs of attribution. Or don't you remember the days of the Tom Swifties:

"I've found a mistake in the answer key," the teacher remarked.

"I'm gonna parachute before we crash," Tom explained.

"Give me the door chimes now and I'll pay later," Tom bellowed.

Unintentionally, attributive verbs can be just as ridiculous.

Another prescription for curing the ailments of quotes: be sure to indicate when and where something was said—and in what mood and in what tone of voice. For instance, a girl running for vice-president of the student body was quoted as worrying about the boy running on the same ticket for president. The story goes as follows:

. . . Hours later, on her way to campaign alone at another dormitory, she said, "If he doesn't win, I'll kill myself."

Did she say it seriously . . . jokingly . . . . sarcastically? The meaning of this statement lies in her mood and in her tone of voice. Without reporting that information, the quote is useless.

But, don't worry. It is getting the quote that counts most. Just as our professional reporter did in the closing piece to this chapter. After

INFORMALITY—Especially when a person's portrait is going to be used with a feature story, informality should be the key to the photograph. It can be achieved easily by photographing the individual in his own environment, or with something symbolic—something with which he feels relaxed. That is what Russel Mur did to get this photograph of a college student at a time when motorcycles had become the fashion. (Photo by Russel Mur)

the professional football St. Louis Cardinals had defeated the Minnesota Vikings, the reporter visited the Cards' locker room. He talked to the coach, to players. He listened; he observed; he noted descriptive material. He used "quotables." And he put it all together for this Monday morning *quote story:*

The Last Laugh

Cards Get Their Revenge

Bloomington, Minn.—Coach Wally Lemm of the St. Louis Cardinals reached to the bottom of the bag of clichés.

"He who laughs last laughs best," he said with a trace of invective.

His team had just walloped the Minnesota Vikings 56-14 Sunday at Metropolitan stadium.

A month ago, the Vikings had gleefully trimmed the Cards 35-0 during a pre-season exhibition.

Lemm referred bitterly to that 35-0 score. "They yakked it up along the sidelines . . . I don't go for that stuff."

So he confined himself Sunday to a few quiet clichés as he perched on a red trunk in the Cards' locker room, cigaret in one hand and bottle of pop in the other.

Lemm said he wasn't surprised at the change of events. A month ago, the Vikings had caught the Cards at an awkward time. "For one thing," Lemm counted on his fingers, "we didn't have our regular guard, Ken Gray, in there. We had a rookie in. Gray is back and has helped us tremendously."

He made it known once again that he considers Gray the best guard in the conference.

"Second, we had just broken training camp and were unsettled," Lemm explained.

He spoke quietly and efficiently. He is short, a little stout, and wears black-rimmed glasses. He looks more like a popular history teacher than a professional football coach.

Last year, at this time, the Cards had lost three of four games.

Today, they have won three of four and are tied for second place in the Eastern Division.

In fact, the Cards are one quarter away from a first place tie with Cleveland and an unbeaten season.

That bad quarter happened last week: Pittsburgh got 17 points in the final quarter to defeat the Cards 23-10.

Lemm explained that quarter. "Three very unfortunate penalties hurt us. One cost us a touchdown. One cost us at least another score of some kind . . . The third was a defensive penalty . . . set up a touchdown for them."

The Cardinal coach tried to account for last year's poor showing and this year's success. "We had a good ball club last year, although we have more depth this year. We didn't get the breaks."

He checked off a list of injuries to key men.

"We were young, too," he continued. "And maybe the boys didn't quite understand what I was after . . ."

Last year was his first as Cardinal head coach.

"And, of course, we didn't come up with Charlie Johnson until late in the season."

Johnson sat across the locker room, rolling a pair of sweat socks. He had been phenomenal against the Vikings, completing 16 of 25 passes for 301 yards and three touchdowns.

He looked up to answer a question from Lemm, then went back to his socks.

Lemm slid off the red trunk. The trunk was plastered with great white letters: "Property of the St. Louis Cardinals."

Lemm looked around the locker room. He smiled at the prospects of success tranquilly.

#

Most interview stories seem to fall into a pattern deadly dull and so mechanical as to lack individuality—and no two interviews really are alike. They consist of paragraphs of quotes strung together. Some textbooks even advise students to alternate direct-quote paragraphs with nondirect-quote paragraphs. Like much textbook advice, it is bad!

Interviews also consist of setting, of action, of interchange between persons, of tones of voice, of nuance of words, and so on. All this as part of the complete report should be included in the story.

Note the "other" material in the story above. HOW THINGS WERE SAID: "he said with a trace of invective." DESCRIPTION: ". . . as he perched on a red trunk in the Cards' locker room, cigaret in one hand and bottle of pop in the other." HOW THE PERSON INTER-VIEWED LOOKED: "He is short, a little stout, and wears black-rimmed glasses." ACTION: "He looked up to answer a question."

All this provides the Dramatic Interview, not just the routine, mechanical interview story. It combines what was said, how it was said, where it was said, what went on while it was said—into a multi-dimensional report.

Chapter XI

THE HUMAN INTEREST FEATURE

How the Student Does It

By BOB KRATTLI

As matter of factly as though he were describing a Sunday school picnic, the president of ZAPU in the United States discussed the events which will be tomorrow's headlines.

Sikhanyiso (pronounced Sick-han-yee-so) Duke Ndlovu leafed through a mimeographed newsletter labeled "The Zimbaway Sun" and pointed to a long list of names. Beside the names was printed a list of what they had done to become newsworthy: One had dynamited a train; another had bombed a welfare office.

"There is an attitude in the West that the Africans are docile—are not active in protests against the UDI," Duke said. As he spoke, the softly booming vowels rolled like a mellow jungle drum—a drum like those which were frequently heard by Duke's father, a drum like those which were the principal means of communication for Duke's grandfather.

"You can see from the paper here"—Duke indicated the Sun—"that we are now dedicated to violence as the method of destroying the Smith regime." Then he picked up some snapshots. "This is the detention camp in which I was held for six months. Here," as he indicated a handsome, heavy-set man, "is Joshua Nkomo, our leader. On the left is the minister of education-to-be."

ZAPU, the name of Duke's party, is an abbreviation for "Zimbaway African People's Union." Zimbaway is the African name for Southern Rhodesia—the real name, according to Duke. Duke is in Syracuse at the expense of ZAPU and the Afro-American Institute. He is studying sociology in preparation for assuming a position in the government-to-be of Mr. Nkomo.

Duke, 29, is reluctant to speak about his life. He seems to be interested only in talking about today—now. Duke spent his early childhood at a missionary station near the city of Bulowayo. His father was a missionary-

116

trained teacher. At 16, Duke went to South Africa's University of Natal and studied there until the University Apartheid Act forced him to leave.

After returning to Bulowayo, he became a welfare officer for the Bulowayo city council. Social services there were services in name only. Duke described the conditions: "Social problems in townships were not catered to whatsoever. If a man would fail to pay rent—because of unemployment which is rife, or because of the political situation in the country, he would be just evicted from his house; the children would starve. No attempts were made to find out the real socio-economic position of the people."

Duke described his position then as "at loggerheads" with the administration. As a result, he continued, "That led to my detention for six months at a remote desert area near the Portuguese border, about 400 miles from Bulowayo." Duke has a snapshot of his wife and three-year-old son visiting him at the camp.

Upon release from imprisonment, Duke worked several months for his party in and near Zimbaway, at one time writing for a revolutionary newspaper. Then he began his travels, the purpose of which he describes thus: "I felt I would contribute to my country by painting the world a picture of what is taking place there."

That the ZAPU is serious—that they are playing for keeps—is obvious from the reports of terrorism and violence which come daily out of Rhodesia. But how long will ZAPU be on the outside, looking in?

In Duke's answer to that question lies the reason for his being a "newsmaker of tomorrow." As he puts it: "An attempt will be made within six months to establish majority rule in Zimbaway. If we should fail to oust Smith within six months, it will mean a much longer delay—which we do not anticipate."

News is made by nature, or it is made by man. Mostly, it is made by man. And even when nature makes the news—tornado, earthquake, freak of weather, animal—it is of importance mainly because of its effect upon man. It follows that news can be best told through man, either how he has been touched by the news (as caught in a tornado) or how he has made the news (as committing a crime). Therefore, the creative journalist tries to report the news through the eyes of a man. Essayist E. B. White once phrased the idea this way: "Don't write about man; write about a man."

And that is what student Bob Krattli did in the feature which introduced this chapter. In the United States, at a time when Rhodesian politics had reached the stage of revolution, Krattli found on his campus an exile, a Rhodesian whose comments could reveal the nature of some of Rhodesia's problems. Krattli interviewed Sikhanyiso Duke Ndlovu, and then let the reader see the interview.

Telling about people in the news is old as communication. Chaucer did so in Canterbury Tales. So did the minstrel and the balladeer. So does, more and more, the modern journalist. James Gordon Bennett, a century ago the editor of *The New York Herald,* the first really successful mass-circulated newspaper, stressed man-in-the-news. Bennett once wrote: "An editor must always be with the people—think with them—feel with them—and he need fear nothing, he will always be right."

If a tornado sweeps a town, the disaster can be told most movingly by someone who survives it. Similarly, for most stories, there exists a man who can tell about the news; if "the proper study of mankind is man," then the journalist had best concentrate on man.

The point is illustrated by a film about reporting, "The Unique Advantage," produced by *Look* magazine. In it, a reporter-photographer team is assigned to a story about high school dropouts and their return to vocational education. They choose the case-study technique. Through the experiences and comments of one student, typical, they tell the story of all. With the comments of one person, they include the facts and ideas they have to report. It makes a readable story, because man likes to read about man.

In the feature opening this chapter, reporter Krattli shows an aspect of the Rhodesian revolution. In parts, he quotes the one interviewed. He describes the interviewee quickly. He briefly backgrounds the situation in Rhodesia. But, mostly, he is concerned with the interviewee.

Another student journalist, after a series of assaults on women at an Eastern university had led to the stationing of security officers in remote parts of the campus, decided to interview one of the guards whose lonely all-night vigil illustrated the state of fear and insecurity. Here is some of the story:

During the evening Corrigan usually stands at the head of the stairs where he can see everyone who comes up. There isn't much else he can do except think, or, if it is cold, walk up and down the steps to keep circulation going. . . .

Leaning against a railing while lighting a cigarette, he explained,

"There used to be a lot of characters just wandering around for kicks." Since he has been working nights, however, he hasn't seen anyone who doesn't belong there. . . .

And when the evening ends—what then? "I feel a little better when it gets up around curfew. I think about getting home, saying hello to my wife, and having a cup of coffee."

Suddenly, the news is more meaningful. Because of violence on the campus, security patrols are necessary, and the story of one such patrolman symbolizes the situation. Straight facts could never have the impact of the revelations of a man on guard.

Thus, the *newsmaker story* should be frequent to publications. The newsmaker feature is used by *Time* magazine for cover stories. *The New York Times* calls attention each day to "The Man in the News," who may vary from Santa Claus to Sheriff Jim Clark of Selma, Alabama, to a little Negro girl deprived of school during a Bronx teachers' strike. Each is a profile and seeks to document the news.

A student publication should publish its own "man in the news." When a teacher writes a book, he should be interviewed. So should winners of science fairs and Miss Homemaker contests—the fact of winning is not so interesting as the how and why of winning. The news story of election results can be accompanied by a story about the new president of the student body. The annual, all-school musical can be promoted through a story about the experiences of the actor who has the lead. A student strike against Food Services should be accompanied by a newsmaker story about the strike leader, or about the head of Food Services, or about both. Editors and reporters must examine every story for its human involvement and assign newsmaker features whenever possible. And remember: the feature is placed next to, or under, the main news story. Thus, a package is created, two stories (and maybe photographs) to report in depth the same event.

Besides the newsmaker, there are other kinds of stories of human involvement. There is the case-study . . . telling a story by using one person as typical of the group. We have already discussed it.

And, third, there is the *human interest feature*. Much that is newsworthy does not have importance nor timeliness. A man collects a ball of string which, as it mushrooms, must be moved from drawer to closet to bedroom to out-of-doors until it obscures the house. The

ball of string doesn't affect the course of human events; it doesn't
even touch the lives of the readers of the newspaper. The story
doesn't fit definitions of news, but readers are interested in it: Why
the ball of string?

Such features have a place in publications, whenever a student or
teacher collects the odd, does the unexpected, advocates the unusual,
experiences the unaccustomed.

(1) The newsmaker profile, (2) the case-study, (3) the human-
interest feature—all are methods of telling news through human involvement. They all represent a philosophy of reporting which de-
clares, "For news that is readable, study the man who makes news."

But in telling about man, avoid the pitfalls:
• Don't try to tell about a person's life in chronological order; it lacks
emphasis.
• Don't turn a lifetime into a dossier of facts and dates; it takes the
living out of life.
• Don't report one side of a person's life.
• Don't try to bring in too many subtopics.
• Don't interview the subject in a vacuum.

Which means, first of all, don't try to tell the story as it happened
first to last. Just as a sportswriter shouldn't start a football summary
with the news, "East high kicked off to start the game," the feature
writer shouldn't start a profile piece with the fact of birth: "Henry
Smythe was born Jan. 12, 1929." Unfortunately, chronological order
is easy to organize, that is why it is used too frequently. *But it lacks
emphasis.* What reader wants to suffer 40 years of dullness to reach
the 41st year of discovery, of prestige, of achievement. There, in mid-
life, is where the story should begin.

And don't clutter the story with irrelevant facts, like the dossier in
an employer's file. A listing of jobs held, awards won, organizations
joined, offspring named, promotions earned—most of it is dull. The
reporter must find out more than what has been done; he wants to
know *how* something was done—and *why.* Ask how, ask why. Report
how and why. Scatter the facts of a dossier among the how's and the
why's.

Don't be myopic either. The story should have focus to it. Select
an area of special interest for the lead, and then concentrate on that
topic in the body of the story. To borrow a term from photography,

the reporter wants to concentrate upon "the decisive moment." Or to borrow a term from bullfighting, he seeks "the moment of truth." One major topic, a handful of minor ones. That is enough. Readers can't travel several roads at once.

And a reporter should talk to all who know about the man before talking to the man himself. His friends, his enemies, his neighbors and business associates, his family, his relatives, his followers and antagonists—all can be interviewed to ensure a clear picture of the subject. If the reporter relies on one or two interviews, he is subject to all the prejudices, biases, ignorance, and near-sightedness of one or two men.

In 1965, a professional reporter, Richard Whalen, wrote a biography about the father of President Kennedy—without ever talking to his subject. From sources surrounding Joseph P. Kennedy, the author pieced together a portrait of a man he called *The Founding Father*. The book rose to the top of best-seller lists.

Lastly, on the stage of the story, the reporter places setting and action. He interviews the subject in his lair, in his natural environment. It helps the interviewee to be confident and relaxed. It gives the reporter color to blend into his feature story. It makes the story more dynamic.

Atmosphere was what the professional journalist was seeking when, as a sportswriter, he interviewed a winning coach at courtside one Monday evening after the team had won a Christmas basketball tournament. The coach could tell the story of the championship with much more gusto than could the usual statistics and box scores and facts. As the players ran through drills, the reporter stood at the coach's elbow, asked the how and the why of things, and got this "newsmaker story."

A Visit with a Happy Coach

Coach Bill Morris of Mankato State was obviously happy, which is a state of mind not readily found among coaches in mid-season.

While the players skipped nimbly through routine drills Thursday, Morris stood at the opposite end of the Highland Campus gymnasium and tried to muster up the normal supply of coach's pessimism.

He didn't succeed.

His team had just returned from winning an invitational tournament at Hastings, Nebr.

"We weren't even ceded," Morris said with pride.

"The boys had to look the best of the year in order to win. We got the rebounds . . . we were worried about that . . . but our defense was the thing that did the most. I don't think we were as smooth offensively as last year."

Mankato had lost its first three games this year.

"We haven't had any consistency in scoring." Morris suggested that wasn't exactly a bad point at Hastings. "John Seifert got hot and just sank Hastings college. Then Les Sonnabend got 26 points against Omaha. He looked like an all-American out there. In the final game. Jim Tetzloff took over. He looked great."

The three wins at Hastings gives Mankato six consecutive victories. In defeating Omaha, Hastings, and Emporia, Mankato subdued teams with combined records of 18 wins and 3 losses.

*   *   *

FRAMING—Another way of focusing attention on one person or on one bit of action is to frame it—by trees or by buildings or by arms or, as here, by heads. Of course, the photograph is given further interest by the fact that the runner is just breaking the string at the finish line. But the photograph is weakened by lack of a sense of motion; the runner, as far as the reader is concerned, looks as though he might be posing.

Lest thunder and lightning strike him on the spot, Morris tried harder to be a prophet of gloom and doom. Failing with the past, he looked to the future—a road trip this weekend to Bemidji and Moorhead.

The thought was sobering.

"Ordinarily, the team that makes that Moorhead and Bemidji trip and picks up more than one game is lucky," Morris said with distaste. "The fans at Bemidji are tough . . . you get lots of fire from them. Bemidji gets a little bit ahead and the house comes down. And distance is part of the problem."

Mankato made that dangerous expedition last winter and won both games . . . handily.

"It doesn't happen very often," Morris said in rebuttal.

He tried to summon up more despondency by looking at the Northern Intercollegiate conference. For a minute, he was in fine form. "I'll still pick St. Cloud. Why, they got more height, and more guys with records as long as your arm. . . ."

But the depression didn't last. Thoughts of the happy Hastings experience returned. It was a moment for the entire team—and coaching staff—to savor.

And so one coach was last seen, standing at the end of the Highland campus gymnasium, watching his champions go through a layup drill . . . and very much at peace with the world.

Chapter XII

THE NARRATIVE STORY

Quotes and description and a sequence of action—put them all together and you have the basis for a narrative style of writing. A strong opening section and then logical organization of the story—and you have the structure used by both short story writer and journalist.

The fictionalist and the journalist follow parallel paths which, in fact, turn at times and converge. Compare the two types of writing:

The Fiction writer	*The Journalist*
Uses dialogue	Uses quotes (those overheard and those gotten from interviews)
Uses description	Uses sights and sounds
Uses sustained action	Uses on-scene observations, episodes, anecdotes—all limited action
Characterization	Human interest features
Plot development	Story structure
Climax and denouement	Climactic order
Opening section	Lead, including extended leads
Imagination plus reality	Reality
Narrative person (I, you, he)	Narrative person (I, you, he)
Documentation	Facts, documentation
Variation in vocabulary from colloquial to formal	Vocabulary—informal
Style of writing—unlimited	Style of writing—economical, written at level of reader
Imagery and figurative language—unlimited	Imagery and figurative language—greatly restricted
Comment and opinion—unlimited	Analysis and interpretation

The journalist, dependent upon his powers of reporting, narrates an event—just as the fiction writer constructs his narrative. For instance, here is a narrative news-feature by a professional journalist. It is based on description, research, on-the-scene observations, and comment, to tell in episodic fashion the story of a student demonstration at an eastern university in 1964. It serves to close out this section about feature writing, the source of the most consistent challenges to the creative journalist.

It was a strange kind of Christmas gathering, several thousand college students massed around the broad, stone steps of the chapel at one end of the campus mall. Nearby, the American flag was hung at half mast. A giant Christmas tree which rose above the crowd was stiff and, though decorated, unlighted. A student promenaded a sign which read, "For Christ's sake, let us go home." It was one of many such home-made signs which added spots of color to the crowd. And at the top of the chapel steps, a clutch of student leaders, wearing orange arm bands, the school color, talked to the crowd.

An issue was at hand—that was the reason for the gathering. For three weeks the student senators and other campus leaders at Syracuse University had been asking for a longer Christmas vacation. They wanted to start vacation on Dec. 18 instead of a mid-week Dec. 23. For three weeks the answer from university officials: "No." There had followed petitions, editorials, finally an ultimatum.

Now, on this deceptively warm (42 degrees) December afternoon, a showdown had been called. As the student newspaper had been headlined (page 1) that morning:

STUDENTS MASS TODAY;
BIG TURNOUT HOPED

An accompanying story began as follows: "Student leaders are hoping Chancellor William P. Tolley changes his mind today, following his refusal Friday to grant an earlier Christmas recess. Student Government President Carl Corrallo has called a mass meeting at 3 p.m. today on the quad. He plans to call for further student action if no change comes today. Corrallo met with the Chancellor Friday morning and gave him a pile of petitions from the students asking an extension of the scheduled 12½ day vacation."

The newspaper asked, too, for orderly conduct—women to wear skirts and men to wear coats and ties, if possible.

And so, at 3 p.m on a Monday, there they stood, estimated variously from 2,000 to 5,000 students—some in skirts and few in ties. They jammed tightly toward the chapel steps to listen to a series of their student leaders . . . and to await an appearance by the Chancellor himself at 3:30.

One of the first speakers told the students that the real issue was student-administration relationships. He said that the students weren't being recognized by the administration, that they weren't being given a proper voice in campus affairs. The university wasn't really interested in the student, he suggested; *there* was the real cause for worry—the student being buried in the complex of the mass university.

(The student paper that day had said the same thing in an editorial: "The issue is the question of the role of the student in the mass university complex, which has been brought to the fore with the seemingly endless runaround given to student officials on the vacation question. . . . If today's demonstration proves nothing else, it must at least show the administration we are here and we care what it thinks about us. We are not ones to be ignored or taken lightly.")

While waiting for the Chancellor's appearance, another student speaker got curious about interest in the Sugar Bowl game coming up on Jan. 1 (Syracuse vs. LSU). "I am really interested in how many students plan to go to the Sugar Bowl," he said. Students had been granted an extra day of vacation Jan. 4 to get back from New Orleans. "All those who are going say aye."

A few scattered shouts.

"All those who aren't going, say aye."

An avalanche of sound. And a sign, "Christ vs. Football" was shoved up above the heads of the crowd. At repeated mentions of football the students booed.

Another speaker hinted that the Chancellor would still say no to an extension of vacation (boos). He suggested that further action might be necessary (cheers). "If the answer is no, how do you feel about having a boycott of classes?" The yeses echoed across the mall, strangely winter-green after a thaw that weekend. The speaker thanked the students for their support. It was gratifying, he said.

Students were given repeated warnings to behave themselves. One speaker pointed to the Christmas tree towering above them and asked that it be left alone. "I think it should stand as a monument to our lost vacation," he said.

By 3:20, time began to hang heavy. The crowd got restless. A few student marshals, appointed to keep order, walked through the crowd. Heavy clouds moved in from the west, heralding sudden snow that would blanket the campus three hours later. Most of the students waited quietly, shifting their feet to keep warm. Most were quiet, except for hecklers who clustered at the bottom of the chapel steps. They continued to whoop it up. Their noise was picked up by the speakers' microphones and was boomed over the loudspeakers. They made a comparatively solemn crowd sound angry.

"We've got 10 minutes to kill," a speaker said. Laughter from the crowd. "Kill, kill, kill," the hecklers chanted. And the chant broke down in laughter. Another speaker suggested singing carols. More laughs.

And then the Chancellor, punctual, arrived on the scene. He was greeted with applause, but when it became apparent he was not going to accede to student wishes, boos took control, sometimes drowning out his talk. In essence, the Chancellor said that he had made a decision (no), that he hoped students would abide by it, even though they disapproved of it. He said that next year's vacation dates had been changed to meet student requests; but this year . . . "No."

"When final decisions are made by the Chancellor of the university, you must learn to live with them," he said.

Down front, the hecklers jeered. A girl cried. Another shook her fist at the chapel steps and shouted imprecations. The hecklers took up the chant, "Boycott . . . boycott . . . boycott . . ."

And as the Chancellor left the steps, talk finished, a student took control of the microphone. "We're meeting again tonight," he said. "We'll decide then what further steps we will take." He called for a singing of the alma mater. Most students sang.

But the mass demonstration had come to a close. The students drifted off to classes and to residences, a few to Marshall Street coffee spots. The snow and Senator Wayne Morse (scheduled to speak that Monday night in criticism of American policies in Viet Nam) drifted in.

And on the next day, Tuesday, a group of students amid swirling snow picketed the administration building and the Chancellor's house. The picketing got little support from students.

And the campus newspaper declared in an editorial: "We'll yell our heads off, and we won't quit yelling and some people somewhere in this university community are going to realize that maybe we're right." It closed in sardonic humor: "The evening twilight is glistening for Syracuse University, and the shadows are falling over the closed windows of the administration building. The Chancellor won't change vacation. Maybe the Pope will change Christmas."

The newspaper put out one more edition, then shut down the presses until after vacation.

And a number of classes for the next week were cut short or were eased off by a great many professors. Officials said attendance was better than it had been prior to Thanksgiving vacation. Boycott—a failure.

And one girl in a hallway between classes said to her friend, "You know, I wrote a letter today to the Chancellor, thanking him for speaking to us."

And her friend said, "Why?"

And the two of them, in their own way, represented the extremes of thinking about a student demonstration.

THE PROBLEM OF CREDIBILITY

The degree of accuracy and the honesty of a newspaper over a period of time leads the reader to a feeling of confidence in what is printed. Or the opposite, if the newspaper staff is careless. A high credibility rating is necessary, and *reporters* more than any other group on the staff build it or destroy it. What causes a credibility gap? Professional editors in 1969 sought evidence by polling legislators, mayors, educators, religious leaders, and others. The major reasons for public distrust, as enumerated by "leaders," were these (and the reasons apply equally to student publications):

1. Visual evidence of unbalanced reporting—such as placement of stories, size of headlines, length of stories.

2. Evidence of unbalanced reporting by failure to cover, in a news story, all sides to an event or controversy.

3. Half-told stories resulting from obviously lazy reporting—not enough background information, not enough detail to answer the questions of readers.

4. Misleading or inaccurate headlines.

5. Too much space given to sensational news, rather than to stories seriously affecting the community.

Therefore, credibility can be better established by reporters unrelenting in getting full information for their stories, by editors copyediting stories with an eye to unbalanced and unfair reporting, by editors being more careful in headlining and displaying stories.

Chapter XIII

MOOD AND TONE

The People Came . . . 400,000 of Them

By TERRY OBLANDER
The Daily Kent Stater

Peace was 400,000 strong.

Peace drove, rode and hitch-hiked from all 50 states.

Peace was 80 years old, and peace cuddled close to its mother.

Peace was black and white and yellow.

Its description knew no bounds and was defined in the minds of those who marched in Washington this weekend [November, 1969].

The 400,000 came to the nation's capital after a week of violence scares. They came knowing there would be up to 35,000 armed troops and police waiting. Many had no idea where they would stay or eat.

They came anyway and were greeted with rain and a bitter wind.

Some came to walk in the four-mile March Against Death. Carrying candles and the names of men who had died in Vietnam, they made their way from Arlington National Cemetery to the Capitol at a rate of 1,000 per hour.

They dumped their signs into coffins.

Others came to participate in Saturday's Moratorium march. They contributed to the peace walk in different ways.

There were marshals whose locked arms kept the demonstrators in order and possible violence out.

There were medics . . . private doctors and Red Cross officials who maintained health.

There were members of the Mobe Legal Corps. They watched and were ready to offer their professional talents if they were needed.

There were other professionals, but the bulk of the 400,000 were those who contributed by carrying signs and walking in the peace march. They contributed their voices and their leg muscles.

129

Their signs supported and mocked.

"Get out of Vietnam" and "Bring the troops home now" were among the most common.

Some carried American flags with peace symbols while others carried the National Liberation Front flag.

Their chants ran from "Peace now" and "All we are saying is give peace a chance" to "Ho, Ho, Ho Chi Minh."

They tried to make themselves heard and seen as they passed the back of the White House, which was surrounded by troop emplacements and a steel barrier of privately owned D.C. buses.

But Richard Nixon did not see or hear. He watched televised football.

When they finished marching, they sat on grass near the Washington Monument. Packed tightly . . . they stretched as far and numbered as many as the mind could imagine.

The sea of bell bottoms, long hair, and peace badges found entertainment there in folk singers, rock groups, country and western singers, and a string quartet.

They sang to the tunes of "Hair" performed by its cast and danced to the "Stoney Mountain Breakdown" by Earl Scruggs.

They pondered and mulled and listened to draft resisters, welfare representatives, and educators. They heard Mrs. Martin Luther King, Dr. Benjamin Spock, and Dick Gregory.

The crowd melted with the dusk.

Washington watched it melt and its head spun from the shock.

It had seen its people in its streets.

It had smelled the perfume of their sweat.

It had felt the soles of their feet.

It had heard their cry for peace.

#

Sometimes Mood hangs so heavily over an event, it is the "fact" you will remember most. Fear. Joy. Tragedy. Boredom. Sometimes Mood is so important to understanding an event, you must be sure to include it in your report. The Mood is one of the facts, as surely as names, statistics, and direct quotes. As Terry Oblander found out at Moratorium Day: "Washington had felt the soles of their feet."

In reporting the German army marching into Paris in June, 1941, American correspondent Quentin Reynolds could not overlook the Mood. France had fallen once again to an invader. Reynolds wrote this in his book *The Wounded Don't Cry*:

There was no dawn.
This was puzzling at first because it had been a clear night. Now the

air was heavy with a smoky fog so thick that you could reach out and grab a piece of it in your hand. When you let it go your hand was full of soot. Then you realized that this was a man-made fog, a smoke screen thrown over Paris to hide the railroad stations from the bombers. But for the first time in its history Paris had no dawn.

At such times in the affairs of man, cold facts become irrelevant. The number of German troops. The names of streets they march down. The time of day. Quotes from French and German leaders, and from the few witnesses to the event. These details would give the story a sense of precision, of course, but it is Mood that is master of the moment. Reynolds therefore reached out, grasped a handful of darkness, and turned the reader's senses to the Mood. The most difficult of writing challenges, but Reynolds tried. . . .

Fog conveying Mood to the reader.

Especially man-made fog used to deceive bombers.

Hotels, restaurants closed.

The rumble underneath of a mechanized army trundling into the city.

One lone elderly lady sitting at a table at a sidewalk cafe. The last refugees leaving on bikes, on foot.

Reynolds finally turned to metaphor to describe the Mood of Paris: "Today Paris was a lonely old lady completely exhausted."

Now, a straight-fact man can report the same event this way:

Paris fell to the Nazi Army this morning, without a shot being fired in defense.

German troops began the march into the city at dawn. Hotels and restaurants were closed. Streets were mostly empty. The last refugees streamed out of the city on bicycles and on foot, going south to Bordeaux.

The drive to Paris culminated the German blitzkrieg that entered France June 5 . . . etc.

That account is certainly acceptable. But it lacks Mood and therefore fails as a true report of the fall of a great city, suddenly, to a traditional enemy. An emotional event, it will be regarded with detachment by an American reader halfway across the world, sitting in a warm armchair, without fears and sense of loss.

Unless . . .

MOOD. The jubilation in the champion's locker room. The suspense of a close election as the final tallies are counted. The fear present at crime and disaster. The sense of loss and confusion as a family at a lake watches sheriff's deputies drop iron grapples into the water to seek a body. The humor and good-naturedness of a lively speaker and audience. Tension in the final quarter. Uncertainty on the first day. All that is part of reporting.

As a sports columnist wrote the morning after a football team had lost a particularly important game:

Defeat puts a sting into the air, as surely as the October wind. Defeat can sit heavily. It muffles noises and spirits.

After the worst defeat in Viking history Sunday, the stadium needed muffled drums and crepe to match the atmosphere. The players crowded quickly into the exit from the playing field. They refused to acknowledge 20 or 30 boys asking for autographs.

One fan yelled at the players: "Whatsa matter with you guys? Tired?" Not a player looked up.

The players soon disappeared under the stands, clacking with echoes down the cement runway to their locker room.

The usually ebullient pompon girls waved their streamers, but listlessly. They tried to smile at the exiting players, but without noticeable results.

Less than two minutes after the end of the game, the electric scoreboard had been erased by the flick of someone's finger. A flick of a switch and the humiliating score was blanked out.

But it wouldn't be that easy for the Vikings.

THEN THERE IS TONE

That is what a writer puts *into* his story, on purpose, to be sure the reader responds a desired way. Tone in a story shows the writer's attitude toward the subject—and toward his audience. It is editorializing. It is influence and propaganda. It is providing the reader with a point of view to respond to, preferably to agree with.

For the editorialist, the columnist, the essayist, and at times the feature writer, tone stands honorably; it is defensible.

The selection of adjectives, for instance, and the planned connotations of words can inject tone into a story. Look at this passage, for instance, written with two contrasting sets of adjectives and other "sensory" words:

Positive tone	*Negative tone*
For three weeks Sen. Henry J. Smythe, a venerable knight on a noble horse, had piled up accusations against his opponent. He overwhelmed him with testimony of conversations, incriminating letters, and a multitude of charges. The whole affair, it seemed, might subside, and Sen. Smythe would ride majestically off on his sturdy steed, and his opponent would get his way.	For three weeks Sen. Henry J. Smythe, an ancient knight on a spavined horse, had roared accusations at his opponent. He bludgeoned him with gossip, crackpot letters, and unsupported charges. The whole thing, it seemed, might subside, and Smythe would clump off on his moth-eaten charger, vanquished easily by his unruffled opponent.

The different tones are obvious. The writers' intentions show clearly, and the attitudes toward the readers are apparent.

Because of possible excesses of tone, reporters often are instructed by editors to ignore the Mood of events. Yet the report of violent death without attention to Mood can seem dehumanized, indifferent, and as routine as items for the police blotter. The journalist gets the reputation of being insensitive—or too much a technocrat. All events, devoid of Mood, would seem alike to the reader. War. Basketball. Jaycee picnic. Fender-bender at Maine and First. Mayoralty election. Yet all of these events are distinctive, largely because of the Moods inherent in them. Therefore, the writer of news must attend to Mood wherever it is of significance. Yet he must exercise restraint to stop short of tone.

Let us look at examples of writing in journalism, in which Mood or tone are of importance. Which represent Mood? Which tone? How do the words play on your senses?

Example No. 1—Outlined against a blue-gray October sky, the Four Horsemen rode again. In dramatic lore they are known as Famine, Pestilence, Destruction, and Death. These are only aliases. Their real names are Stuhldreher, Miller, Crowley, and Layden. They formed the crest of the South Bend cyclone before which another fighting Army football team was swept over. . . . (Grantland Rice writing about a football victory by Notre Dame)

Example 2—'Twas a drizzly, boggy Dublin sort of night with the gutters all slushed and the snow all muddy and the elms ganging bleak and drippy over the wee white church at 50th Street and Girard Ave. S. . . . (Dick Cunningham of the *Minneapolis Tribune,* in a lead to a story about an Irish Bagpipe Band)

Example 3—At the swimming hole in Black Creek the sun was warm today, but instead of ringing to the usual shouts of swimming, diving children the area was so quiet that the chirp of a bird deep in the brush could be heard. . . . The change was symbolic of what has happened in this suburban town since two teen-age girls were found murdered Wednesday. (From a lead in *The New York Times*)

Example 4—These were New Yorkers on a spring day, their only mission to enjoy the city. They watched youngsters playing basketball in the playgrounds, and they promenaded along the thoroughfares, holding their children's hands. There were baby carriages and strollers, and there were men walking dogs. The fountains flowed, and in Washington Square the amateur and professional painters were out and beatniks strummed guitars and sang. (From a feature story about spring, in *The New York Times*)

The sources of Mood in a story become apparent. Partly, what the reporter observes and then chooses to report can condition the story. (From a story about antiwar moratorium: "They carried knapsacks and sleeping bags. Many of the males had beards. Most of the girls had long hair.") Partly, Mood results from the words selected to tell the story. Partly, from what is stressed by repetition or by placement at the top of the story. Partly, by the metaphors and references (such as the Four Horsemen metaphor). Sometimes, by the style (short, staccato sentences for impact or by run-on sentences for informality).

By the specific details reported. The weather. Blood and gore. Clothes and styles. Appearance of persons. Specific actions, such as reporting the V-sign, or a clenched and upraised fist. The violence of language at the event. Description of scenes, as the flames or silhouettes of firemen at a fire. Unfortunately, by selecting only negative details, a reporter can tone a story away from the truth; if he sees a few hippies and describes them only, he leaves an impression with the reader that no white collars or blue collars or other kinds of people were there. The reporter could be constructing Untruth just as surely as if he were to lie.

Subject matter of story. Children and animals generally provoke pleasant and sentimental reactions from readers. Picnic. Commencement ceremony. All have inherent pleasant emotional values.

Evaluative adjectives used. For instance, if a meeting were closed to the press and outsiders, it might be described variously as "a secret meeting," "clandestine meeting," "mysterious meeting," "private meeting," "meeting conducted in ominous seclusion." Each adjective or phrase conditions a different response from the reader.

The action verbs selected. Compare "He moved across the room firmly" with "He stomped across the room" with "He clomped and clacked across the room" and you will get three distinct impressions of what happened.

Level of vocabulary and style of writing used. A reviewer for *Time* magazine wrote a 364-word commentary about a book, all 364 words in one sentence to make this final point: ". . . may well wonder if the whole book is not simply a typographical catastrophe caused by the absence, on the author's typewriter, of a . "

Figures of speech. When Wordsworth referred to old age as "serene and bright/And lovely as a Lapland Night," he certainly meant in his metaphor something much different from the poet Yeats when he compared an aged man to "A tattered coat upon a stick." Both figurations evoke strong images. In writing for journalism, you use figurations infrequently—and only with the utmost consideration of their effects, and possible interpretations.

Lead stress. The first few paragraphs of a story are like first impressions gained from meeting a person—they tend to stick. Lead with a negative impression and that may stick throughout the entire story. For example, this:

A group of college students broke into the President's speech this morning with hoots and catcalls. . . .

Even if that event took up just two minutes of time and did not seriously affect the whole course of the speech, it sets a dominant impression hard to escape.

Word exploitation. By using certain levels of words you can establish certain appreciations or dislikes in the reader's mind. For instance, a law enforcement official can variously become a security officer, policeman, cop, fuzz, and, in the language of the left, pig.

Conscious style. Staccato sentences have one effect: He turned. He gasped. He reached out his hand. He staggered. And fell. He had had his.

Run-on sentences create another effect: It is in the spring you feel glad, and a walk down the street can reconstitute your soul, and the world seems in its very best spirits, and it is at such a time you are glad to be alive.

Put these elements together, in varying proportions, and you establish Mood or tone. As for Mood, it should mean the reader responds to your story exactly as he would have at the event itself.

You Must See and Hear and Sense

For certain, a reporter must "feel" his story as well as accumulate valid information about it. The modern American novelist Walter Van Tilburg Clark (*The Ox-bow Incident*) clearly defined that necessity when he once wrote: "A writer uses his ears and eyes better than the average person. As a result his memory is keener and he remains more concerned about life, continually making associations between his past and his present. The ability to feel deeply and to express that feeling is an essential quality of the journalist."

One of the great American reporters, Lincoln Steffens, more specifically called for the sensitive, as well as mechanical, writer of news. In his *Autobiography* (1931) he warned about the dangers, as reporters, of becoming cynical. He preferred, as he wrote: ". . . the fresh staring eyes to the informed mind and the blunted pencil." Steffens also wrote: "When a reporter no longer saw red at a fire, when he was so used to police news that a murder was not a human tragedy but only a crime, he could not write police news for [our newspaper]."

Steffens, of course, saw journalism as an art form. He wrote in *Autobiography*: "We dared to use such words as 'literature,' 'art,' 'journalism,' not only in the city room itself, but at a fire or in the barrooms where the Press drank. The old hacks hated it and ridiculed us. . . . But we did not care. . . . they likewise were laboring at the art of telling stories." (Quotes not consecutive.)

Steffens had no interest in beating other newspapermen to the story. He wanted a good story, truthfully and memorably told, and he sacrificed the "scoop" for extra time in which to get it done. One of his reaches was for Mood, as well as facts. Mood, he found out, could be more honest than the fact.

But there are pitfalls to Mood writing. Overwriting, for one. Too much sentimentality. Too heavy with phrases and adjectives. Reaching too far and desperately for humor. In all such situations, the too-intense stories become maudlin or bathetic. Clichés, too, tend to pile up: "fell into depths of despair . . . was a Black Day for . . . the fear pressed heavily onto . . ."

And the writer can allow his bias too free a rein, turning legitimate Mood into unacceptable tone. Or he forgets reality and lapses into fictionalizing at the typewriter.

All of those problems can be easily overcome—by keeping emotions under control, by copy-editing your own work carefully (be a "taker-outer"), and by letting someone else edit the final draft.

FINAL WORDS ABOUT TONE

In this discussion, tone has been purposefully played down. A lower-case tone and an upper-case Mood. Yet the commentator, the reviewer or critic, and the writer of light features must use tone to accomplish their appointed tasks. Tone—what the writer consciously puts into a story to create a specific effect, or to cause an emotional reaction by the reader. Recently, one of the most effective users of tone has been a Vice President of the United States, Spiro T. Agnew. In frequent speeches about college students and antiwar protesters and political liberals, he delivered such toning phrases as these:

They are vultures who sit in trees and watch lions battle, knowing that win, lose, or draw, they will be fed. . . .
An effete corps of impudent snobs. . . .

Tone excites emotion. It enlists reaction, mostly visceral. It draws attention and holds it. What the permanent effect on the reader will be, however, cannot be accurately predicted. Tone, without doubt, does provoke immediate reaction.

Time magazine at times has been accused of tone in its political reporting, thus reducing news to personality conflicts.

They saw Ike, and liked what they saw. They liked him for his strong, vigorous manner of speech . . . and for an overriding innate kindliness and modesty. But most of all, they liked him in a way they could scarcely explain. They liked Ike because, when they saw him and heard him talk, he made them proud of themselves and all the half-forgotten best that was in them and the nation.

In an excellent study of possible bias in one publication, Dr. John C. Merrill of the University of Missouri showed how attributive phrases (especially the adverbs) lead to severe toning of the news:

About President Truman: . . . said curtly . . . said coldly . . . barked Harry S. Truman . . . preached the Truman sermon . . . grinning slyly . . . with a blunt finger he probed . . .
About President Eisenhower: said with a happy grin . . . cautiously pointed out . . . chatted amiably . . . said warmly . . . paused to gather thought.
About President Kennedy: President Kennedy said (used most frequently) . . . concluded the President . . . the President urged . . . he suggested. . . . Kennedy insisted . . . The President promised.

The attributive phrases tended to portray Truman negatively, Eisenhower positively, and Kennedy neutrally.
Such words could be called "tones of voice."
There are tones of style, too. A flippant, semiliterate style demeans the subject. Satire, parody, and sarcasm belittle the subject by accentuating its weaknesses and failures.
Pleasant tones are possible, too. Pleasant words, symbols, and images. Praise, nostalgia, humor. Even a hoax can be enjoyable at times.
And finally, then, let us examine a Moodpiece and a tonepiece. The first, dominated by Mood, is a news account of war in Vietnam. The second, heavily toned, is a review of a biography of Y. A. Tittle, one of the great quarterbacks of all time who played well into his 30's—an age when most men have given up gamesmanship as being mere passing fancies.

Mood: Bombed by Mistake

It was shortly after 8:30 a.m. yesterday when one of those terrible accidents of war happened.

I was sitting in the command bunker, a mound of dirt screening us from communist snipers.

Suddenly, I felt a searing heat on my face. An American fighter-bomber had misjudged the communist positions and dropped a load of napalm in the wrong place. The flaming jellied gasoline, impossible to shake or scrape off once it hits the skin, splashed along the ground in a huge dragon's tail less than 25 yards away.

Screams penetrated the roar of flames. Two Americans tumbled out of the inferno, hair burned off and clothes incinerated.

"Good God!" Col. Hal Moore yelled. Another plane was making a run over the same area. The colonel grabbed a radio.

"You're dropping napalm on us," he shouted. "Stop those damn planes."

At almost the last second, the plane pulled up and away, its napalm tanks still hanging from the wings.

One soldier was a mass of blisters. The other wasn't quite so bad, but he had breathed fire into his lungs and wheezed for air.

A medic asked me to help get the men into the medical helicopter when it arrived. There were no litters. Tenderly as we could, we picked the soldiers up. I held a leg of the most seriously burned man.

But I wasn't careful enough. A big patch of burned skin came off in my hand.

—Joseph Galloway, at Chu Pong Mountain, for United Press-International.

Tone: Hooray for Y. A.

Y. A. TITTLE—I PASS!—as told to Don Smith. Franklin Watts, Inc. 290 pages. $4.95.

I am 35. I am for Y. A. Tittle.

He is 38 . . . and still number one quarterback for the New York Giants.

Reading about Tittle's indestructibility is better therapy than my whole cabinet of Geritol, Carter's Little Liver Pills, vitamin tablets, dietetic soda pop, and pep pills. I want to throw away my Metrecal wafers and my midriff harness and join the kids in a neighborhood football game.

Only tired blood prevents me.

Let me tell you about this Tittle . . . or at least about what he reveals in his new book. First of all, he takes care of himself—on the field and off. That's his secret to longevity. On the field he relies on his passing arm, not his running legs. Now, that's smart. Legs give out fast. So Tittle conserves them.

He writes that football is a passing game anyhow. He puts it outright—without any shame: "To me, football is passing. I am a passer before everything." There it is, on page 68. While other quarterbacks like Fran Tarkenton and Roman Gabriel are skittering all over the place, Tittle is saying to himself, "Legs, take it easy. Arm, do the work."

For a while as quarterback at San Francisco, he had to run bootleg plays. The 49ers tried to make Tittle do Frankie Albert's old stuff. Well, Tittle got smashed up like Stunt O'Reilly's jalopies. By the time he was 35, he was pretty much through at San Francisco.

So in 1961 they traded the guy to New York. A lotta people were amused. Tittle, 35, goes to the Giants to help out another old-timer, Charlie Conerly. He was 40. It got so only antique dealers took the Giants seriously.

Well, Tittle and the Giants won three straight Eastern Division titles. No one says, "Tut, tut, Tittle" anymore. He's a community hero now. People see him for his bald head and his reading glasses and his 2,000 completed passes . . . and they love him. In New York he's a bigger thing than Jimmy Walker ever was.

Tittle loves football. Only once did he get sorta disgusted with it.

That was when Red Hickey and Red Strader coached him at San Francisco. Tittle doesn't come right out and say it in his book, but he suggests that Hickey didn't have much time for a quarterback who couldn't run. Strader was too much an organization man. Neither coach was much tittle-ated by Y. A.

But he wouldn't give up. At age 35, he set out to really get into great shape. After a few bad weeks trying to get the Giants to accept him—well, you know the rest of the success story. Championships for the Giants.

Tittle is great. His book is pretty good, too, mainly because he's an athlete who has had to overcome real obstacles.

Some of these jokers to try to make a plot for a book or movie have to make up problems—a sore toe or a father who was only middle class or a Hollywood starlet who turned him down. Despite all that, the joker makes it to the big leagues . . . and then Sam Huff grinds him up.

But not Tittle. Here's a real guy with guts who overcame real problems. . .

But then, I'm prejudiced. I'm 35 and Tittle's 38.

Hooray for all of us old indestructibles.

—Bill Ward

The Light Essay

Chapter XIV

WRITING THE LIGHT ESSAY

How the Student Does It

Thoughts

. . . at Graduation Time

By DeeDee MAIR

Then too it was spring. True, the world had yet to hear of Sputnik, compact cars, Viet Nam or Selma, Ala., but the grass still grew and the leaves still came out to bathe Minnesota with warming salve for the winter wounds.

It was new patent leather Mary Jane shoes that squeaked, a new friend who owned a two-wheeler, the first sunshine-scented laundry and the first taste of sadness.

For me as a six-year-old, the spring in 1955 came on tennis shoes, trike wheels, and angle worm backs and the whole world—except across the busy street—needed my constant attention. For my brother and sister, however, the spring came in a whirl of yearbook pages, college catalogues and graduation robes that smelled of dust and confidence and about 100 years of mothers' tears.

That night of their high school graduation, I was scrubbed and groomed to an itchy, un-tomboyish state and stuffed into a grandmother-gift dress which crinkled like paper bags and showed the scabs on my knees.

I was shoved into a stiff-backed chair in the first row of the balcony and ordered not to chew any of the gum which was stuck precariously to the underside of my uncomfortable perch.

There was unhappy crying music as the graduates filed in like a huge, solemn choir. From my seat I heard the click of a purse being opened and the ineffective stifling of a tear into a Kleenex. An old man with rheumy eyes beside me fingered a goldfilled watch chain and ignored a glistening tear at the corner of his eye.

My mother smiled, bit her lip and recreased her rumpled program with her thumbnail. My father smoothed the hair which wasn't there, shook hands with my brother and kissed my sister.

No one said much but still no one could find steady, unquavering words to answer my questions on why they all had on bathrobes and why everyone's eyes were rimmed with red.

For the family of four adults plus a restless six-year-old, there was just the night and the thoughts.

Summer passed with the urgency and finality of an ambulance. Leaves blushed and fell off as if embarrassed by the hints of winter. At the same time my brother and sister closed our homey front door for the last time in preparation for opening their own "golden doors to the future."

The years passed too quickly and suddenly that restless six-year-old was a Brownie Scout, a ballroom dancing recruit, a cocky ninth grader, a humble tenth grader and finally—a quivering-on-the-brink senior.

Two weeks from tonight another huge, solemn, yearly choir will include me and the class of '65 will be scrutinized by other itchy six-year-olds, other melancholy grandfathers and other misty-eyed mothers.

#

Writing humor is serious business. And those journalists who have specialized in the informal essay (Russell Baker, John Gould, Art Buchwald, and others) must approach their work with all the dead-pan calculation of a mathematician.

Why?

Because a writer owns just one device for setting off a laugh. He has the word—printed and dry on the page.

A comedian is much wealthier in resources. If the word fails Jerry Lewis, he can stagger, stork-legged, across the stage, pop out his eyes, pop open his mouth, and get laughs. If the audience is unresponsive, Jack E. Leonard can change his subject matter in midjoke. Some comics are imitators; some recite in falsetto; some throw custard pies. Where all else fails, a pratfall succeeds.

But the essayist has just the word—printed and dry on the page. He cannot add visible gestures; he cannot change the topic on the spot to accommodate the audience; he cannot even bring in the Keystone Kops. For the essayist, every word counts. That is why writing humor is a most serious business.

Let us compare: the baggy pants comedian comes on stage. He slips on an imaginary banana peel. He leers at the audience. Already, three laughs and not a word spoken. He has trouble with his belt and his pants turn from droop to drop. Red Flannels underneath. He is embarrassed. More laughs.

Finally, he says in a ridiculous tone of voice, "Why does the chicken cross the road?" He may even stammer. He rocks from side to side and rolls his eyes. His grin is lusty. "To get to the other side," he says, and falls over backward in a dead faint. He, the baggy-pants comedian, got a laugh with the oldest joke in the business.

But the writer! What does he have to work with? Words must carry the load.

"Why does the chicken cross the road?"

"I don't know—why?"

"To get to the other side."

Tain't funny, McGee.

So how do the Buchwalds and the Bakers, as creative journalists, get the audience to respond to humor? Two ways—through a thorough understanding of life and its foibles and thorough knowledge of how to deploy words.

The essayist to say the least must be disciplined. For one thing, he must confine himself to a topic, universally experienced and appreciated, a topic with which the audience can identify. Some examples: trying to withdraw from a record club . . . putting up a lawn chair . . . passing a driver's road test . . . proving identity to a bank teller . . . or taking the topic from some newsworthy event which is timely and has size to it (Buchwald's favorite device).

The informal essayist confines himself, too, in such ways as the following:

In style, he must write so clearly, directly, and simply that there is no confusion. If the reader is confused, he can't very well be amused.

The essayist must write in "visuals"—those elements which put pictures into the reader's mind. Dialogue, anecdotes, description all create pictures and sounds.

Like the 880-yard runner, the essayist must start fast, settle quickly into a strong pace, and then finish with fervor—so that the reader gets interested quickly, maintains his interest, and finishes on a point to be remembered.

The essayist can present an unexpected point of view about the topic. Examples: I miss highway billboards now that they have been banned; they served many useful purposes to the motorist . . . laundromats have replaced drugstores and luncheon counters as settings for neighborhood gossip. The essayist takes a common topic, and gives a twist to the tale.

So, the informal essay must be carefully planned, worked and reworked, and finally polished to perfection. So much for the egotist who believes he can write humor with a spontaneous outflowing of phrases and ideas. You can find more laughs at a funeral. Or at final exams.

Yet, the informal essay, if handled with a disciplined attitude, is surprisingly simple to write. Let's trace the case history of one:

Inspiration. You, the writer, in a camera store cannot help overhearing an argument between salesman and customer. Customer has bought a new, automated camera and he claims it won't take pictures. Clerk keeps insisting that the camera is foolproof, that it is so simple even an ape can take pictures. You are amused and you listen for a while; yes, it seems that those simple things too often turn out to be baffling. Everybody has been told, "It's easy as falling off the log." Everybody has discovered the opposite. A promising topic for a humorous essay; it passes the test for commonality.

Building up content. For a period of time—hours to some, days and weeks to others—you, the writer, piece together anecdotes about times when the simple proved exasperating. Some incidents happened to you; others, you get from friends who, when asked, recall them. Maybe, you have a clipping or two about the topic in your *tickler file.* Still other incidents you recall as having happened to others, and somewhere in the past were told to you. For some topics, you will track down facts. Unexpectedly soon, you will have a hill of anecdotes, dialogue, facts, incidents.

Developing style. You wonder whether the essay is best told in first person (I), second person (you), or third person (he); you choose one point of view. You also decide whether to be slapstick silly about the topic; or to be restrained and subtle. You pick a style of writing, too. You even work up some lines of humor, some catchy phrases.

Opener and closer. You try to pick a strong anecdote for opening the essay . . . and save the strongest one for the closing. In between you spread out the other material.

Twist of the tale. You see if you can find an unexpected twist to the story—in structure, in ending, in odd point of view (remember: billboards were good things; too bad they're gone).

Write and rewrite. You stop only when *every* word (600 to 1000 at most) is perfect.

You wind up with this general outline:

> You remember in grade school, told you couldn't miss the place where erasers were cleaned—never found it.
>
> The incident in the camera store—"You can't miss getting a perfect picture every time." Someone missed.
>
> The time in Montana when, asked for directions, the man on the street said something was "plain as the nose on your face." It wasn't.
>
> All the things advertised as simple enough for a child to put together.
>
> The friend who was bothered because everyone told him he couldn't go wrong getting married.
>
> Several other incidents.

As for style, with mostly incidents to narrate, you decide to use anecdotes with some connecting comments between them.

As for twist—not much. You decide to call this the You-Can't-Go-Wrong syndrome. And the catch is, assurances are frightening. Your life has been a series of failing to do the obvious.

For the opener, you pick the grade school incident about not finding the cleaning room—you want to point out that this failure has been with you all your life.

For the closer, you will use the marriage bit, because most people have the same sense of impending disaster when marriage is near.

The rest consists of anecdotes, interspersed with commentary.

And, so, here is your informal essay: "On Missing the Obvious" (first appeared in *The National Observer;* later reprinted in *The Observer's World* (Dow-Jones Books, Princeton, N.J., 1965).)

Reflections

. . . *On Missing the Obvious*

It started many years ago when I asked the custodian at our elementary school where the erasers were to be cleaned. He pointed down the hallway. "Go down to the far end, turn right, four doors down and there you are. You can't miss it, young man," he said.

I missed it. Down the hall, to the right, and four doors down was the incinerator, so the erasers got cleaned by my leaning out a window and clapping them together.

Since that ominous episode, my life has been a series of failing to do the obvious. It is called the You-Can't-Go-Wrong syndrome.

For instance, the camera dealer in our neighborhood recently sold me a completely automatic camera. It had automatic meter, automatic aperture and shutter adjustment, automatic film advance. "Point the camera and—click—you just can't miss getting a perfect picture every time," the salesman said.

I should have refused on the spot to buy the camera. But I bought it, and my first roll of film looked like something the dog had chewed. The dealer probed the camera from lens to sprocket and shook his head in disbelief. "I don't know what you could have done wrong."

I tried to tell him it wasn't what I had done, it was what he had said that had caused the trouble. I tried to explain to him about the time in Hardin, Mont., when I asked an old-timer how to get to the high school. "Jes go upta the nex' block and jog offta the right. There it is . . . plain as the nose on your face," he said. I finally found it: by parking my car, getting out, and hailing a taxi to take me there.

The people who write directions for assembling backyard barbecue spits have not taken me into account. The directions conclude somewhat like this:

"(23) Just follow these simple directions; even your child can put together the E-Z Cookout."

The Cookout, of course, is piled—unassembled—in a corner of the garage, along with an easy-to-assemble lawn chair, a family tent, and a collapsible trailer.

The most frightening assurance of all, however, is the statement, "It's easy as falling off a log." Delivered by the self-assured and the over-righteous, it is deadly as a python's embrace. Many years ago, a cousin said, "It's easy as falling off a log"; yet, I spent a summer learning how to ride a bicycle. Learning to set the margins of a typewriter, to tie a Windsor knot, to shift gears, to get used to contact lenses—all were, as predicted, as easy as falling off a log (and breaking a leg).

Evidence piles up. At the carnival stand where "everyone is a winner I never get a prize. At the movie "all America will love" I walk out in the middle. At the race track "sure things" are sure losers.

But the most insidious of all assurances was handed point-first to me recently. I had proposed, was accepted, and looked forward to a life of marital bliss. Then a pal slapped me on the back. "Friend, I just heard the good news," he said. "Congratulations."

We shook hands.

"Yes, sir, you've got a mighty fine woman there."

Then he ruined it.

"You just can't go wrong."

The essay is light. It tries for a gentle laugh or a smile. As one writer of humor suggests, "Don't go for the belly, try for the lip."

And it is written *to a degree* by formula. Much of journalism is loosely defined by formula. Not a barbed-wire boundary with sentry towers every 300 feet and with police dogs on patrol, it is a loose boundary, twine strung casually from stick to stick. There is ample room in which to move and to be independent; yet, there is the rope beyond which lie quicksand and undergrowth and other traps for the wanderer.

For instance, you cannot use a formal vocabulary, not because the reader is a mental defective but because with an increase in difficulty of vocabulary there is an increase in difficulty of reading. Forget the rock-and-gulley route over the mountain when a smooth and level trail cuts around it. If a reader is faced with the *necessity* to read—such as you do with textbooks—then he will pick his way among the obstacles, retracing his steps, moving carefully, and even stubbing toes at times. A man of ideas—such as a philosopher—will, too, with a work of abstractions. But when the essayist is trying to be light, he shouldn't make the light a fantastic trip.

Journalism shuns the needlessly complex sentence and the needlessly pompous phrasing. The principal of a school sent a news release to the local newspaper to announce: "The Senior Class and the Eighth Grade graduating students are occupying much of their times polishing their motor skills to debouch the traditional 'Pomp and Circumstance.' "

A sportswriter reported, "The halfback launched a successful expedition to hit pay dirt." Which is to say that Henry Smythe ran for a touchdown.

To be pretentious in style goes along with being a city slicker, a snob, a drummer. It is preferable to enlist the reader on your side.

Besides, the story to be told is what is important. The style—the manner of telling it—is secondary to content. Don't try to change the order of things.

Similarly, sentences move forward, from subject to verb to complement, the natural order of transmitting thoughts.

And paragraphs! In newspaper journalism, for good reasons, the short paragraph is stressed. First of all, newspaper format demands brevity. With columns about two inches wide, words quickly form a deep measure of gray tape. Caught in that gray mass, the reader easily loses his way. But each indention of a paragraph provides a landmark for the eye—a place to mark his way.

Psychologically, short paragraphs set a quick pace for the reader. He moves rapidly forward, resting briefly at each indention. He feels compelled to continue reading.

The journalist paragraphs for other reasons, such as the following:

(1) For dialogue, with each change of speaker. Example:

The greatest tribute to Charlie, the ice-fisherman, was this story often told about his dedication to the sport.

The old man was squinting uncomfortably into his fish-hole one blustery, uncivilized day.

"What's wrong?" a friend asked him.

"Dropped my glasses down the hole," Charlie answered.

"Wanta go home then?"

"No," Charlie said. "Don't hafta see to catch a fish." Charlie sat there, on the ice, in his fuzz and fever world for another hour.

At noon, the friend suggested lunch.

"Ain't hungry," Charlie said. "Besides I dropped my lunch down the hole."

Charlie glared fiercely out-of-focus, so the friend left. But he came back in a few minutes with a peanut butter sandwich. Charlie refused it.

"Go ahead," said the friend. "It's good. You can have it."

"Nope, can't eat it," Charlie said.

"Well, holy cow, why not?"

"Just dropped my teeth down the hole."

(2) For impact, for effect, the writer can isolate a sentence by itself. Example:

Six-man football. It has become scarce, unfortunately. During the 1930's and 1940's in midwestern prairie hamlets, it flourished like sunflower stalks. Whenever a high school was too small to generate a full complement of ends, tackles, guards, centers, and backs, six-man football was the answer.

It was better than putting Agnes Skolnicky into the lineup.

(3) Paragraphs can be arbitrarily broken up to eliminate a mass of gray type. Example:

(More formal paragraphs with topic sentence and climactic sentence in italics.)

There's a canoe in your future. For tomorrow's vacation, you will paddle along the Minnesota, the St. Croix, the Big Fork and the Little Fork, the Pigeon. You'll consult a river map, not a road map, and you'll put up for the night at a campsite, not a motel. That prospect is less a hope and more a reality every day, with several states promoting themselves as "the outdoors state." Marine dealers are mapping canoeable streams and lakes. Vacationers are buying canoes and packs and tents and reflector ovens. *The vacation of the future will consist of fresh air, sore muscles, improvised menus, and freedom.*

(The journalist will paragraph it for pace and readability.)

There's a canoe in your future. [Lead isolated for impact.]

For tomorrow's vacation, you will paddle along the Minnesota, the St. Croix, the Big Fork and the Little Fork, the Pigeon. You'll consult a river map, not a road map, and you'll put up for the night at a campsite, not a motel. [End of first subtopic.]

That prospect is less a hope and more a reality every day, with several states promoting themselves as "the outdoors state." Marine dealers are mapping canoeable streams and lakes. Vacationers are buying canoes and packs and tents and reflector ovens. [End of second subtopic.]

The vacation of the future will consist of fresh air, sore muscles, improvised menus, and freedom. [Last paragraph isolated for impact and final effect.]

(4) You noticed in the previous example the paragraphing by subtopics: that is the basic rule for journalistic paragraphs, indenting for each subtopic. The topic sentence, as a formal structure, generally is absent. It is replaced by a feeling that the whole paragraph, easily grasped in one look, is in itself a separate subtopic.

(5) Occasionally, a sentence is isolated to serve as an introduction to a new topic. These paragraphs serve as transitions.* Example:

(After a series of paragraphs telling about a tornado in Kansas, there appears this sentence):
Elsewhere in the nation, other natural disasters have been reported. (Then follow stories about hurricanes in Florida and fires in California.)

Another example:

During the speech, General Smythe listed several reasons for defending Taiwan from the Red Chinese. They were as follows:

(6) Sometimes for lead impact, the first paragraph is artificially cut short—even though following sentences could fit with it. Example:

You can bet that a new word war is starting today. According to a story from the wire services, Frank Ramsey, a guard for the Boston Celtics, has been censured for unsportsmanlike conduct. Ramsey, says the story, is the source of an article in Sports Illustrated about how to draw fouls.	You can bet that a new word war is starting today. According to a story from . . .

(7) To establish a rapid pace of action, paragraphs can be short and fall one upon the next: Example:

The fog was impenetrable. We had never known the world to be so silent.
Crack!
The fog quivered with the sound.
Danny almost fell out of the boat.
Three souls were frozen solid.
Burt finally shook his salami at us. "Sonic boom."
The world had caught up with us at last.

Agreed: you would rarely use these rules of paragraphing for formal writing—the term paper, the dissertation, the formal essay.

But these rules are fundamental to the journalist, the informal essay-ist, the advertising copywriter, the radio and television script writer, and frequently the writer of fiction.

The journalist is defensive about his paragraphing when a teacher says, "You do terrible things with paragraphs!" It is like being ac-cused of wearing brown shoes with a blue suit. Yet, the journalist—like all professional writers—has reasons for what he does. And, after all, a successful writer is one who knows how to reach a par-ticular audience—and does so consistently.

Essays don't always need to draw laughter. They can be sardonic. An essay can point out the unpleasant side of life in a shockproof manner. The reader will feel uncomfortable, but he won't suffer from revulsion or terror, moods which render the reader emotionally in-capable of coping with the message.

Here is a simple example of what is meant by the unpleasant nature of an informal essay:

He stood before me. Goon slacks, shirt opened to the belt, sweeping ducktail, sneer set on lips . . .

The biggest hood in school.

"Say, man, s'pose I could get some pads?" Swagger was all I could see.

"Nothing for you, Kallen."

"Man, whatta ya pickin' on me for. Whatta ya got against me?"

He was hefty, thick-shouldered, quick.

"No room for trouble-makers on this squad," I told him. I explained that football demanded a different type of toughness.

"Hey, man . . ."

"Coach," I corrected.

"Coach, I wanta play football. Serious, hey. I'm as tough as any of those squares you got out there."

I made a deal. He could come out. "Don't expect favors," I warned. "And promise me one thing—if it gets too tough for you, quit. Don't hang around and make trouble."

He promised.

No player ever worked as hard as he did that night at practice. He collapsed during the umpteenth wind sprint. He got up and finished. He lit on his rear while back-pedaling during agility drills. The players laughed. He got up and pumped his knees a little higher. A veteran knocked him down with a scissory body block. He got up slowly. On the next play, he was sent flying again. He panted and staggered and never said a word. His lips thickened, his eyes hardened. He gritted to hang on.

The pomp and bluster had been thumped out of him.

When the ordeal was over and the team had showered and gone home, he limped out of a corner of the locker room, plumped down his football gear in front of me and didn't look up. I waited for words. He had none. He pivoted and walked away, head sunk into shoulders.

I never saw him again. A month later, he was in reform school.

Note the narrative style:
Dialogue: "Hey, man . . ."
    "Coach," I corrected.
    "Coach, I wanta play football. . . ."
Description: He stood before me. Goon slacks, shirt opened to the belt, sweeping ducktail, sneer set on lips . . .

ACTION—Lineman Jim Prestel of the Minnesota Vikings closes in on quarterback Roman Gabriel during a professional football game. To get the action (see the look on Prestel's face), the photographer kneeled in the end zone behind the play. Besides the unusual angle, the photographer worked for a closeup of the action, using a 300mm. lens. A news photographer must be like the feature reporter: he must look for unusual viewpoints to the routine event.

Action: He lit on his rear while back-pedaling during agility drills. He got up and pumped his knees a little higher. . . .

The introduction with its touch of mystery; the buildup to the climax with its unexpected result.

All in a few words.

Those are elements of fiction writing, too. The informal essay is a proper training ground for fiction writers. The principal difference is the origin and then the translation of the content. The essay rises out of reality without much change. Fiction is more the product of change —reality is put into the hammermill of the imagination and recast; same material, but different shapes and textures.

The essayist, in looking ahead to fiction, learns to perfect his style, to develop a sense of rhythm and pace through words and plot buildup. He has chances to work with moods and effects upon the reader—all in abbreviated pieces. He sharpens his perception of people and events. He does in 600 words what any short story writer does in 10,000 and a novelist does in 100,00.

Student writers are not generally capable of the novel nor the short story. They haven't had experience at extended plotting. They can paint a room, varnish the floors and repair the ceiling, but they can't be the architect of a skyscraper. And they haven't developed enough insight into human character to develop one fully enough for fiction —or to reasonably cause a change in characters, which is the essence of plot construction. To know and understand people takes years of sheer living.

The short short story, yes. And the light essay. The student can handle them both, and they lead to a future.

As time and experience pass, the young writer learns to use repetition to accumulate effect, to select words carefully to establish mood, to hint at things but never to bring them into the open until the climactic moment. He learns to back into the action rather than telling in chronological order (which lacks emphasis), or to use flashbacks, or to slide into the action sideways, like Faulkner. He learns to surprise the reader with the unexpected adjective. He learns to reveal a character by what is said and done, rather than telling the reader outrightly that a character is "that way."

He learns to shift gears by changing sentence and paragraph structures, by slowing down the reader and then, with quick paragraphs, sending him pell-mell down the hillside, unable to stop himself for fear of falling on his nose. He learns to portray characters who talk like people, and with each one distinctive in pattern of speech.

He learns to make readers laugh and cry, to feel uneasy about the rustle of the curtains, to make them feel the rush in of happiness or the ebb of sadness. He learns to make them love a character like Ichabod Crane or to feel compelled to sing aloud the words, as Dylan Thomas does.

Somewhere, the young writer must start, and the informal essay is a proper place.

So, let's see what a high school journalist can do with it.

Inspiration. Clague Hodgson, when a high school junior at Rochester, Minn., was fascinated by a remote control for the television set. Zap!—and the channel was changed. As Clague toyed with the gadget, his mind—that of a writer—began to seek humor.

Development. In the next few days, at idle moments, he speculated on what he could do with a remote control. He decided he could refashion the whole electronically-inspired world. He brought into play enough of his science background to give his essay pseudo-scientific authority. "A book on electronics taught me by squaring the voltage ($3^2 = 9$), I could also square the effective range of my control (150 ft.$^2 = 9000$ ft.)." He began to see his essay as a series of incidents, each one showing his build up to power.

Twist to the tale. He decided his power would benefit mankind. By eradicating from the air the inadequacies of television he would pose as the saviour of the human race. He would not be a villain.

Narrative point of view. First person. But he had to be careful to laugh at himself; he could not sound egotistical.

Opening and closing sections. He used chronological order leading to the present . . . with a suggestion of suspense in the opening: "I suppose it started last spring." Clague's opening section is weak in that it doesn't cause enough curiosity in the reader. The closing section is very weak because it doesn't resolve the situation in the most humorous section of the essay. Instead, it takes a doubtful, vague, easy way out of a dilemma. Most light essays have the same fault. They build up—to nothing. They let down the reader, leaving him with a touch of disappointment.

Here is the essay, satirical more than anything else, about "The Aero-Control Tyrant."

A Satire

The Aero-Control Tyrant

By CLAGUE HODGSON

I suppose it started last spring. I was in the hospital recuperating from a skiing accident, and they had strung me into a jungle-jim contraption that restricted everything but my mind. When I asked the nurse to turn on the TV, she informed me that all I had to do was punch a button at my side.

I spent the remainder of the evening experimenting with the device. By rapidly flicking the row of buttons, I sent the various channels whizzing across the screen. Now darker, now lighter, now on, now off, but always the Aero-Control held the pace.

Perhaps my greatest thrill that night came when I chopped off that repetitious Aspirin commercial.

Later that night, I couldn't sleep because the idiot in the next room had the late movie turned on full blast. But Aero-Control came to my aid. By aiming it at the radiator across the hall, I discovered I could reflect the waves back into his room and chop the power to his set. But I didn't quiet him for long. With his Aero Control, he revived his set. Soon a full scale duel was in progress. It was a fight to the bitter end. In a final coup d'état I inserted a fresh three-volt battery into my control unit and nailed his channel selector to a test pattern.

The next day he was transferred to the psychiatric ward.

My near escape in the duel taught me one thing. My three-volt battery was not nearly powerful enough.

That was when I discovered the nine-volt battery. A book on electronics taught me by squaring the voltage ($3^2=9$), I could also square the effective range ($150ft^2=9,000$ ft.).

Now I had all the TV sets in town at my mercy. The night after my first nine-volt test, this little obscurity appeared in the evening paper:

Freak Incident Baffles Police

Eighty-two home owners reported that their radio-controlled automatic garage doors mysteriously opened and then closed again. The chief of police is unable to explain last night's incidents.

Two more tests brought equally astounding results. On the third test the signal was strong enough to set off the automatic timing on a bank vault.

By now I was adding to my arsenal. I had installed a directional antenna and a beaming rotor, and I perfected a frequency modulator which enabled me to operate garage doors, TV sets, bank vaults, and radio-stop-lights without bolixing everything at the same time. By this time I had tapped the street current (440 volts), and thus extended my domain over the entire tri-state area.

As my first sovereign act—just to prove my power, I removed the Beverly Hillbillies from all Aero-Control sets and substituted runs of famous pain reliever commercials. I admit I had to shed a few nostalgic tears as I watched the old hinged flap once again pump B's into the bloodstream. Next I called on the concentrated stomach acid that burned a hole in an asbestos handkerchief. As a finale, a pill traveled through a spiral glass esophagus and slowly flaked away into a nebulous milky residue.

It was very moving.

For a time, under my rule civilization reached a practical high plane in Rochester. Fattened oafs again went for walks when I chopped off their TV sets. Homeowners stepped from their cars and pulled garage doors up by hand. Bankers returned to the combination lock. Cops threw away their crazy radar equipment and again screeched out from behind billboards, lights whirling, sirens screaming, to chase the speeding car.

Almost overnight I became famous as a saviour of the human race. People from all over started coming to see my rig. One man even came all the way from Washington to see me.

"My name is Javits," he said. "I represent the Federal Bureau of Investigation. May I inform you that you are in very serious trouble?"

One strength of the light essay is its devotion to fact. The details in Clague's essay are specific—exact TV programs, exact voltage, sights (on the TV screen) common to human experience and emotion.

And the essay is based upon a simple experience everyone can understand and enjoy. The style, too, is quick, lean, and disciplined.

For a 17-year-old writer, it is an exceptional light essay. Professional essayists would be hard-pressed to do better.

One last comment about the light essay: it does not have to be humorous. It can make use of such other emotions as sympathy, happiness, nostalgia, excitement, suspense, reverence, security.

Mood is important. At Christmas, for instance, a happy time of the year, light essays must be carefully drawn to depict the proper mood. One journalist wanted to write about violent moments in the lives of the Santa Clauses of the world. He had collected a file of anecdotes about Santa Claus being mugged, being assaulted, dying of heart attacks, absconding with funds. But the essay would have insulted the spirit of Christmas—and along with it the reader. His story awaits a cynical magazine.

Another essayist turned to the religious experience that Christmas provides. He recalled a story told him by a friend who had visited in desert Africa. The essayist recast the story in narrative style, adding description and dialogue to cast pictures for the readers:

> On the far side of the camp, the camels snuffled in half-sleep.
> "Have your eyes seen the star that shined the night your God was born?" the desertman asked.

Here, in a light essay, a not humorous but still pleasant experience, is how one professional writer handled Christmas:

The Desertman Who Saw the Star

Far into the desert of North Africa, a camel track winds up from the heart of the continent and plods across the sands toward the Holy City of Mecca. It is etched into the desert floor by centuries of camel trains. Time is stationary. It is now as it was then.

And it is there that an American, a Christian, had reaffirmed for him a few years ago the full meaning of Christmas.

As a night fire threw quick shadows into the desert, a desertman plied him with questions. "Have you been to your Holy City?"

"No, but I shall go as soon as my wife joins me."

The desertman, a Moslem, laughed uproariously. "But one does not take his wife to the Holy City," he protested. "I shall go to my Holy City as soon as my sons are old enough to watch over my belongings."

On the far side of the camp, the camels snuffled in half-sleep.

"Have your eyes seen the star that shined the night your God was born?" the desertman asked.

Answers had to be carefully thought out and phrased. The American finally answered that he had not. It had happened many centuries ago.

"Ahhh, but my eyes have seen the star that shined on the night your God was born." The humble desertman stared into time. "I am part of my father, am I not? And part of my eye was part of his, is it not? And was not my father a part of his father?"

He traced his ancestry down the centuries.

"Therefore, my eye is part of the eye of my ancestor who gazed upon the Great Star that rose the night your God was born."

He was grave. Only the camels touched the silence of the night.

"It is strange," he said finally. "Your eyes have not seen the star. I am but a humble man, and yet my eyes have gazed upon that star. And my camels have seen it and have followed it to the land where your God was born.

"It is strange," the desertman said.

JUXTAPOSITION — Relationship of unexpected objects creates interest. Here: Abercrombie, plus chain, plus lock, plus blackness. Sometimes a mood picture such as this can be used to illustrate an article, or to call readers' attention to an unusual "sight" on campus. Sometimes, the aesthetic alone can carry a news photographer's work.

Chapter XV

EDITING AND DISPLAYING THE LIGHT ESSAY

When and where can the informal essay be used in student publications?

Sometimes in the yearbook—when it is used to summarize the year or to recall some exceptional event of the year, such as the Biggest Blizzard in 50 Years.

Extensively in the literary magazine—with little fiction of value being written by students, essays provide the bulk of the prose. Formal essays provide the profundity; informal essays provide the entertainment and thoughtfulness.

In newspapers, columnists regularly use informal essays. Otherwise, essays can be published on periodic literary pages or in literary sections which are inserted into some issues (see illustration 13: an example of a special literary page taken from *The Rocket* of John Marshall High, Rochester, Minn.).

An informal essay also can be used on the editorial page, which is customarily a place for opinion. There, newspapers should try to publish an essay per issue, selecting the best submitted by the staff or by students elsewhere in the school. The essay should be given a set heading like this:

It Seems to Me

And then a line or two should be included each time to describe the content and the mood of the essay, like this:

It Seems to Me
Time to Buckle
Down to Safety

159

A familiar essay

One cat's family

(or happily Yul-tied')

By SUE COOPER
Rocket Staff Writer

Yul Brynner would not like our cat . . . even though the cat was named for him.

Yul is a Siamese cat, but not just any Siamese cat. He has features that no other cat could possibly have . . . or want. Nature gave Yul a pair of the most beautiful blue eyes—the color poets write odes to. Then as an afterthought nature crossed them. Yul also has his own war club. It is his tail. The way he swings it when he's angry is very effective. He has conquered all these defects, however, with an unmatchable personality. He imagines himself a human being, and no one can tell him differently.

IN HIS THREE YEARS of life he has gone through several different stages. The first was the clothes-chute stage. It consisted of running up two flights of stairs, jumping into the clothes chute, and after giving a war whoop sailing two stories into a pile of dirty clothes. Once in the clothes he lay on his back, purred contentedly, and imagined himself the Wilbur Wright of the cat species. Two minutes later he was again running up the two flights of stairs.

Once I found him purring in the clothes and screamed, "Out!"

"Meow," he retorted and burrowed farther into the clothes until only his beady eyes showed. Then he blinked and settled back purring. Battle at the clothes chute lost.

Another early stage was bird fright. Yul was absolutely petrified by birds because they always outsmarted him. He finally overcame the phobia. One day he found a dead bird, picked it up, and carried it around for the rest of the day. To him it symbolized that birds were not invincible.

He is fascinated by paper sacks and loves to run around with a sack over his head. The day that he applies for membership in the Ku Klux Klan, we may have to break the habit.

HIS LATEST STAGE is watching television. If no one else is watching, he whines until someone turns on the set. If the program is not to his liking he complains until someone changes the channel. His favorite program is "Huckleberry Hound." He idolizes the lion Snagglepuss and has set him up as the Elvis Presley of the cat world. If that lion ever makes records we will undoubtedly go broke buying records for the cat.

Until that time we may go broke buying steaks and chicken for his well developed appetite.

If an outer spaceman knocked on our door and said, "Take me to your leader," I'd take him straight to Yul. Who knows . . . maybe he'd be so fascinated he'd take Yul back to his planet.

And Yul of course, would immediately think he is a Martian.

A Rocket review

A fuse blows . . . and machines
push the world near to war

By ANN POUGIALES
Rocket News Editor

FAIL - SAFE, by Eugene Burdick and Harvey Wheeler. McGraw-Hill. 286 pages. $4.50.

"U. S. President Averts Accidental War" could well have been a newspaper headline on the day the Fail-Safe system failed. In this novel, authors Burdick and Wheeler express their skepticism of the Fail-Safe system and the men who control it.

The "system" supposedly employs all possible means to avert an accidental war, largely through the use of reliable machines. When a fuse blows unnoticed in one of the machines and sends a convoy of six bombers to Moscow, an atmosphere of suspense is created which permeates the whole book . . . who will win? man or machine?

THE ACTION TRAVELS from the War Room in Omaha, to the Pentagon, to the White House, to the Kremlin, to New York City in a "meanwhile back at the ranch" style. Yet, the fast-moving pace retains the reader's interest. The style is outwardly objective, but there is significance between the lines.

The book, a current best-seller, provides entertainment, information, and for the discerning reader, a challenge. Can man entrust his future to a machine?

The authors have also criticized the Pentagon, that organization which aims at the mechanization of men. At one point, a lead theorist on preventive warfare divulges a long concealed thought. "Knowing you have to die, imagine how fantastic and magical it would be to have the power to take everyone with you . . . the person with his finger on the button is the one who knows and who can do it."

IN A LAST ATTEMPT to prevent war, the young U. S. President establishes a conference line with Khruschev. The two leaders realize they have put too much trust in the Fail-Safe system. "You can never trust any system, Mr. President," Khrushchev says, "whether it is made of computers or of people . . ."

"But we did trust them—that's what made us both helpless when it broke down," replies the President.

The two then agree on a new policy: "The computer proposes: man disposes."

The art corner

Photograph by Tyler Monson

JM SENIOR EDD CLARK reverses the usual integration pattern as he is outlined by black gowns and white tassels at last year's graduation. The picture was taken in the JM gymnasium where Clark sat as a junior marshal surrounded by graduating seniors.

Photographer Tyler Monson says about the picture, "I was just playing around with a 23-year-old Leica 35 mm. camera . . . . The picture's only aesthetic values are the contrast of black and white and the pattern with the tassels."

A soul yearns

A soul yearns.
a fire burns.
A whispered thought,
a method sought.
Then running feet,
a measured beat.
The rattle and clank
of the moving tank.
A secret war
and then no more
the soul yearns.
No fire burns—
where freedom ought
to be.
—John Pearson, '63

Exile (?)

tree whistles, silver and blond,
a night song over yellow lake,
warm water ripples the dawn's
death trapped with a glower snake

toy moons swing under black sails,
purple light stalks shadows in no day,
end comes to watch wearing tails,
those under grey leaves won't stay

lantern goes out minus sound,
Change amber waves into blue-white
sand,
soft arrows long last have found,
this my own, my fatherland.
—Linda Forest, '63

Storm

I stand on a hill with the
moon burning down,
and the sea like a silver
whipped dream.
Sea spray in my hair and
salt on my lips,
and the wind blowing by
with a scream.
I shall dance with the waves
~~~~~~~~ ~~~~ the wind
and stand to the force
of the gale.
—Cindy Shick, '65

I have love

If I saw
The sun rise on a beautiful day,
The children coming out to play,
The vast magnificence of all of God's
creation,
And did not see them through love,
I saw nothing.

If I heard
The beauty of a new born's heart beat,
The people laughing on the street,
The praises that his people sing,
And did not hear them through love,
I heard nothing.

If I felt
The hurt of what someone had said,
The loneliness 'cause someone now was
dead,
The closeness of my God when I take the
time to pray,
And did not feel through: love,
I felt nothing.

If I have
All the riches of the earth,
All my life to be filled with mirth,
A God who has promised me everlasting
peace
And do not have them through love
I have nothing.

I have seen, I have heard, and I have felt
The evils of men that love can melt,
And I have gifts given from above
For I have love.
—Gary Winter, '63

Time heals
al wounds

Time heals all wounds so they say—
Fools!
It only digs deeper—gnawing out
more and more.
Time tears at the soul—'til mind and
body are almost diverged.
It reflects the memories that once
held so much promise.
Time and the memories remain—only
you must change.
—Laurie Sues, '63

Rochester

Medical Center for the World,
Educator, Manufacturer,
Food Producer, Shopkeeper;
Strong, merciful, prosperous
City of Wealth:

They say you are a healer, and I believe
them; for I have seen your Mayo
Clinic and the people who have hopefully sought help there.

They tell me you are beautiful, and I
agree; for I have seen your wide
streets, subways, and clean buildings,
your lovely parks and well kept
homes.

You are strong in your youth, faithful in
your religion, and proud to be Educator, Manufacturer, Food Producer
and Shopkeeper: A City of Wealth in
the Land of Lakes.
—Chris Billings, '65

Sad parting

Sleet and snow
Dark and drear
Strong winds blow
There is no cheer
To help my heart
Hold back a tear
When we part.
—Ron Struckmann, '63

Sketches

THE POLITICIAN
The politician, a learned man is he,
Kissing young children upon his knee;
With an honest record, free from a
smear,
And a friend to all at this time each
year.
The party works hard, raising funds
To finance his speeches of jokes and
puns;
As he rambles on, long and loud,
In front of his ever diminishing crowd.
From the rostrum, promises galore,
Only to be left on the platform floor.
In the Southern States he speaks with a
drawl,
While in other states you can't hear it
at all.
A somber suit with a wrinkle or two,
A bow tie and a hole in his shoe,
So the common man can plainly see
He is not from the aristocracy.
He definitely has that well-fed look;
In parliamentary procedure he follows
the book.
Laying cornerstones, planting trees
Is obviously not a life of ease.
When in the city, a plug for labor,
While on the farm, a friendly neighbor.
He certainly knows how to play the part;
Being a politician is quite an art.

THE DOCTOR
The grey old doctor, a kindly gent,
Service to others his life has meant.
From early morning'til late at night,
He continues in his constant fight
Against germs, disease, and injuries too.
Staph and cancer, to name a few.
Much of his learning is not from books
But gained from questions, prods and
looks.
Over the years his fund of knowledge
Has greatly increased past that of
college.
Because at night with the day's work
done
He turns to his books for his evening's
fun.
Or joins his coworkers for a chat
On medical problems of this and that.
For greater stimulation he can be found
Visiting doctors for miles around.
Too bad this man, so skilled with a knife,
Cannot be trusted with a patient's life,
As shaking palsy has afflicted his hand
And diminished his talents to the average
man's.

THE BOXER
Long on brawn, short on brain;
The way to win is to train and train.
Month in, month out, what a pace
He must keep up to win the race!
Fifteen rounds once a year
For a half million free and clear.
Two minutes six seconds is all it takes
For him with a build like an oversized
ape's.
With arms so long and strength so great,
He made short work of his little play-
mate.
All over the land his picture is known,
Including mug books most frequently
shown.
—Paul Lipscomb, '63

Illustration 13

The essay should also get a two-line byline to identify the writer and his background, such as this:

By Tom Magerkurth
A sophomore at East High

The Rocket of Rochester, Minn., which was named All-American nine consecutive times, used a light essay in every issue, always on the editorial page, placed in the upper right-hand corner under the set-head, "Thoughts," including a second headline about the content of the essay. It became an institution because of its regularity and its quality (see illustration 14).

On full pages of literary matter, the light essay can be treated in headlining and in layout exactly like features (see chapter 6). The one variation: the essay lends itself to label heads, which give a thought in abbreviated form, like a title:

One Cat's Family

Whereas, the usual sentence headline demands subject-verb treatment for sentence sense:

The Head of Our Family Is—a Cat!

A label head in most newspapers is unexpected fare—just as the informal essay is exceptional. Therefore, in mood, the two go together.

On rare occasions, when the essay is especially timely, it may be used in a *package** with a news story on the news pages. In the professional press, the humorous essays of Art Buchwald are split off from a breaking story, but rarely, and only when the essay is almost news in itself. For instance, the essay which opens the chapter about writing the light essay could have been linked with a news story about graduation.

Artwork is a necessity for light essays, especially if they run long. The staff artist can do half-column inserts to go with the story (see illustration 14, the artwork under "Thoughts"), or he can do one- and two-column illustrations to appear on literary pages (see illustration 13, the artwork used with "One Cat's Family"). Photographs rarely fit.

Topic for the week: 'images' of JM

Vandals give JM black eye, says Mayor

A car parked at the **Rochester Post Bulletin** was marked with the number "63," the entrance to the National Food Store reads "64" and a water tower has been sprayed several times with "63."

The vandalism outbreak is a source of disgust for many city and school officials.

"We don't want this . . . I deplore this," said Rochester Mayor Alex Smetka last week about the markings.

JM's Student Council President Tom Mahler said, "I'm disappointed in the few students responsible for these actions."

James J. Macken, Jr., Rochester chief of police, remarked, "Only about one percent of the students

"Now, no one can say there's anything wrong with our school spirit"

are causing this trouble, but they're giving all of John Marshall a black eye."

The writings appeared in late October. "We never had any such trouble before," commented Mayor Smetka.

He continued, "I felt that with the background and with the type of city Rochester is, students at John Marshall would take it upon themselves to police and discipline the very few who think it smart to paint numerals on various buildings."

The police are investigating the vandalism. Chief Macken said, "These people will be caught and soon."

Mayor Smetka said those responsible will be charged with willful damage of property.

Both Mahler and Mayor Smetka have ideas about how to handle the problem.

Mahler said, "I feel the student body should put pressure on those responsible. I hope they stop before they get caught. They will be in deep trouble."

Mayor Smetka said, "I'd put them to work scrubbing those numerals off. It's unfortunate that a few are giving a black eye to the city. Really it's not so much the city who is getting the black eye as it is JM."

Assistant JM Principal Jennings Johnson and Mayor Smetka felt that the writings were done as a prank. Mr. Johnson remarked, "It is always wrong to do something, playful or not, that causes damage to someone else's person or property."

All officials agree on one point that possibly other students or outside parties are responsible to some extent for the writings.

"Certainly we don't feel John Marshall students are the only ones responsible for this," Chief Macken said.

Finally Mayor Smetka reminded JM students of taking greater pride in their school. "Constantly I hear people from all over the country referring to Rochester as having one of the top public school systems in the country. I sincerely hope John Marshall students show respect befitting such a school system."

Letters to the editor

Val Gould assembly draws fire

The recent appearance of "Mr. Quaker" at a JM assembly has brought about two letters to the *Rocket*. Both are criticisms of his message and technique. Other students are encouraged to write further letters; they will be published in next week's *Rocket*.

Rocket Editor:

"Well, did you expect me to be shot from a gun?" shouted Mr. Quaker to an all-school assembly Oct. 24. Such action would have aroused more patriotism than his lengthy speech did.

"Now listen here." By commanding their attention, Val Gould, representing Mr. Quaker, insulted the intelligence of his audience. His melodramatic use of stage whispers, heaven-imploring gestures, and background music do not belong in a serious presentation of a high ideal.

"I represent the Quaker Oats Company." Val Gould's authority depends on his employment by the manufacturers of a hot breakfast cereal as a public relations man. This authority is not strong enough to support an emotional speech.

"I'll skip over these facts . . ." By skipping over the economic, social and political ideals, he missed the basis of our democracy and also our patriotism. Instead, he appealed to our religious conscience to inspire patriotism.

As Americans, we feel our patriotism is independent of a dramatized, unauthorized, religious speech. We have a rich history and heritage. This is our country . . . to have and to hold.

Sincerely,
Sue Hokanson and Vickey Noser
JM seniors

Rocket Editor:

Mr. Val Gould, alias Mr. Quaker, made an impression on JM. With his corny jokes and funny dress, Mr. Quaker thrust himself physically upon his captive audience here at JM.

The audience was captive, and he knew it and played upon it. His only problem was to keep the attention of the unfortunate people before him.

He kept their attention well with his loud voice and waving arms, while he filled their minds with his meaningless speech.

Mr. Quaker filled the auditorium with his wonderful generalities as "We will skip over these . . ." He skipped all right—right over the important fact that the American system is based on the people. He skipped over to appeal to religion. He made it sound as though the American Constitution was given to the Founding Fathers by the hand of God.

He mentions that Benjamin Franklin moved that the Constitutional Convention pray for guidance, but he did not mention that the motion was voted down!

Mr. Quaker skipped over the fact that the only way that America is going to beat the Russians is by military, economic, and political means. God is not going to step in personally to wallop the Russians.

Mr. Quaker made an emotional appeal, rather than a rational appeal, to sway his audience. He must have felt that his audience was very stupid. Does he think that the students of John Marshall are unable to reason for themselves and must be told what to think?

Sincerely,
John Pearson
A JM senior

The John Marshall Rocket

is published on Fridays, except for exam weeks and holidays by the Journalism I and II classes at John Marshall High School, Rochester, Minn. The publisher is the Schmidt Printing Company of Mankato, Minn. The newspaper is distributed free to all students.

HONORS: All-American in 1961 and 1962; Columbia Medalist in 1962; Quill & Scroll International Honors in 1961 and 1962; George H. Gallup award in 1961; Best Printed Newspaper Northwest Interscholastic Press Association; 1962 national best-sportswriting plaque (from ANPA) in both 1961 and 1962; six Quill & Scroll national writing awards, 1961, 1962; All-Columbian for literary excellence (1962).

At a recent football game at John Marshall, a junior high girl walked by the fence surrounding the football field. A little boy ran up behind her and grabbed her hair. It came off.

Fortunately, she was wearing a "wig-hat," better known as "wig-wags."

In the past, wigs could be purchased only by those who could afford the high price. Now anyone can have black, platinum, red c h a m - pagne, gray, blue, silver, or green hair for $2.98.

This modern wig is economical in other ways, too. A girl can remove her "hair" at any moment and shake it into a hat.

Stores in Rochester are unable to keep up with the demand for wigs, said a clerk at Penney's. The brown and the champagne shades are the most popular, she added.

Wigs are versatile. They can be combed, brushed, or sprayed. Naturally, they should be dry cleaned, not washed. If they are washed, they can lead to the anguished shrieks of "I can't do a thing with my wig today."

It is interesting and amusing to watch customers shop for wigs. Some dash to them with cries of delight. Others slip up to them rather nervously.

Some g i r l s with o l i v e complexions like to wear blue hair whereas some fair-skinned girls favor stark-black w i g s . Once the big step is taken and the wig is on, customers generally react with laughter. Nevertheless, they buy them.

Girls often appear self-conscious wearing their wigs. Other people's reactions to them vary from winks and smiles to guffaws.

The wigs are sold to all age groups. The sales clerk at Penney's said she has sold wigs to very young children and to an 87-year-old woman.

Wigs can drastically change an adult's appearance. One mother achieves the Cleopatra-look by wearing her daughter's raven-black wig. In it, the father bears a shocking resemblance to Adolf Hitler.

Wigs are worn everywhere—while driving, in the house, and at football games. They seem to tease little boys into snatching them.

Shots & tho'ts:

Gail Franke, a senior: "He liked the 'Tea for Two Cha-cha' the best of the dances, but he really enjoyed the w h o l e evening. He was especially impressed with the mature conduct of

Sue Cooper, a junior: "He got a chance to show off his twisting ability, which is sort of modernistic."

Jackie Antenthie, a sophomore: "He liked the dancing best of all, especially the twist. He does a sort of odd step to the slow dance."

What did your father like best about the Father-Daughter Dance at JM

Brenda Tuttle, a senior: "He is a fabulous dancer, so naturally he enjoyed the dancing most. This is the second year we have won the prize for best dancers."

Girls find wigs a boon since they can be worn to cover a ravaged hair-do, or as warm hats, or as attention getters (though the attention is not always favorable), or purely for fun.

Although boys may snicker at artificial blue or red hair, girls may have the last laugh. A wig is now being produced exclusively for boys.

—By Sue Crawford, '63

Illustration 14

Lastly, to get essays, the school must be searched for good writers. Teachers of English can provide leads to writers and to individual essays already written for class. The teachers periodically must be asked for information; they usually are too busy to worry about the needs of the publications issue by issue. Editors should know personally all the good writers in school and regularly ask them for their best work, or ask them to do special essays, much like assigning stories to reporters. But the best source is the staff, itself. The essays column can be held out as a type of reward to them.

Some school publications sponsor contests. One mimeograph paper conducts a "Riter's Roundup" in each issue, on one page publishing the best essays submitted to the editor. Another conducts a creative writing contest and awards cash prizes. There are many ideas to be explored. But in each case where the publication seeks outside contributions, a prospectus should be mimeographed, listing specific requirements for length, for subject matter, for style and organization. It should be distributed widely.

Prospective essayists should be directed for guidance to fine professional work: the Reflections column in the weekly *The National Observer;* the Phoenix Nest in *Saturday Review;* the Accent on Living section in *Atlantic;* the columns of Russell Baker three times weekly on the editorial pages of *The New York Times*; the columns of the syndicated Buchwald, Vaughan, Gould and Harry Golden.

The efforts pay off—in variety for the publication, in prestige, in service to the school. And most important of all, in encouraging writing among students. As a literary magazine, the *Pride of South Park* (in New York state) summed up the philosophy in a preface: "In an age when 'Johnny can't read' or 'Johnny can't write,' it is heartening to find we have some Johnnies, and Marys, too, who can both read and write. We hope, by producing our anthology, we are doing something in a small way, to encourage our students to write."

Literary Content

Chapter XVI

REVIEWING POPULAR ARTS

HOW THE STUDENT DOES IT—THE REVIEW

By DOTTIE CANNON

Our Lady of Mercy H.S., Rochester, N.Y.

No Plea for Equality . . .

'The Fire Next Time' Evaluates Racial Problems

The Fire Next Time by James Baldwin is a shocking, penetrating evaluation of the racial problem in America by an educated American Negro.

Baldwin's approach is neither radical nor sentimental, nor does he plead for Negro "equality." For him, equality does not mean the measuring of one individual against another to compare intellectual capabilities or moral eligibility. There is no need for the Negro to work for equality; he has been equal for 400 years!

Working on this assumption, Baldwin transfers the "problem" of racial equality to white Americans. According to him, it is the white who must re-evaluate and re-adjust his moral values and correlate the black standard and the white standard into one pattern of thought, from which he can rationally assess the racial problem.

His sequence of thought is clear, unemotional, non-political. He blames the treatment of his race not on separate white individuals but on the basic immaturity of the American people as a whole. He theorizes that America is mesmerized by its own brainwashing, and until it recovers its identity we are destined to misery, heartache, hatred, and war; in his own words: "Rather the white man is in sore need of new standards which will release him from his confusion and place him once again in

165

fruitful communion with the depths of his own being. And I repeat: The price of the liberation of the white people is the liberation of the blacks —the total liberation, in the cities, in the towns, before the law, in the mind."

This liberation does not mean the nominal freedom by the passage of laws obliging integration, explains Mr. Baldwin. Nor does it include the offensive, patronizing congratulations extended by whites to blacks—or by whites to whites—on the approval of such laws.

"For example," he says, "white Americans congratulate themselves on the 1954 Supreme Court decision outlawing segregation in the schools; they suppose, in spite of the mountain of evidence that has since been accumulated to the contrary, that this was proof of a change of heart— or, as they like to say, progress." He describes these meaningless gestures as "tokenism."

Solution begins with the deep, heartfelt conviction that the Negroes are of equal worth as human beings, however different their psychology as a race may be.

This book should have a special significance for Christians, for Baldwin's analysis contains a special bitterness for the hypocrisy of Christians who preach love and yet irrationally hate. In this cloud of bitterness, he equates America to Christian Germany during the Third Reich, saying, "From my own point of view, the fact of the Third Reich alone makes obsolete forever any question of Christian superiority, except in technological terms."

This and many more earth-shattering, shockingly credible statements are made by Mr. Baldwin in *The Fire Next Time*. It is a thought-provoking, intuitive summation of a problem whose solution is so crucial to the well-being of America.

* To be a critic, authority is needed.
* To be a reviewer, knowledge is needed.

Thus, it follows that student journalists can serve as reviewers, but rarely can provide legitimate criticism. That statement will insult those egocentric writers who think that reading a handful of books or that completion of a unit of study in critical writing entitles them to professional stature. Hardly! It requires years of concentrated study, of close contact with an art to become an experienced critic, the person who can praise and attack, who can explain and analyze intelligently and honestly.

It takes much less to be a reviewer, and that is where the student journalist should start.

For instance, the novels of J. D. Salinger for several years have been popular with student readers. A student reviewer could report several things about them—a brief summary of the plot, the book's relationship to previous works by Salinger, facts about the sales success, perhaps a few comments about how the professional reviewers and critics have greeted it, newsworthy details about the book and its authorship. Such material is basically objective in nature. The student reviewer might even be somewhat subjective in reporting—gently—his personal reaction to the book, good and bad. He might even compare the book—like an essayist—to his own experiences as a teenager.

But when the student tries to discuss the book as a contribution to art, interpreting its symbolism, analyzing its styles, determining its place in contemporary literature, even to outrightly accepting or rejecting it, he may be overstepping his qualifications.

● Remember, the student journalist can be knowledgeable, but rarely authoritative. Oh, yes, in English class he is asked to analyze and to explicate prose and poetry, but that is a learning exercise, not a semi-professional effort to be distributed publicly under the guise of expertise.

At this point, let us, step by step, look at the process of writing a book review—not a critical essay.

Selecting a book. The selection is determined by the interests of the audience, which consists of young people concerned with learning. Thus, books about youth would be of interest (in the past, such books have been *The Shookup Generation,* by Harrison Salisbury; *Teenage Tyranny,* by Grace and Fred M. Hechinger; *Society and the Adolescent Self-Image,* by Morris Rosenberg; hundreds of such books every year).

Or, books about schools and the processes of education (such as, *The Schools,* by Martin Mayer; *High School English Textbooks, A Critical Examination,* by James J. Lynch and Bertrand Evans; the novel, *Up the Down Staircase,* by Bel Kaufman; *Campus, U.S.A.,* by David Boroff).

Or, about teenage or student culture (Salinger's novels; *Too Far to Walk,* by John Hersey; *In His Own Write,* by John Lennon).

Books about teachers, about rock 'n' roll and its heroes. Books by teenage authorities (*Who Has the Answer?,* by Dorothy Gordon, moderator of radio's Youth Forum); about life at college (*Revolution at Berkeley,* by Michael V. Miller and Susan Gilmore).

Also, new books by the established authors, especially those whose books represent literary values.

Somehow, the book must be of *considerable* interest to students. And, above all, it should be contemporary—even immediate—in its interest to the public. There rarely is a reason for reviewing a book out-of-date or out-of-discussion; yet, in student publications, reviews are written about *Silas Marner, The Old Man and the Sea,* and even, as noted not too long ago in a high school paper, *Goodbye, Mr. Chips.* Such reviews could be accepted if something new and local has happened to the book; maybe it has been added to the course of study for senior English (such as *Lord of the Flies*) or has incited new controversy (as *Catcher in the Rye*) or has begun a comeback as a paperbound book (works of Nathanael West, of James Agee, of Daniel Fuchs).

Otherwise, that seemingly eternal triumvirate of news values is triumphant: proximity to the reader, timeliness, and importance.

Some books *must* be reviewed. For instance, when in 1965 *Up the Down Staircase,* a novel about a first-year teacher and her students in a slow learner's class, placed on the list of best sellers for over a year, it should have been reviewed. And when in 1962, the Hechingers' *Teen-age Tyranny* claimed that teen-age culture was permeating adult society, the book should have been commented about. And, in line with the Beatles' fad (or was it fashion?) in the middle 1960's, the books by one of the group, John Lennon, should have been reviewed.

Where do you find leads to such books? The best bet is to assign a student to read each week *Publishers' Weekly* or *The Library Journal,* which in ads and short reviews list new books prior to publication. Any likely prospects can be listed in a future book and assigned for reviewing at the most newsworthy time, generally at the date of publication.

The school and city librarians are good sources for ideas. If they know the school publication is interested, they will watch for suitable books—and most likely be happy to reserve each new book as it comes in. Teachers of English, too, are familiar with new works. Other good sources include book sections of the Sunday newspapers.

By directors

Three facets of drama discussed

By Barbara Faulconer
Rocket Staff Writer

Who is a director? If you are an actor you fear him. If you are a playwright you depend on him to make your play a success. And if you are a playgoer you probably couldn't care less about him. But a director has to care about the playgoer. Along with the actor and the playwright, he considers the audience one of the three major influences on his work.

"Most people prefer comedy,"

Mr. Burdette Moeller, JM director, stated. "People come to the theater to get away from daily tragedy."

Mr. Dwain Johnson, JM's other director, agreed with Mr. Moeller. "People prefer comedy, although pseudo-sophisticates are attracted to tragedy. There is more social prestige in it. More and more we go to see what we want to be seen seeing and less and less to what we want to see. The theater is a symbol of sophistication."

A second thing a director must consider in his cast. Mr. Johnson stated, "In comedy there is a constant demand on timing, which is difficult for the amateur actor. Timing must be very controlled in this type of play.

"In comedy, timing must be instilled in a person," commented Mr. James Cavanaugh, director of the Rochester Civic Theatre. "Anyone can count three before they cry in a tragedy. But in comedy, each night dictates the timing. In drama the actors are more easily led through their paces." One of the most important jobs a director has is choosing the right play. "I have chosen my plays for their themes," stated JM English teacher, Mrs. Claire Van Zant, who has had much directing experience in England.

"I like the challenge of comedies," explained Mr. Johnson. "Tragedies draw better but comedies are harder to direct. I chose to do 'Charley's Aunt' because its value was so universal."

Mr. Moeller also tends to do more comedy. "I think comedy is more realistic," he stated.

All in all, these directors seem to feel that the majority of playgoers prefer comedy, which is challenging for the director and difficult for the actor.

Descriptions by two seniors
portray animals' movements

(The following essays were written as assignments for the senior advanced placement English class when the class was told to describe the movements of a person or animal.)

* * *

The water is clean and cool, and the two fish dart through it in search of prey. The sun is already going down, and they have eaten nothing but water plants since morning. It is a bad time of year for them for the first frost has killed most of the summer bugs, and true winter, when the fish will need less food, is still a month away. **Suddenly their** patience is rewarded as, with a small splash, a faded, left-over ladybug drops into the water. She struggles frantically, attracting the fishes' attention. The two fish pretend indifference to each other, but each watches the other with a wary eye. As if doing a dance, the fish begin to circle the victim, searching for the best angle of attack.

Now the larger fish pounces —not at the ladybug, but at his partner, sending the smaller fish racing to the far side of the small, man-made pool. Here he hovers uncertainly behind a rock, outraged but timid.

With his competition disposed of, the conqueror returns to the ladybug and notes that she is growing weaker with each kick. There is no hurry. He pretends nonchalance and swims over to nibble a water leaf. In ten leisurely seconds he is back, again studying his victim. Almost casually he darts at her and misses. Now his impatience is aroused. He charges viciously and sucks the morsel into his puckering mouth. After only a short struggle he swallows her and then swims over to his companion to gloat.

Bette Goldstein '66

* * *

The step was, perhaps, three feet wide and eight inches deep. It was only a part of the long stairway, but to the tiny albino

hamster this step and the carpeted cliff he must climb was all that mattered. He sized up the obstacle.

Back and forth, the length of the step, the hamster paced. He jerked to a stop—then moved on. His white-furred rump swiveled with each step of his pink hind paws. His ears stood up stiffly. The faint twitching of his nose attested to his alertness. He stopped again and scratched his chin with his right hind foot.

He marched up to the wall and, with his front paws on the vertical barrier, pulled himself upright. He dug his claws into the worn carpeting and stretched himself to full length. He was several inches short of the top. He lifted his left hind foot and scratched for a foothold. The nails caught the frayed fibers and he pushed his front feet farther up the surface. The other hind foot sought a hold as his hands held to the worn pile. For a moment he hung with three feet clinging to the wall. Nothing moved but his one foot frantically trying to grasp the face of the cliff. His nose twitched; he blinked his red eyes. His right front paw slipped. His left one released its hold. He rolled over on his back but promptly righted himself.

Following two more similarly unsuccessful attempts, the hamster tried the step's opposite side and quickly dropped over the edge. Perhaps there is always more than one way out of a situation.

Bob Ridenour '66

Nature is everything. It is the flowing of a mountain stream, the turning of leaves in the fall, the singing of a bird and the scream of a dying rabbit. Even in this day of the space age people still want to be with nature. To reject nature is to rebel against yourself.
—**Doug Ondler '66**

Rocket Literary Page

Number 2   November 24, 1965

Contributors: Barbara Faulconer, Marsha Forest, Bette Goldstein, Doug Ondler, Rita Pougiales, Bob Ridenour, Andrea Saint-George, Lynne Smith

A Rocket review

Kaufman describes different world

Up the Down Staircase
by Bel Kaufman
Prentice-Hall, Inc.

Copyright 1964   340 pages

Bel Kaufman uses vivid dialogues, stodgy curriculums, bright intraschool communications and long, tired letters to a married friend in suburbia to tell her story of going "Up the Down Staircase" in a large New York City high school.

The title explains the plot of this book. A young teacher fresh from college and a master's thesis on Chaucer, Miss Sylvia Barrett, trys to teach

English to students who are classified as special-slows in a room with a broken window that isn't fixed because the one-man custodial staff sends back messages like "There's nobody down here. Try after lunch."

Inside the deteriorating walls of Calvin Coolidge High School, she enters a world that was never mentioned in classes on "Meeting the Adolescent." A world where a boy skips school to marry a girl he doesn't like but whom he might have gotten into trouble and apologizes to the teacher. A world that makes a tough boy scream silently, "Love me back" and run out of

the room, damning a teacher who didn't realize his real need soon enough. A world hemmed in by brick walls, missing drawers, locked doors, paper work and students looking for answers they can't spell.

It is the offer of small classes, a good salary, and respect from a small private college that tempts Sylvia Barrett to leave Calvin Coolidge. It is a student who writes ". . . You know you can't get along without us, ha-ha" that convinces her to stay.

Andrea Saint-George '66

the campus poet

Photograph by Rita Pougiales

Come away with me

Come away with me
And watch the fertile valleys grow
And watch the open white-capped sea
And watch the gentle breezes blow.

Come away with me
And watch the flowers bloom in spring
And watch the leaves fill out a tree
And watch the birds lift into wing.

Come away with me
And hear the sound of war no more
And hear the sound of being free
Hear not the sound of shutting door.

Come away with me.
—**Marsha Forest '66**

Illustration 15

Weekly magazines carry sections of reviews (*Time* and *Newsweek*). Lists of best-sellers are found in most of the journals mentioned.

Where to get the book? The school library receives it too late, generally ordering it for delivery from six months to a year past publication date. Timeliness evaporates. Neither will publishers send review copies to student publications; the circulation is neither big enough nor the influence strong enough to merit free copies. The best bet is the community library, which often orders quickly—and receives quickly. Another possibility would be to make arrangements with a local bookstore so that a reviewer can quickly get a book at list price —or maybe free. Publishers, too, are generally willing to ship a book at list price by publication date, if an editor requests it on letterhead stationery. But, at the current high costs of books, the investment mounts too heavily too soon. Perhaps, the school library can rush-order a book because the newspaper wants to review it. And, then, there is borrowing the book from someone who has purchased it.

Getting the book at the most newsworthy moment can be difficult, but most good things in journalism are hard to come by.

Who should review a book? Match the book to the reviewer! If someone on the staff has read all of—and about—Salinger, let him work with the new Salinger novel. Science books go to the student scientist. *Up the Down Staircase,* about teaching, to a teacher. Remember the demand for authority, so match a book with the most logical near-expert, if possible. Otherwise, give it to the best general reviewers, proven by past work.

Where to publish reviews? For the newspaper, two possibilities.

(1) Reviews can be used on a full-page of literary matter run periodically (see "A Rocket Review," illustration 15, a literary page taken from an issue of the Rocket, John Marshall High, Rochester, Minnesota).

(2) As part of the editorial pages where opinion matter of all kinds is collected (see "Critic's Choice," illustration 16, from The Chariot of New Hyde Park, N.Y., Memorial High School).

Some staffs publish a literary insert, sometimes letterpress or offset, sometimes mimeograph. It is circulated with the regular papers (see illustration 17—the Weekend section of the Daily Orange at Syracuse

2 — Editorial THE CHARIOT Friday, October 18, 1963

Kick in the Teeth

Gladiators have been playing a different kind of football this season, wherein it's not a football they've been kicking around but rather N.H.P.'s pride and ideals.

Points To Ponder

"Don't worry about failure, unless it comes through your own fault."

F. Scott Fitzgerald

Critic's Choice

A Question Of Faith

by Anita Charney

When that certain rare occasion presents itself and I do have the time to read a book for sheer enjoyment, I, ironically and perhaps unwisely, decide which of the millions of books to read by a scanty glance at their covers. But no matter how fruitless past choices have proven themselves. I found **Remember Me to God** a most gratifying selection.

Written as a simple narrative by Myron S. Kaufman, this novel held more for me than I ever dreamed possible. The story takes place in and around Boston and Harvard University, constantly switching from one locale to the other.

And who are the players on this stage of life? Adam, the conscientious magistrate who clings to his Jewish heritage hoping his children will do the same; Bessie, his wife, the determined and devoted mother who can't bring herself to believe that their son is rejecting Judaism and its ancient concepts; Dorothy, fifteen-year-old Dorothy, who through her search for happiness brings herself only misery; and Richard, her twenty-year-old opportunist brother, son to said Adam and Bessie Amsterdam, who has had it with the Jewish faith, who has found himself only stifled by it, who is sure he is doing the first smart thing in his life, who is looking for a more profitable, more meaningful life, and has found a future in Christianity.

Through the Amsterdam's, Kaufman brings to life a prominent struggle in modern-day society. He describes the little squabbles and the big family friction in such moving and pointed detail, that it's hard to believe the arguments, as well as the beautiful scenes, aren't happening right before you.

These four people, their relatives and friends, are all so real, it's frightening! I've often wondered, as I'm sure most teenagers have, what role religion is going to play on my own stage of life. I don't say that Kaufman's novel will answer your questions; however, it may. But I do insist that no matter what your faith, you'll find much meaning in **Remember Me to God.** For although it is the story of the Jewish Amsterdams, its appeal is so universal that it could touch the lives of any one of us.

THE CHARIOT
"Carries The News"

All-Columbian—1961 First Place, Columbia Scholastic Press Ass'n

ESSPA School Service Award

Advisors .... Mr. Bernard Wallerstein, Mrs. Vivian Fishbein, Mr. Harry Kristy, Mr. Grant Steinhauer
Editor-in-chief .... Carol Landau
Managing Editor .... Ann Sparanese
News Editor .... Stuart Gardner
Editorial Editor .... Anita Charney
Feature Editor .... Sue Rovner
Sports Editor .... Carol Schomberg
Art Editor .... Ginny Ruffert
Business Manager .... Ronnie Kogan
Public Relations Manager .... Howard Berrent
Photographer .... Mark Jacobson
Staff .... Ellen Bebko, Mary DeRose, Helen Donigan, Merilyn Elkin, Rhoda Frank, Sandy Freiman, Sandy Fried, Fran Henschel, Janet Kurtter, Fred Lipkin, Noreen Navazio, Dee Pollack, Judy Scheider, Helen Strassner, Judy Wong.

Vol. 8—No. 3 CHARIOT Oct. 18, 1963

Foot-Brawl

It has always been assumed that every Gladiator nurtures a deep-seated pride for Memorial. And it's pretty shaky business when this formerly accepted-as-natural pride has to be questioned; when the foundations of that "Memorial feeling" are tainted, not by the minority, but the majority of the student body.

Obviously, Memorial realizes we are talking of none other than our first two football games. Yes, congratulations, Parkers—you're batting (or kicking) one thousand! Sure hope you're proud of the way that "Memorial spirit down in your feet" has been roughly transported to a number of swelled heads!

It's a crying shame that at the Herricks clash, English wasn't the right language with which to impress the visiting Gladiators that the throwing of confetti was not allowed. Unfortunately, we left our mark at Herricks.

But this might have gone undiscussed, had not the Parkers lost complete control of themselves. Oh, yes, it's understandable. The "pier six" brawl was inescapable — we were challenged. We're not chickens! Oh, no, we couldn't let them think that!

Don't you think it's about time we reevaluate the meaning of "spirit" and "pride"? It's inconceivable that supposedly "intelligent" people can still walk with swelled heads held high. Yes, congratulations, Memorial, for a wonderful display of showmanship and sportsmanship.

• • •

Healthy Attitude

Just as in our childhood "telephone" game, it's easy to get a statement twisted and distorted when everyone talks about it and no one really knows the facts. This is the case with the administration's new health policy and we'd like to clarify it with info that comes straight from the top.

Effective with the Class of '66, all sophomores will be required to take a one-half credit course in health. Although this procedure is recommended by the State of New York, the regulation permits individual schools to substitute health with an advanced biology class for valid reasons. In former years this was done in Memorial, but the administration now feels that health can, and should, be included in every sophomore's schedule.

However, this ruling is not retroactive. Health will be compulsory for the current juniors and seniors, who have never taken it, only in the event that it does not interfere with any elective or major subject. It will be included only in these upper classmen's schedules where there is room for it.

In this way, no student will have to eliminate subjects because of a ruling which was not imposed upon him a year or more ago. We feel that the policy stated here is a fair one, and hope that it continues to apply, without modification, to next year's seniors.

• • •

Weak Or Week?

You seniors have clamored loud and long for your Senior Week. Now, if you'll stop shouting long enough to hear us out, we think there's a solution to all your gripes.

We know that you want a complete Senior Week all your own. We hope that you realize that you don't get anything for nothing. If definite plans are drawn up by the senior class and then presented to Mr. Goldman for approval, it is most likely that Senior Week will be yours.

At a loss for ideas? How about a Senior-Faculty Square Dance? Come on, don't skeptically say, "square." After all, how many of you have ever seen Mrs. Flannery whoop it up at school dances?

Gather 'round girls — How'd you like a repeat of last year's Sadie Hawkins Dance? Now, now boys, stop complaining. We know you love that boost to the ole male ego!

Kidding aside, though, when you come right down to it, there's no limit to the number of terrific ideas that await uncovering. All you need is a little bit of elbow grease, ten cents worth of ingenuity, and an interested senior class. On your marks, get set, GO!

Caroling . . .

What's So Funny?

Carol Landau

The trend has shifted from adult westerns to medical shows and movies. We no longer want to hear our "hero" speaking in gruff tones to the saloon keeper. Our hearts are warmed, this year, by the good looking psychiatrist who charms his patients with sugary phrases.

But while we are staying up late at night to watch these "touching" melodramas, we fail to realize that real dramas are taking place. What is accepted on the screen as "normal" is looked down upon in real life.

There is no shame attached to a physical breakdown. But people have made fear a part of a mental breakdown of any kind. It has become a sort of nervous joke, when passing a mental hospital to make a comment such as, "That's where you belong."

I fail to see the humor of the "men in white coats coming." And yet children can be heard spouting this phrase daily.

The mass media have done their part in showing that mental illness is no more shameful than physical illness. Television has been showing the "average American" lying on a couch.

Some people who really need help, walk for a part of their lives in the darkness of depression. They fear what others will think of their undergoing psychoanalysis. It is sad that our society should create this menace to itself.

It's high time people opened their minds instead of their mouths. It is not impossible that the people who snicker at the mention of the proverbial "head shrinker" will be needing one some day. And, as the old saying goes, "He who laughs last . . . "

Howz About It?

—Hmmm . . . Don't know what to make of this weather. One day it's freezing cold and the next it's as warm as a December day in the Amazon River Basin!!! Sure wish Ol' Mother Nature would make up her mind.

—Boy, oh boy, am I angry. Last week when I wanted to make a great suggestion to Student Council, I went to the place where the suggestion box used to be and I found that it doesn't be there anymore. Well, this certain **BIRDIE** got so upset that he forgot his suggestion!! My advice to you big Student Council wheels is to reinstall that box 'cause you know what happens when a government doesn't allow the little creatures (notice how neatly I fit into that category) to have their say . . . Remember the Bastille!!!!

—**Mr. Engert,** tell me if you can answer this joke — QUESTION: Why did thirty little elephants each write five elephant jokes for homework? ANSWER: 'Cause the nasty **Green Giant** made them . . . Some people just go through life without room for fun or laughter in their tall souls . . .

—We're behind you all the way, **Jules Fried.** But did you have to throw your chem book at **Mr. Goldman?** Look, it happens to the best of us—**Mr. Goldman's** perennial bird bath (or should I say Biblical Flood?).

—**Mr. Starapoli,** may I please take this opportunity to explain to you — three bells mean a fire drill is in progress. With that in mind, we wish you better luck next time!

—Whew! I just took my Regents Scholarship Test. Naturally I walked off with three scholarships. Some people, though, are jealous. They think they're so funny when they call me a bird-brain . . . yuk, yuk.

—Hail to our new motto: Fire drills followed by fire drills; clean halls; and high attendance.

—I have a cousin. Her name is **Bertha.** For short, we just call her

BIRDIE

Roamin' Runner:

Senior Hunts Mysterious Man; '63 Grad Thanks Former Prof

Dear Mystery Man,

Have you ever heard of the book **Address Unknown?** Well, I am in the position that not only is the address unknown to me but also the person to whom I am writing.

Last summer I worked at Camp Deerwood in Massachusetts. Sometime in July we had an inter-camp baseball game with the neighboring Camp Kadima. I was on my day off and as I was returning, a busload of Kadima boys was leaving. A boy stuck his head out the window and shouted to me, "Hey, I know you." Before the bus was out of sight he managed to also yell out, "You go to New Hyde Park Memorial."

Please, whoever you are, make yourself known by answering this letter.

Judy Silverman

Ed. Note: Mr. Louis Anastasio, language chairman at N.H.P., recently received the following letter from one of his former students and last year's CHARIOT Editor-in-Chief.

Dear Mr. Anastasio,

Just a note of thanks to tell you about my Spanish Placement Tests at the University of Massachusetts. I have been placed in Advanced Conversation, a course normally offered juniors. Accordingly, I am receiving six free credits for the courses exempted. I was led to believe that of the 2300 in my class, I was the only freshman to be placed this high.

I thank you, Mr. Anastasio, from the bottom of my heart, for giving me such a firm foundation in Spanish. I'll never forget you!

Lorna Sass

Illustration 16

University; it contains reviews on page 4), and it provides the logical place for a full page or a section of reviews.

In the school's literary magazine, reviews would be best placed in a section of literary comment, rather than scattered throughout the magazine. (Incidentally, reviews should be mandatory for magazines.)

For purposes of illustrating the reviews, you can use several items: a picture of the author requested from the publisher or taken from the flyleaf of the book, an illustration reproduced from the book, or an illustration executed by the staff artist (but be sure it fits the nature or theme of the book).

That brings us full circle back to How to Review. Let's first look at a prize-winning review; this one by a student at Our Lady of Mercy High School in Rochester, N.Y. Dottie Cannon's review of a book by John Lennon was named best of the year among New York state schools. She also wrote the review which opened this chapter.

Beatle's Book—'A Sad-Happy Look at Life'

By DOTTIE CANNON

Of The Quill, Our Lady of Mercy H. S.

Much of the original popularity of *In His Own Write* can be attributed to the popularity of its author, John Lennon, a Beatle. However, now that the Beatle hysteria is dying down, people have had a chance to form an objective opinion of this unusual book.

Your first thought on opening it is that it is going to be an organized collection of take-offs on Lewis Carroll's "Jabberwocky." *In His Own Write* is more than this; it is the sad-happy observation of life by a man who has greeted success with amazing indifference. John Lennon mocks every phase of life—and a little more. He laughs at his English accent by "sound-spelling" every word; thus "I" becomes "Oi," might becomes "moight," and so on, until you find yourself speaking with an English clip yourself.

He injects his own peculiar humor into his stories by ending an apparently serious story with an ironic sarcastic twist—in a way which destroys the whole plot and framework built up so carefully in the preceding parts. The best example of this shock treatment would be "Good Dog, Nigel." In this, he conjures up an image of the perfect dog —and ends it with,

Clever, Nigel, jump for joy
Because we're putting you to sleep at three of the clock, Nigel.

BIG WILD WIDE WONDERFUL WEEKEND

April 29, 1966   SYRACUSE DAILY ORANGE   Page 5

Concerts, Games, Dances, Parades

Greek Week Starts Monday

By DAN SCHLOSSBERG

It should be quite a week: Dick Gregory, chariot races, a football game in the middle of baseball season (with Charley Brown, Pat Killorin and others wearing enemy uniforms), a formal, an informal, several parades, and an outdoor dance.

Monday Syracuse University will be celebrating Greek Week, an annual week-long series of games and events sponsored by the University's fraternities and sororities.

Festivities begin at 6 p.m. Monday with the traditional torch run and parade. Tuesday's schedule features the faculty tea in the afternoon, followed by the housemothers' card party Wednesday. Exchange dinners are slated for Thursday and the big Greek Week Ball for Friday.

Students will be offered a frenzy of activities once classes end Friday, May 6. That night, at 8:30, the Greek Week Ball will be held at the Country House. At 9:00 a.m. Saturday, the Greeks will have chariot races in Walnut Park, followed by a car parade. The varsity-alumni football game begins at 2:00 p.m., with a dance on the quad listed as post-game entertainment. In between, will be the Greek games in Thornden Park.

AN INFORMAL party at Drumlins Saturday night and the Ernie Davis Scholarship Fund Concert at 2:00 p.m. wrap up the weekend.

Top entertainers have been signed to appear in conjunction with Greek Week. Negro comic Dick Gregory, a leading figure in the civil rights struggle, is the top star of the Scholarship Concert Sunday. The Isley Brothers and SU's Otis and the All-Night Workers also are on the program.

Comedian Nipsy Russell, a formal band, and the Del Satins will entertain at the Friday night formal, which is open only to Greeks, as is the Saturday party.

GREEK WEEK Chairman Neil Schlesinger said, "We have top-name entertainment. It should be attractive to both Greeks and students, especially for the Ernie Davis concert."

Full proceeds of the Sunday afternoon concert go into the Ernie Davis Scholarship Fund, a tribute to the late football star who died of leukemia. The fund will also get half the proceeds of the varsity-alumni football game Saturday, with the other half going to University Union.

Greeks will compete with architecture pavilion when their modernistic Trojan horse, denoting the arrival of Greek Week, rears on the quad this afternoon. The horse was designed by the sculpture department.

A HUGE BANNER hanging near the Corner Store will remind SU students and visitors of the occasion and the weekend concert. The orange-and-blue banner is 24 feet long and four feet wide.

Greek Week's Monday starts with a twilight caravan of torch-bearers, cars, motorcycles, bicycles, pedestrians, and anything else with means of locomotion. The paraders meet at the base of the mount on Comstock Ave., swing left down University Pl., then down and around Walnut Park, where a band will be on hand to initiate the week of the festival.

Tuesday's activity, the Faculty Tea, is planned from 3 to 5 p.m. in the Colonial Room of Hendricks Chapel. Each Greek house is asked to invite a faculty member of his own choice to the tea, an exchange meeting for student and faculty.

Housemothers will play cards Wednesday in the Alumni Lounge of the Women's Building from 7:30 to 9:30 p.m.

EACH OF FOUR sororities sends two girls to four fraternities Thursday night, and, in turn, two boys visit the four sororities for exchange dinners. Thursday drew a relative blank in the Greek celebrations since most students will be catching up on sleep (who said work?) which they will probably be doing without over the weekend.

On Friday, things pick up speed, especially for the Greeks. The formal Greek Week Ball will be marked by the crowning of Miss Aphrodite, this year's Greek queen. Contestants must be Greeks and will compete on the basis of charm, poise and personality, as well as of beauty. Greeks will meet the winner Friday night, but the queen will also make an appearance between halves of the Saturday football game.

As of tomorrow's 6 a.m. awakening of the campus by the Goon Squad weren't enough to disturb the peace for one semester, the Greeks will also perform the friendly service of rousing the population at 9 a.m. Saturday. That's when the chariot races begin in Walnut Park.

FRATERNITIES will be grouped into five-team heats, with finals taking place during half-time of the afternoon football game. A float parade, which would have been an innovation this year, was scrapped because tomorrow's Spring Weekend parade would undoubtedly hinder participation if another were scheduled only a week later.

After the races, the Greek Games begin in Thornden Park. They include a burlap race, rope pulling and a surprise event.

Football game tickets sell for $1.50 each. Senior athletic stars such as Charley Brown, Pat Killorin, Ted Holman and Ron Oyer will play for the alumni, opposing the varsity regulars led by Mr. 44, Floyd Little.

DICK GREGORY

But Meanwhile

It's Spring Weekend

Torches of red, orange, and yellow . . . white gowns with colored sashes . . . the green hanging ivy of Hendricks Chapel and twilight open what is traditionally one of the most colorful festivals of the year.

As the ninth Festival of the Arts draws to a close, tonight marks the beginning of Spring Weekend on the Hill with the Eta Pi Upsilon, senior women's honorary, having a processional and presentations at 8:15 p.m. today. Twenty outstanding senior women will be honored at the on the Hendricks Chapel steps, Saturday morning the color key changes to red with the strawberry breakfast set for 7 a.m. at Sims Dining Hall, sponsored by Lambda Sigma Sigma, the junior women's honorary. Tickets are $1 each.

JUDGES for the Float Parade which begins at 10 a.m. in front of Newhouse Communications Center, will be a panel selected by Tau Theta Upsilon, senior men's honorary.

Banking on a helping hand from the weather, the Newhouse patio will be the scene for those who wish to make the scene, frug fashion after the float parade.

At 3 p.m., everyone packs his bags and moves to Lake Onondaga for the Crew Race, and that evening, the Senior Ball, sponsored by the senior class, will be held in the LeMoyne Manor Flamingo Room.

Also on Saturday, are remembrance of William Carlos Williams and an emotional view of New York City, two films by Albert Watler, will be shown in Kittredge Auditorium at 4 p.m.

A LECTURE on dance will be given at 1 p.m., Saturday in the Women's building, and at 8:30 that same evening, "The Fire bugs," will be shown at Machinery Hall and the Krasner Chamber Ensemble will perform in Gifford Auditorium, HBC.

Sunday marks the close of both the Festival of the Arts and Spring Weekend with a performance of "Time Cycle" by the University College Orchestra at Crouse College Auditorium,

BROADCASTING IN WAER's Spring Weekend music marathon are, from left, Dick Kunkel, Wes Tree, Bob Mendelsohn, Jeff Greenblatt and below, Bob Einhorn.

Illustration 17

Such incongruities take you completely by surprise, and your immediate reaction is stunned laughter. And we can be fairly sure that laughter was John Lennon's chief motive in composing *In His Own Write*.

One reason for the complete enjoyment derived from John Lennon's book in his avoidance of any morbidity. In fact, he refuses to be serious about anything at all; his treatment of death, socialism, and the racial problem are all pervaded with the same good-humored optimism that everything will turn out all right (if you just laugh at it).

There is little cause to suppose that *In His Own Write* is merely a coverup for a maze of philosophical concepts; Paul McCartney tells us in the introduction that only "thickheads" will search for hidden meanings. There are none. The author sums up the purpose of it when he says, "None of it has to make sense and if it's funny then that's enough." And it is funny.

First, Miss Cannon makes it clear that John Lennon is a Beatle, thus insuring greater readership. A good journalist, she has her reader in mind—and the necessity to interest him from the outset.

She next, gently, summarizes the book: "the sad-happy observation of life by a man who has greeted success with amazing indifference."

She follows with more statement of content, accompanied by examples.

In the next to last paragraph, she states her opinions. And at the close, she quotes the author's own opinion of the book.

It is basically an objective piece, but woven together by bright writing and concrete examples. She has reviewed properly, without injecting too much unstable authority.

All reviewers, in telling the reader about a book, must find a theme of interest, a theme to be developed throughout at least half the book. Some themes might be as follows:

A great number of facts and ideas are presented in the book; here is a resume of some of the more important ones.

The book presents a distorted picture of the student and the situation (the review points out the discrepancies).

The book provides solutions for a common problem (review summarizes solutions and discusses them).

Somehow, someway, the reviewer must be conscious of a reading audience which is asking, "What would be of greatest interest to me?" The answers to that question would most likely provide the reviewer's themes. Review 20 books, try for 20 themes. A rule of thumb to remember—the theme should be brought out in the opening paragraphs of the review, and if worthy, it should take one-half to two-thirds of the review to develop. As for the remaining fraction, it can be devoted to commonly included information such as:

Background of the author. Example: "Professor Rivers is well qualified to write a comprehensive book. He is now a teacher of communications at Stanford. He has a Ph.D. in political science. He was a correspondent for *The Reporter* magazine. He has worked with NBC news."

The response by the public to the book thus far.

The reviewer's own response to the book. Example: "Finis Farr's book is as much social history as biography. It chronicles quite fully the rise of Jack Johnson and the championship years, but is weakest when tracing his fall; Farr dismisses Johnson's life after 1920 quickly and disinterestedly. Perhaps Farr found the pattern of disintegration too familiar, too typical of athletic heroes, and therefore not worthy of intensive treatment. He leaves us, nevertheless, with a burning image of a tragic character trapped between his own temperament and an inimical society."

Any interesting details about the writing of the book or the reasons behind the book.

A secondary theme or "other matter" to be brought into the last part of the review. Example: (about a biography of Bob Cousy, a professional basketball player):

After 20 years in basketball, Cousy has developed a gritty philosophy. His views are tough as a basketball player's legs.

Here are some Cousy-isms:

". . . You're more likely to win when you have to fight to live." (Cousy calls himself a New York slum kid) . . . "I've been willing to bet on a hungry kid over a well-fed kid ever since."

"The best place to watch a basketball game is from the balcony, not from floor level."

"If you aren't hitting, keep on shooting."

"You don't get breaks, you make them."

"I'm a lousy loser. I don't hold with these Pollyanna theories about the game being the thing. That may be the right and proper thing to do, but it doesn't go with me. When I lose, I don't feel like congratulating the winner and shaking his hand. I want to go into a corner and mope. I do all my hand-shaking and congratulating later, after the heat of the game has dissipated."

There you have it: a combination of Jack London, Friedrich Nietzsche, and Red Auerbach.

Anything special about the typographic or visual presentation of the book.

And, somehow, the basic facts about the publishing of the book must be included. They generally are found in two places:

Death -- and the voices of dissent

They Will Be Heard, America's Crusading Newspaper Editors—by Jonathan Daniels. McGraw-Hill Book Co., 1965. 336 pages, $6.50.

Lovejoy: Martyr to Freedom—by Paul Simon. Concordia Publishing House, St. Louis, Mo., 1964. 150 pages, $3.00.

FIVE BULLETS STRUCK Elijah Lovejoy, but he managed to get back into the warehouse where he and friends were protecting a printing press. Three other presses of his were at the bottom of the Ohio River, broken up and dumped there by pro-slavery mobs.

Now, the mob was after the fourth one. But they didn't really have to worry about the press, for the edi-

Illustration 18

(1) Most commonly above the review (see illustration 18); included are title and author, publisher and his address, year of copyright, number of pages in the book and its retail price.

(2) Sometimes that information can be boldfaced and placed within the review but set off by Ben Day rules—or if a two-column lead is set to the story, the bold paragraph can be placed beneath the shoulder of the second column. It could also be placed at the end of the story, in parentheses and before the 30-dash.

There is no best way. A publication should select the most convenient method of layout and conform to it.

Best advice of all in writing a review: stick to one theme if possible. The reader cannot juggle too many ideas at one time. If the review is centralized, the reader can master one idea—which is infinitely better than confusing two or three. A reviewer cannot tell everything —and he shouldn't want to. One of his tasks is that of condensation. His problem is to settle on the best possible theme and restrict most of his review to it.

As an example of building a theme, let's take this professional review, in the *National Observer,* of a novel by the controversial Jack Kerouac, who in the era of Beat writers (1950's) was widely read, if not acclaimed.

From the Road to a Rocker, Kerouac
Finds Destiny in 'Peaceful Sorrow'

After 11 novels, that long, long road traveled by the Boswell of the Beat Generation, Jack Kerouac, apparently has come to an end. And what does he find there? Incongruously, a house with a back porch, and Mother around to provide company. What could be more bourgeois! But for Mr. Kerouac's perennial autobiographical character, Jack Duluoz, it is destiny.

"A peaceful sorrow," Kerouac/Duluoz calls the end of the journey. In the final paragraph of his latest novel, *Desolation Angels* (Coward-McCann; 366 pages; $5.95), he writes: ". . . Now we're (The Beats) famous writers more or less, but they wonder why I'm so sunk now, so unexcited as we sit among all our published books and poems, tho at last, since I live with Memere (Mother) in a house of her own miles from the city, it's a peaceful sorrow. A peaceful sorrow at home is the best I'll ever be able to offer the world, in the end, and so I told my Desolation Angels goodbye. A new life for me."

This disillusion of the roadrunner, Kerouac/Duluoz, is no surprise, however. In *Big Sur,* a novel published in 1962, he had already plunged to alcoholism, drug-induced paranoia, and a fear of impotence—far from the exuberant "life to burn" impetus that made famous the first of Mr. Kerouac's novels, *On the Road* (1957), and the Beats themselves.

But what caused the change from road to rocker? From *Desolation Angels,* evidence seems to point to such eternals as age, success, and marriage and family responsibilities: Age most of all. Kerouac/Duluoz says in the new novel: "All my friends growing old and ugly and fat, and me too, and nothing then but expectations which don't pan out— and the Void'll Have Its Way."

Give credit, though: In *Desolation Angels* he tries to go through it all one more time. He makes a final check of the old haunts, the cities of America where the Beats in the late '40s and '50s burned furiously in search of full expression and in rejection of society. But the cities have changed, and the Beats too. Where Kerouac/Duluoz once drank and drugged for the sheer sensation of living, he finds he is a bleary bloopy (his words) alcoholic. He recalls over and over again his youth on the road, exciting days. Now, all is hangover, a constant shudder at age.

And so, off to the back porch.

This novel will discourage the college-age hipsters who have looked to Mr. Kerouac's writing as a scripture of social revolt. Equally, it will delight the citizen of conventions who has always frowned on the principles of the Beat.

Yet another chapter is to be written, at least. In the introduction to *Big Sur,* Mr. Kerouac, 43 this year, wrote three years ago: "My work comprises one vast book. . . . (the books) are just chapters in this whole work which I call The Duluoz Legend. . . . The whole thing forms an enormous comedy, seen through the eyes of poor Ti Jean (me), otherwise known as Jack Duluoz." That last unwritten chapter could possibly report Duluoz' salvation; it could be simply death. Whatever it is, though, the era of the Beat Generation has passed.

In *Desolation Angels* Mr. Kerouac comments more than ever about his philosophy—or lack of it—of writing, something he calls "absolute spontaneity." He refuses to allow restraints on his style: "schools of writing limit men," he writes. So he pours out words—and when available words fail, he creates new ones. His model is the improvisation of jazz. He is a Babel of every revolutionary stylist in English prose—Thomas Wolfe, Dylan Thomas, James Joyce, John Dos Passos.

At times so many voices are heard in Mr. Kerouac that the result is din. Yet at other times he is highly distinctive. In this novel, as in 10 others before it, he is a master at describing the exhilaration of life on the free road. In a sense, one will miss that exhilaration.

Theme: end of the road (paragraphs 1 and 2); with some history of it (paragraph 3); back to the end of the road theme (paragraph 4) and the theme concluder, "And so, off to the back porch."

Secondary themes: the future (paragraph 8); comments about style (paragraph 9); concluding comment of the reviewer (paragraph 10).

The primary theme takes up half of the review. The second half is given to several other comments.

Above all, don't try to narrate the plot. It twists and turns too much to be told intelligibly and interestingly. The reviewer might as well try to give directions to a secluded neighborhood across town. The plot may have to be quickly summarized—but in the review it should be avoided as a theme.

Themes can be fitted into several categories:

Polemical: the reviewer, in his opinion, strongly agrees or disagrees with the author's ideas.

Informational: the reviewer basically reports the facts and figures found in the book, a theme generally reserved for non-fiction books.

Biographical: the reviewer sketches the life of the person as he is treated in the book.

Emotional: reviewer concentrates on the humor or anger or sympathy or tragedy revealed in the book.

Style: the reviewer discusses the writing style or organization of the book.

Analytical: the reviewer analyzes and evaluates the book, usually a demand too advanced for the student reviewer. This is the first step to criticism.

Essayistic: the reviewer, inspired by something in the book, sets off on his own recollections, such as a teacher when reviewing *Up the Down Staircase* might write about her own experiences. This is not really a review!

As for the reviewer's background—his authority—that surely must be included with the review. Perhaps, a second-line to the byline will suffice:

By Henry Smythe
Chronicle Literary Editor

By HENRY SMYTHE
A Junior at East High

Better still, to convince the readers about the authority of the reviewer, details should be included, perhaps in a bold or italic paragraph placed with the review, such as follows:

At East High, Henry Smythe is in the Senior Honors English program, where he has been specializing in the study of J. D. Salinger and his novels. He is a Merit Scholar finalist and a straight A student in English.

He has written reviews for both the Chronicle and the Leaves, the school's literary magazine.

The more you can establish the credentials of the reviewer, the more the reader will accredit the review.

Like any piece of fine writing, the review is divided into three parts —the introduction, the body, and the conclusion. The same structure is followed for the essay, formal and informal; in a sense for the short story; for the editorial; and even for the feature story.

In the introduction, the theme is set down in a manner that will engage the reader's attention; it can be extended over several paragraphs if necessary. Here is an opening section of a review about a book about Mark Twain:

> This is Mark Twain writing at the dusk of his life: "How poor I am, who once was so rich. . . . I sit here writing . . . to keep my heart from breaking. How dazzling the sunshine is, flooding the hills around. It is like a mockery. . . . I am bankrupt and my life a bitterness."
>
> The last leaf on the tree, Twain died shortly afterward, leaving literary critics of the next 50 years a problem: how to reconcile Mark Twain, great American humorist, with the latter-day Mark Twain who composed the preceding dirge.
>
> [And thus, the theme of the book about Twain is introduced.]

The body, of course, carries out the theme by adding details and explanations.

The conclusion is as difficult to construct as the introduction. For certain, the review must not dwindle into nothingness. It must leave a lasting impression, a final point of strength, a final whack on the noggin that will be felt by the reader. Here is the concluding paragraph of a review about Herbert Hoover's "Fishing for Fun—and to Wash Your Soul":

> Mr. Hoover's book is not more than an essay. It is thin as a crappie, tidy as a bass, perhaps as enduring as a muskie.

Here is the concluding paragraph to a review of three biographies of sports heroes:

The world presented in these three books is demanding, brutal and often dehumanized; it defeats most who live in it. The enduring athlete must be something more than a man and these books testify that his greatest victories and most ignoble defeats are never seen in the arena.

The closer can be a restatement of the theme, or a bit of style to be remembered, or a final and strong opinion, or a summation of comments. It should be the final word in attitude, in style, in intensity.

Thus, the reviewer must either sketch an outline for his review or see one in his mind. "This is my theme, and here is how I can go about organizing it. Here are the elements about the theme I want to bring in . . . 1-2-3-4-5. Here is a good strong point I want to conclude with. I have saved it for dessert."

Writing a review is like planning a trip for a vacation: you choose the starting point, you know the destination, and you carefully map out the stop's and go's between the two.

What has been said here about books can apply generally to motion pictures, to television and radio, to phonograph records and tapes, to the theater—wherever there is something of special interest to student readers.

Here are some performances of the past which deserved attention by the school press:

Motion pictures. James Dean and "Rebel Without a Cause." "Blackboard Jungle." The whole genre of Bikini and Beach flicks, good and bad. Maybe "David and Lisa" in that the film was concerned with teenagers with special problems. The pop singers turned actors (Presley, Avalon, Dee, Boone, Ann-Margret). The Beatles' films. The film that is of such quality it shouldn't be missed. The Oscar winners, good and bad. The problem here: reviews are published after the film has been shown, and they cannot serve as guidance for the reader.

Radio. Review the most popular disc jockeys, about the only radio items of interest to the student generation.

Records. No comment needed here; most popular records are directed to the teenage market. It is a matter of editors sorting out the newsworthy, and the worthy records, the latest by Big Names, the rise of New Names, the case of Overlooked Names. And attention must be directed to classical records and to records of drama and readings. Record reviews are built around guidance—buy the record or don't—and the writer of the column must be capable of fine judgment. No room here for a person of exotic taste who will bankrupt his readers with esoteric records. A reviewer wants to elevate the taste of his readers, but in doing so, he doesn't want to try to revolutionize taste. He shouldn't try to force the listener into a diet of candied grasshoppers and chocolate-covered ants. At the same time, the writer must give the audience what it should know, as well as what it wants to know.

Television. Of the areas other than books, the reviewer must attend most of all to television. The present student generation, raised with TV, is acutely aware of it. More of their general conversation is derived from TV than from any other form of popular arts. TV demands comment by the student press.

For instance: a documentary about the teenager, or about students, merits reviewing. So does a series about the typical teenager, or one that is popular with students (such as the movement in the mid-1960's to satirical drama—"Get Smart" or "Man from UNCLE"). Or, perhaps about a series students should be watching ("Camera 3" on Sunday mornings). Or perhaps a popular series which is so low esthetically that it merits attention (hillbilly comedies, for instance).

The problem of reviewing television, as with film, develops from time: the review is retrospective. By the time the review appears, the performance is over, forever. Everything is hindsight, leaving little opportunity for those who missed the program to see it.

Perhaps, a beforehand is needed, too. Each issue of the paper could advise students of significant programs coming up. A later review would evaluate or summarize the program. Prewarned, students may watch, and mindful of a review to appear may watch more attentively. One of the attractions of a review is the chance for the reader to pit his ideas and responses against someone else's.

Beforehand information can be gotten from the local station officials, who are well aware of upcoming programs of special interest to students. They generally have plenty of press information.

Besides the sports writer who criticizes the coach or the editorialist who challenges the administration, the most daring writer on the staff is the reviewer who comments about the school play. He walks unarmed into a cage of lions; he plays in a cyclotron; he flirts with Circe.

You must admire the student journalists who review the winter production of the Drama Club. But there are those who respect no sign of Danger, who stroll against red lights. One such reviewer is Fred Steinberg of Monroe High School, Rochester, New York. He reviewed the school's fall comedy, in part as follows:

Jim Thompson who played Phelix Ducotel seems to have a good deal of talent for playing old men. As I remember he has been at least 55-60 years old in his past three plays.
John Seegler . . . did well in his first play, although I often found it difficult to understand Seegler. He could have been more effective had he been told to dispense with the accent.
While I felt it fell short of excellence, the play seemed to provide a pleasant evening for many.

Bravo! A Legion of Merit to him.

The question is, you see, whether a student has authority enough to review student drama. One highly successful director used to argue this way: "I don't want any high school student judging one of my plays. He doesn't know enough about dramatics to be responsible. The only person in this school qualified enough is me, and I am not about to evaluate our play for the public. I'll do that backstage."

The director wasn't bathing in ego; he was being matter-of-fact—and probably very right. He would say, "If the school paper wants to publish a review, I'll accept one from the director of community theater or from the reviewer for the newspaper, but not from a student."

Employing an outside writer would be one solution, or forgetting about the whole thing would be better—except that a school is supposed to provide, as much as possible, learning situations. Just as a student dramatist learns from experience, so can a student reviewer. If there is a student who has been interested in theater, who has seen many plays, who perhaps has been on the amateur stage himself, if he has fully researched the play being presented, and if he has carefully followed its progress from rehearsal to finale, then just perhaps he can be trusted to write a knowledgeable review. He, in a sense, would be as authoritative as the cast. In flirting with danger, however, he should be aware of the following weaknesses which beset all beginning reviewers.

Don't be hypercritical. Asked to be reviewer, the writer may feel the need to be critical. Being critical: it is an easily-assumed stance.

It leads the reviewer to such comments as "Jane Magerkurth was not assertive enough to get across to the audience the strength of the heroine" which can be crushing to the amateur actress and may be very much wrong. The reviewer must be absolutely sure he is on solid ground before attempting criticism. He must not only state his point of criticism, but defend it, explain it fully, back it with logic and specific examples and references. The reviewer should, in this amateur situation, look first for the praiseworthy, and only in the case of severe weaknesses, the uncomplimentary.

And he must present criticism with a positive value in mind, so that it in itself will lead to the betterment of the actor and of the director and of the drama department. How? If the setting was ineffective and inappropriate, perhaps it was because of the limited budget which put materials in short supply. That fact should be brought out. If the cast lacked depth, resulting in weak acting in supporting roles, perhaps too few students tried out and that fact should be reported. If an individual performance was weak but the play successful, perhaps the weakness is unimportant and unworthy of comment.

Don't give credit where credit is not due; you are not expected to eulogize a bomb. But be honest with facts and fair with opinions. There may be just reasons, even for failure.

Don't be role-centered. Too many reviews praise John, Joan, Mary, and Henry for their performances and criticize Jack (can't be heard), Marilyn (wooden lines), and Hardy (poor character acting)—then give an overall rating to the play (good, fair, one of the best, if not the . . .). The success of the play results from scenery design, acting, lighting, staging, and audience response, all interacting. All should be recognized where important.

The play was a comedy. The audience laughed uproariously. The play achieved its purpose. Why the audience appreciation? Clever pacing and timing of gag lines (who is responsible?). Some expert slapstick acting by Henry Smythe in the role of the stumbling, bumbling "hero." Some wild costumes dug up (literally?) by the props committee.

The play was a musical. It fell flat. The audience responded politely, but not enthusiastically. Singing—dancing—orchestra. Much too complex for cast and musicians. Maybe the musical shouldn't have been tried. Obvious that practice time was limited. Choreography difficult on small school stage. Too many remember the real play, and the comparison with scholastic theater was unfortunate. Maybe it all leads to a discussion that, despite best efforts of cast and crew, circumstances at the school are not conducive to such plays. Should sights be lowered? Should school system develop better facilities?

The play was a melodrama. It froze the audience with its terror. Why? Brilliant use of stark lighting. Ingenious makeup. Perfect underplaying of horror scenes by well-advised cast. Especially fine Dracula in Henry Smythe (what did he do to prepare?).

The play, "The Night of January 16th." Play got off to slow start because audience was startled by the unconventional setting: curtains open, jury selected from audience, cast working from the audience as well as from the stage. But the audience by the second act began to enjoy the parade of fine character parts. An interesting point— two endings were prepared by the cast, and the jury found the accused guilty one night and innocent the next and sent the cast into two different scripts. The success of such innovations in theater are important at this point because success means future drama groups can range confidently through the unconventional, as well as the conventional, theater.

Don't be cute. Professional reviewers in a professional world can afford to be clever, to use wit and parody and barbed phrases, to hatchet with words an actor or a play. It is tempting to be witty, like the reviewers who have written . . .

"She covered the gamut of emotions from A to B."

(About Uncle Tom's Cabin) ". . . the brace of Siberian bloodhounds was badly supported."

Professional theater can survive, even tolerate, wit.

Amateur theater cannot. The attack can discourage the actor, dispirit the cast, discredit dramatics.

If the reviewer cannot control the urge to be sarcastic, which is a type of exaggeration, then the editor must exercise discretion and authority, and strike out the supercilious comments.

And just as severe are attempts to be the literary poseur, the student reviewer who insists on allusion and references and critical exposition far above his student audience.

Reviews can be well-done and can serve as inspiration to readers. But editors must select responsible reviewers—and be sure that cast and director are notified far ahead of time that a review is planned.

One last word—if no review is planned, then each play should be "reported." A straight news story can report attendance, profit or loss, and comments of director and cast about the performance. Or a feature story can tell about Tom Magerkurth playing his third major role of the season; or about the director looking back from his 100th play presented at East High; or about the difficulties of rigging the stage for intricate maneuvering (such as flight); or about a very difficult role executed flawlessly but at the expense of tremendous preparation and practice. Into the feature can be scattered all the facts about attendance, profit, loss, etc.

And the photographs taken at dress rehearsal can provide illustration. Don't shoot them on play night; a flash can upset the cast and a photographer shooting by natural light at the apron of the stage can distract the audience.

PEOPLE—As much as possible, get people into news photographs. This is not a bare wall, but rather a painting (the straight line) on the wall of the Museum of Modern Art in New York City. The photographer waited until a person came along to give the photograph a final effect. And to draw further attention to the "line."

Chapter XVII

POETRY

Poetry is not prose. An elementary distinction, to be sure, but none-theless one to which I am driven by the current (and sadly estab-lished) state of student poetry. Students themselves, though, are not entirely to blame. The literary hybrid they produce as poetry is a result of forces beyond their control. I am not speaking here of the creative force (though that needs control too). Students forget that creativity must first assume a definite form.

And the student is bucking obstacles right from the start. The very first nemesis is encountered in almost every high school English class. In a zeal to make poetry appealing, teachers rely too heavily on the *emotional* sensitivity of teenagers. True, at an age when reactions are violent and perceptions intense, students feel more at ease reading highly personal, emotionally charged poetry, but unfortunately the student absorbs a feeling that "good" poetry is achieved by a soulful outpouring.

Students seem to have a built-in sensitivity to tone, the unstated position of the poet. They think that if the tone is recognized, then the poem "says something." Teenagers are more interested in feel-ings than in footnotes. It is not surprising, therefore, that John Milton should be way down on the list of high school favorites, and that John Keats often ranks in the "top ten."

This enthusiastic response to emotional commitment is not in itself damaging. No one would argue that a poet should not be involved in his subject. The trouble is that an awareness of form seems to fade in comparison. Students seem interested in the total effect of a poem; the matter of *how* that effect is achieved, however, seems to emanate the intolerable odor of pedantry. And, by and large, English teachers are content to let matters rest there. They argue that it is hard enough to generate even a superficial appreciation—let alone instill a critical discrimination. Practically speaking, this is a strong point. Better to create slight interest than restless boredom.

But we are not addressing ourselves here to the uninterested student. The person who dislikes poetry is not going to write it (although I fear some modern poets are attempting sabotage from within). We are concerned with the direction which is given to the young creative writer. To become a poet, interest itself is not enough; enthusiasm is too often equated with talent. Some of the worst poetry ever committed was produced by people too urgent to be artistic.

Thus, while the student is not expected to master all the intricacies of form by age 17, he should develop a respect for them. Any athletic coach instructs his players in the rules of the game. He demands the skills which result in maneuverability. A player unwilling to abide by the rules is not even considered for the team. No letters are awarded merely for uncontrolled enthusiasm. Yet English teachers are swayed by the degree of interest shown by budding poets. In this area, the standards of mental discipline lag behind those of physical discipline. It is, for instance, assumed by the coach that a skilled and interested student will apply himself to mastering the necessary techniques. And although intellectual pursuits do not command the fevered loyalty of sports, they should not be reduced to a condition of anarchy.

The anarchy of student poetry can be described in a phrase: free verse. This is the amorphous excuse for most of the poetic content of student literary magazines. Having discarded the obvious restrictions of stanza, rhyme, and meter, free verse should ideally maintain the subtleties of cadence, rhythm, and precision. Yet subtleties of form are exactly those elements for which students are *not* prepared. It takes a very good poet indeed to write decent free verse.

You might argue that this position does not give due credit to the imaginative resources of young people. You might say that some highly sensitive and perceptive ideas have been expressed in student poetry. You might say that the balance of phrase and idea is so delicate that a strict adherence to form would destroy it. The teen-age mind is a spontaneous one; impede its interests and other outlets will be sought . . . and probably found. But teenagers also respect a challenge; discovering a proficiency is one of the rewards of growing up.

Poetic expression should be encouraged, but not at the expense of development. It is more thrilling to say "I have become" than to say "I always was."

Teenagers have a way of knowing when they are kidding them-selves—or being kidded. There is no discouragement so permanent as that which results from being "put on" by someone. The adult who applauds every poem as an imaginative masterpiece is fooling no one, least of all the student. There is a certain finality to accepting the immediate talent, as if the subject were closed.

Poetry is an art and should be respected as such on any level. The person who composes a blows-flows-glows-shows epic might not win the Pulitzer Prize, but—unlike the careless free versifier—he at least exhibits an inkling of the way poetic language interacts. If words must rhyme, then each line is made to incorporate a particular word; and the poet concentrates on the poem rather than on himself. On a basic level, he is beginning to coordinate his abstract idea with a physical mode of expression. This combination of elements alters the original inspiration, encloses it within a new form. The poet has manipulated experience by transposing it into symbols. Students do not often realize that an experience can be just as trite as a phrase. There is an absolute burden of poems "To Spring," each complete with its brand new robin. A poem is not worthwhile merely because the poet has recorded something. Journalists do that, as do cameras, or seismographs. It is the *manner* of recording which distinguishes poetry.

But if experience alone is not enough, neither is emotion. If, to achieve poetic coordination, the student must subordinate himself, well and good. Poetry is not therapy. The plague of poems about "Loneliness" indicates that students are equating their own feelings with what goes on in the world.

Good poetry cannot rely on any single inspiration—experience, emotion, or idea. It combines all of these within the forms of the art. Once the student is aware of the necessity for a discipline of form, there is but one obstacle remaining: content. Exhorted con-stantly (and with good reason) to "write about what you know," the teenager reinforces a natural inclination toward the modern. Very little high school poetry deals with ancient Rome or the Pharaohs. This is a credit to the student's own selectivity. By basing a poem upon personal experience, the writer immediately holds a more pre-cise control over his emotional response to it. Unity of tone is more likely to result when words are chosen to describe a particular experience.

If the subject is beyond personal knowledge, the tendency is to fit the experience to the word. Emphasis scatters with adjectives as the writer tries to make something vivid to himself. The student who writes outside these boundaries is very often left with a cliché as his primary inspiration.

There is a strong tendency to confuse first-hand experience with that supplied by secondary sources . . . experiences which the author would like to have had first-hand, but (by some quirk of fate) didn't. A television program about jazz musicians might develop a strong and accurate atmosphere, but this should not be confused with immediate perception. A person who draws his ideas from this source has taken a big step away from reality. He has interposed a barrier between himself, the experience, and the language. A movie might beautifully depict life on a Pacific island, but this should not be substituted for actual experience. The writer should not sacrifice his own perception and powers of description by allowing others to present the world to him in a pre-arranged form.

The difficulties of authenticity apply equally to the student's technical use of the language. Most students naturally prefer the modern poets. These are the people who draw from available attitudes and influences. It is highly worthwhile for teenagers to be familiar with poetic descriptions of the contemporary world. By association, the young writer is able to recognize the representative detail, the telling action, the true turn of phrase. But too often he fails to relate these sensibilities to his own life, and thus to his own poetry. Admiration for a poet very easily turns into imitation. Instead of learning from the examples of favorite authors, students become confined by them, molding personal response after the manner of the poet. The young writer becomes set in his ways before he has experimented with different styles and before he has developed an attitude of his own.

To make matters worse, the most extravagant effects are noticed first—and make the biggest impression. This is most obviously seen in the mass of student poetry patterned after the stanzaic conventions of E. E. Cummings. Form and content were tightly controlled by Cummings; his innovations made possible new poetic combinations. But the style is emphatically not suited to all subjects, all attitudes, or all writers. Furthermore, Cummings was constantly adapting old forms to his new style. Thus the ballad reappears in modern form, as does the sonnet. Beneath the informal style is an acute awareness of the methods of poetic expression. But the triumph and possibility of these expressions is often lost upon students. They imitate instead the superficial characteristic of unrestricted punctuation. However, neither capitalization, punctuation, nor the physical "look" of lines automatically made poetry of Cummings' work—and will not do so for student work.

An appreciation of detail and subtlety is necessary before impressions are ready to be set in poetic form. Though the young writer might recognize these qualities in established poets, student verse is too often devoid of such graces. And these qualities are usually the ones which distinguish good poetry from bad. The problem is, in fact, even more difficult: the poet must not only choose representa-

SYMBOLS—In previous photographs in this book, fall has been represented by barren trees and by geese silhouetted against a setting sun; winter has been represented by the blur of swirling snowflakes. Here, spring is represented by symbols, mainly the foreground branch laden with buds. The photographer has been asked to get pictures of spring; it is a warm day in April in the northern states. He begins his drive and walk, his hunt for a story-telling picture. He finally finds it in youngsters going boating, with spring-bare trees in the background and spring-fresh buds in the foreground.

tive detail, he must also be able to weed out extraneous material. His selectivity must work to discard the vague, the ambiguous, the unrelated. The art of poetry is condensation. The poet who relies on a sweeping generalization to get his point across overpowers both his subject and his form.

All students have been told to "qualify statements," to back up opinion with examples. This warning is equally well-adapted to the writing of poetry and should, in fact, be carried out even further. That is, don't make *statements* in the first place. Let the details, the tone, the descriptions do the work of clarifying an idea. If you want to say, for instance, that memories are sad (or happy, or anything), don't settle for writing, "Memories are sad." *Why* are they sad; what experience is your opinion based on; which details are the most important. Whittle away everything that isn't absolutely pertinent . . . and then pare the details down once more. An idea which goes in too many directions loses its emphasis.

Once the framework of material is settled, then you can begin to construct a poem from your idea. As soon as that point is reached, the only tool a poet has is language. A particular thought of feeling cannot be brought to the page in its original form. The poet must try to recreate the subject in words, symbols; to phrase it in such a way that the language itself becomes an experience. In this way, the poem will elicit a genuine response from the reader. If the poem offers only an outright statement phrased in conventional language, it is essentially no more poetic than a newspaper story or a commercial. Just because something is written in the shape of a poem doesn't mean it is a poem. The language is everything. One "right" word will say more about the subject than 15 vague ones.

Words are as varied as experiences; just as some experiences are more meaningful than others, so some words are richer than others. Choose the precise description and you will get as close as possible to the original experience. If you want to write about a beach in summer, was the sun merely yellow—or was it gray, or copper, or crystal, or green for that matter? Was it the sky that was blue, or the air, or the wind? Each combination alters the dimension of your poem.

Writing poetry is not easy; it is one difficult choice after another. But the poet is better equipped to draw the subtle distinctions. He is more sensitive to the world, more able to describe it. More important, he is able to relate language and experience in such a way that both seem clearer. Part of his job is to make the things he describes vivid. To do this, he should be able to present things in a new way. Some descriptions become so worn that they cease to bring any image to mind. Can't a dawn be anything but "rosy"? Must all oceans "roar"? Does lightning always "flash"? The person not interested in poetic expression is excused for using these phrases. They get the bare meaning across well enough. But poetry demands something more: it requires the poet to care *how* he is expressing himself. The expression is all that will remain of the experience. Not that ordinary language cannot be poetic; on the contrary, highly effective poems are written with the simplicity of everyday speech. But the poet must still exercise a careful scrutiny of the words.

If a poem is written simply, is there a word which draws attention to itself? A common fault of many student poems is that they pin words on a page like a collection of butterflies: a big, beautiful specimen dominates the entire poem. When this happens, the balance of a line can be destroyed, or the whole effect of a poem can be lost. Words must be precise not only in meaning, but in tone as well. In "Stopping by Woods on a Snowy Evening," Robert Frost begins with the line: "Whose woods these are I think I know." Had he said, "Whose woods these are I am cognizant of," the line would be lopsided, weighed down by self-conscious phrasing. Rhyme and meter aside, using the word "cognizant" disrupts the smooth flow of the poem; the effect is too stiff to meet the requirements of simplicity.

Artificial words work against the poem in another way. Besides being unwieldy, they make the reader acutely aware of the poet's struggle. Vocabulary which does not suit the experience obscures, rather than clarifies, what is being described. A barrier is set up between the audience and the experience of the poem. Language becomes an end in itself, and not a means to communication. When watching a movie, for instance, you are not aware of the camera's intervention. The camera, in fact, becomes your own eye: it selects what you see and how you see it. You may find the subject ridiculous, but you accept the idea that you are seeing the action as it occurred. The audience is not conscious of the camera as it follows the subject. In the same way, good poetry does not show the poet at work. He remains out of sight, choosing the action, focusing the image— never taking a picture of himself. If he intrudes, the immediacy of the subject is lost. By using strained or unnatural words, the poet blocks the audience's view.

The poet should remain invisible not only in the technique of language, but also in regard to subject matter. A poem should reflect attitudes without stating them outright. The poet who provides all the answers cuts his reader off from the experience of the poem. The dangers of generalization threaten the effectiveness of material as much as they undermine a precision of language. In fact, control of language will proceed naturally from control of subject.

Although there is no guaranteed formula for writing a poem, it is a generally successful idea to limit the topic (externally) as much as possible. You can say more about an abstract idea by letting the reader make his own generalizations. If you write a poem about love, don't take on the whole theory at once. Pick a situation which incorporates the idea as it functions in the world. Relate philosophy to actual operation, and the poem will be valid on more than one level of meaning. Most students commit the crime of bludgeoning a poem to death. They feel that an idea must be stated directly in order to have any force. But there is actually very little relation between the size of a topic and its importance. A poem about ants can mirror the world of human relations; while a poem about Human Relations may relate to nothing but itself.

The poet who relies on theory rather than on experience is undermining his own art. He should be able "To see a World in a Grain of Sand/And a Heaven in a Wild Flower." Further, he should concentrate on translating his experience into a form available to the world: the form of poetry.

The following poem was written by a high school senior. It displays a few common weaknesses of student poetry, some not-so-common ones, and much genuine talent.

LEMON SUMMERS [1]

Lemon summers were the mind of childhood,
Now banished (almost before I knew)
From my mind by "busy" and "important" but still
Sugaring a random night or second.

[1] By Ellen Murray of Our Lady of Mercy High School, Rochester, New York.

Yellow, round and warm they welcome
My retreat, my lazy (not "idle") moments,
My gulping of lemonade (too sweet),
My clinging to sweet dirty dirt.

They give me long clear nights to shout when
My voice carries up to the stars (not so far);
And they thrust me up on the ferris wheel, so far, so fast,
Then down, and I am dizzy.

They give me short and softly black nights
To think and think and think while being warmed,
While a little bit a little girl and
A larger part (and still too soon) a woman,

While holding my breath as long as I can (not forever),
And squeezing the warm air too tightly.
In short, softly black, thinking nights
My lemon summers continue to slip away

And turn to old, to wise, to cold, to mature, to gray, to compromise,

To bittersweet.

The poem lends itself to an analysis of the way language works in poetry. The word "lemon" is a good example of how precise wording will enlarge the meaning of an entire poem. "Lemon" triggers a variety of images: the taste of the fruit, the sweet-sour aroma, the peculiar texture of the peel, the pure vivid yellow of the color. Because the word is combined with "summers," the latter word takes on the association of the first. The summers need not be directly described any further; nor does the author try, but relies instead on indirection to amplify the meaning.

A contrast is set up between the image of lemon summers and the image conveyed by "busy" and "important." The direction of thought is outlined by that conflict, and is maintained throughout the poem. The student's awareness of the levels of language is indicated by her use of "busy" and "important." The words are employed as nouns, both by the poet and by the adult world to which she alludes. She refers to them as labels, intellectual symbols which contrast strongly with the sensory perceptions of childhood. But the point is not belabored.

The poem is not cluttered with poignant moralizations about the loss of spontaneity (sigh). The student only organizes the elements of the estrangement and lets the labels alone to trigger their own response in the reader. Since she is using the words in their most public sense, there is no need for private elaboration.

The third verse offers an example of the way words can change within themselves. The same words, when repeated as an echo, add another dimension to the meaning. By itself, the phrase "not so far" in the second line can be interpreted two ways. It can mean that she now realizes wistfully that her voice did not actually reach to the stars. Or it can mean that the stars were not as distant then, so it was possible for her voice to carry. Whether accepted individually or jointly, both interpretations describe an action which complements meaning. In the next line, however, the words "so far" are echoed. When applied to the height of a ferris wheel, the phrase takes on still another aspect. The imagination of childhood made physical distance appear immense, yet brought infinity within reach. She was closer to the stars than to the earth. By repeating carefully chosen words, the student was able to combine an echo of language with an echo of childhood, thus reinforcing the unity of the poem.

The tone, though, is not unified throughout. It gets lost occasionally in a delicate extravagance of word-mongering. The lines, "My gulping of lemonade (too sweet),/ My clinging to sweet dirty dirt," do not coordinate well with the rest of the poem. After setting up a mellow tone of sound and image, these lines appear too harsh and naturalistic. They evidence an urgent quality which is not maintained, and so is not justified. Neither is repetition of "softly black" justified. This choice is not nearly as felicitous as the "so far" echo. "Softly black" produces a pleasant pattern of sounds, but is not vitally connected with the meaning of the poem. It has the added disadvantage of being a rather predictable combination—not yet trite, but dangerously sentimental. When repeated, the phrase gives the impression of having been used for its own sake, and not for the poem.

The last two lines of the poem are unconsciously ironic: they incorporate fine poetic expression into a dismal relapse of content. By overtly summarizing the poem, all the previous subtlety is overwhelmed. The physical structure of the lines does not help. It draws even more attention to the overstatement. The lines stretch out at the end like a flag in an eager breeze.

The moral of the story, however, is phrased quite well. The selection and arrangement of words exhibit a quality rare in student work: rhyme. Combining the words "old," "cold," "wise," and "compromise" displays an appreciation of the poetic functions of language. The words are related in sound, as well as being pertinent to sense. The inclusion of "gray" is a perceptive touch. It fits into the sound pattern while serving to break up the slightly premeditated effect of the four words above. Having few emotional connotations, "gray" works also to lessen the sentimental impact of the conclusion. The choice of "mature," though, is another matter. The word not only disrupts the tentative internal rhyme of the lines, but also closes the door on restraint.

The ending is a paradox: the author says quite well something which need not have been said at all. The poem needed no footnote.

The graces of "Lemon Summers" are many. Images are uncluttered; wording is directed to both sound and sense; meaning is amplified by economic words which operate on multiple levels. Literally and figuratively, the poem is under control. The student was aware of the poetic possibilities of experience, and transcribed that sense into authentic symbol. The interaction between the reality of the subject and the clarity of the language imbues the work with a natural grace: the grace of poetry.

BIBLIOGRAPHY

(The following books are carefully selected to provide the creative journalist with instruction, examples, and—most of all—inspiration. Starred books (*) should provide the core library for the classroom or the journalist; they are especially recommended.)

FEATURES

Breslin, Jimmy. *The World of Jimmy Breslin* (The Viking Press, 1967). Also in paperbound. Collection of columns—mainly human interest and from personal experience.

*Talese, Gay. *Fame and Obscurity* (World, 1970). Collection of pieces by the finest feature writer of recent years for *The New York Times*. Includes the full text of *A Serendipiter's Journey,* a series of human interest sketches of New York; the full text of *The Bridge,* a kind of feature story in depth.

*Ward, Bill. *Writing in Journalism* (National Scholastic Press Association, 1969–71). A study in detail appearing in *Scholastic Editor* first and then recast into book length.

The following collections are invaluable, even priceless, but long out of print: Meyer Berger's *New York* (Random House, 1960); *The Best of A. J. Liebling* (Methuen London, 1965).

Also see card catalog for various collections and books by Joan Didion, Hal Boyle, Saul Pett, Mike Royko, Jim Murray, David Halberstam.

REVIEWS

Kauffmann, Stanley. *A World on Film* (Harper, 1966). A collection of reviews by a critic for *The New Republic*.

*Kael, Pauline. *I Lost It at the Movies* (Bantam paperback, 1965). Collection of controversial essays by the brightest reviewer of them all. Several other of her collections also available.

*Wolseley, Roland E. *Critical Writing for the Journalist* (Chilton, 1954). The best of the few instructional books.

Also see card catalogs (and magazines and newspapers) for works by

198

Walter Kerr, and especially Melvin Maddocks, Michael Anlen, and Richard Schickel. Also see front-of-book reviews in *Life* magazine, review sections of books and film and art in *Time* magazine, in the Sunday *New York Times*.

POETRY

Brooks & Warren. *Understanding Poetry* (Holt, Rinehart & Winston, 1960). Popular college text for basic study.

*Ciardi, John, editor. *How Does a Poem Mean?* (Houghton-Mifflin paperbound). Commonly used text for college courses. Also read Ciardi in *Saturday Review* magazine and in other books.

Engle & Langland. *Poet's Choice* (Delta paperback). Poets choose their own favorite poems and comment on them—startling and revealing.

Jarrell, Randall. *Poetry and the Age* (Vintage paperback). Collection of inspired and inspiring essays.

Hundreds of paperbound collections of poetry to learn from.

SHORT STORIES

Mirrielees, Edith. *Story Writing* (Compass paperbound). The best, most succinct advice about writing fiction.

Writers at Work, volumes 1, 2, and 3 (In Compass paperbound and The Viking Press). Outstanding collection of interviews with world's foremost authors, prepared originally for *The Paris Review*.

Brooks & Warren. *Understanding Fiction* (F. S. Crofts & Co., 1948). Instruction and examples.

Also see each year the various collections of the Best Short Stories of the Year; also paperbound collections of campus writings and new-generation writing as found—depending upon the current series being published—in such books as *Intro, New Directions,* and *Countdown*. Watch paperbound listings (*Paperbound Books in Print*) and paperback shelves at university bookstores.

PHOTOGRAPHY

Feininger, Andreas. *The Complete Photographer* (Prentice-Hall, 1965); *Total Picture Control* (Crown, 1970), and *The Creative Photographer*. Not only general information about techniques of photography but also specific concern about the more creative image and photographic techniques.

Life Library of Photography. A series of at least six volumes issued in

1970 so outstanding in their presentation of basic and advanced photography—visually—that no other resource can compare with it. The distributor is Atlantic–Little Brown.

Lloyd, Irving. *The Photo.* Really, a collage of dozens of special techniques every photographer and editor can use in varying photographic presentation—from high contrast prints to screened printing. Lloyd has produced several other such books of immense value to students (see *Books in Print* for listings).

Also see the photography yearbooks (*Popular Photography, U.S. Camera, German Photography Annual*). Also see *The Family of Man*, the most famous collection of all time. Also see in the library photographic books by Henri Cartier-Bresson, David Douglas Duncan, W. Eugene Smith, Dorothea Lange, Margaret Bourke-White, Alfred Eisenstaedt. Also, *Life* magazine and *National Geographic*.

ARTWORK

Little of value to the student, outside of collections of the works of Herblock, Bill Mauldin, and other professional cartoonists.

ESSAYS

See collections of essays—light and satirical—by Russell Baker of *The New York Times*, John Gould of *The Christian Science Monitor*, Harry Golden of the *Carolina Israelite*, and Art Buchwald.

See collections of essays—more of commentary, more serious—by James Reston of *The New York Times*, William Buckley of *The National Review*, Vermont Royster of *The Wall Street Journal*, Sidney Harris, Nicholas von Hoffman of the *Washington Post*, Eric Sevareid and Edward R. Murrow of television popularity.

Also see collections of the more classical Stephen Leacock, Robert Benchley, H. L. Mencken, H. Allen Smith, and E. B. White.

Also see contemporary light essays published in *The National Observer* (Reflections), *The Atlantic* magazine (Light & Lively), the *Saturday Review* (Phoenix Nest), *The Christian Science Monitor* (The Home Forum page and People page).

INTERVIEWS

Gunther, John. *A Fragment of Autobiography* (Harper & Row, 1962). Gunther discusses his methods of interviewing for his best-selling "Inside" books.

*Webb & Salancik. *The Biggest Wheel in Town* (Journalism Monograph series, University of Texas, School of Journalism). A short but revealing discussion of problems of getting truth out of interviews.

Also, see the card catalog for collections of interviews by John Gruen and Studs Terkel, two of the best at the challenge.

EXAMPLES OF CREATIVE JOURNALISM

Agee, James. *Let Us Now Praise Famous Men* (Houghton-Mifflin paperbound). With photographs by Walker Evans. Outstanding representation of the sensitive reporter and writer in depth, here about sharecroppers. Also, see collections of film criticism by Agee.

Hemingway, Ernest. *By-Line: Ernest Hemingway* (Scribner's, 1967). A collection (also in paperbound) of the newspaper and magazine reports of the great novelist. Expert in sights-and-sounds reporting.

Hersey, John. *Here to Stay* (Bantam paperbound, 1964). Outstanding collection of interviews and observations, including *Hiroshima,* Hersey's widely praised interview account of what happened there.

Steinbeck, John. *Travels with Charley.* Classic reporting by one of the greatest American novelists.

Von Hoffman, Nicholas. *Mississippi Notebook* (David White Co., 1964). Little noted but brilliant account of a summer of civil-rights workers in Mississippi—a classic of style and of reporting viewpoint. His *We Are the People Our Parents Warned Us Against* (Quadrangle, 1968) is a brilliant example of life-style reporting, couched in the jargon of the culture being reported. Also, a collection of his work (often called erroneously New Journalism), *Left at the Post* (Quadrangle Books, 1970).

Wolfe, Tom. *The Kandy Kolored Tangerine-Flaked Streamline Baby* (Noonday paperbound); also several other books. A controversial reporter/writer who has developed an echoic, pop-culted, impressionistic style to go with hard-core reporting.

The most dynamic and controversial new writing is found in the so-called underground press (if there can be such in a free society). Here reporters and writers have violated all the traditional advice, have gone to highly personalized styles and techniques. For starters, go to *Notes from the New Underground,* edited by Jesse Kornbluth; *The Open Conspiracy,* edited by Edith Grodzins Romm (both in paperbounds); *Famous Long Ago,* by Ray Mungo (The Beacon Press, 1970), the autobiography of one of the first new-style college editors of the 1960's.

*The best, most innovative "aboveground" reporting and writing is to be found currently in *Harper's* magazine, *Life* magazine, *Sports Illustrated,* in microfilms and old files of the now defunct New York *Herald Tribune,* *Time* magazine for the dramatic narrative, *Fortune* magazine for depth stories.

GENERAL TEXT BOOKS

*Charnley, Mitchell. *Reporting* (Holt, Rinehart & Winston, 1969). The best of its kind, by a highly respected professor from the University of Minnesota.

Newspapering, a 100-page paperbound guidebook to better student newspapers, now in its 17,000th copy. By the author of this book, Bill Ward (from N.S.P.A., University of Minnesota).

*Three other detailed books about writing by Bill Ward: *The Student Journalist and Common Story Assignments; . . . and Writing Editorials; . . . and Depth Reporting* (Richards Rosen Press), all written to the student journalist.

ABOUT STYLE AND GRAMMAR

*Strunk, William, Jr., and White, E. B. *The Elements of Style* (The Macmillan Co., 1959, paperbound). So much in a booklet—a must reference for even the "grammatical" writer.

Bernstein, Theodore. *Watch Your Language* (Signet paperbound). A pastiche of advice about style, structure, and grammar as prepared for staff members of *The New York Times* by one of its associate editors.

Several dictionaries of style seek to resolve conflicts among words and phrases: most famous, of course, is Fowler's *Modern English Usage.* More specifically directed to journalists is Roy Copperud's marvelous *A Dictionary of Usage and Style* (Hawthorn Books, 1964) and Theodore Bernstein's *The Careful Writer* (Atheneum, 1965).

TYPOGRAPHY, EDITING, LAYOUT

*Arnold, Edmund C. *Modern Newspaper Design* (Harper & Row, 1970). The classic study—stunning. Also for the history of graphics, see Arnold's *Ink on Paper.*

Two much-needed books about editing appeared in 1970 and 1971: *Modern Newspaper Editing,* by Robert Root and Gene Gilmore (The Glendessary Press); *The Art of Editing,* by Floyd K. Baskette and Jack Sizzors (Macmillan).

Also: *The Design of Advertising,* by Roy Paul Nelson (Wm. C. Brown Co., 1966).

FOR GENERAL READING

Capote, Truman. *In Cold Blood* (Random House, 1965). Art of the novelist combined with the art of the reporter. Norman Mailer also has combined reporting and the novel form in recent books.

Talese, Gay. *The Kingdom and the Power* (World, 1969). A newspaperman writes a biography about a newspaper—a classic in biography.

*Snyder, Louis L., and Morris, Richard B. *A Treasury of Great Reporting* (Simon & Schuster paperback, 1962). The finest collection of pieces from journalism, from the past 200 years.

Hohenberg, John. *Foreign Correspondence: the Great Reporters and their Times* (Columbia University Press, 1964). The finest account of the history of journalists, especially of ingenuity at getting out the news. Also, *The New Front Page*, examples of outstanding reporting in recent years—mainly in depth.

Best Magazine Articles of (the Year), edited by Gerald Walker (Crown). A collection issued each year of the best reporting and writing in American magazines; each is a textbook in importance.

Ward, Bill. *The Student Press* (Richards Rosen Press). An annual volume summarizing the year, including outstanding writing and reporting by students.

Also, for examples of outstanding reporters and stylists, although not necessarily journalists, see: Ernest Hemingway's novel *The Old Man and the Sea*, Stephen Crane's novel *The Red Badge of Courage*, and Henry David Thoreau's essays about *Walden*.

For autobiographies of outstanding literary journalists, see Lincoln Steffens' *Autobiography* and *Autobiography of William Allen White*.

*Also, read regularly *The New York Times*, *The Christian Science Monitor*, and *The National Observer*, all newspapers that strive for perfection of reporting and of style. Read *The Nation*, *The New Republic*, *Harper's*, *Esquire*, *The Atlantic*, and *Life*, which use fully the journalist's work within their magazine columns.

Most of all, read the collections of writings by Ernie Pyle, the greatest reporter and writer—in this author's estimation—of all American journalism.

A reporter-writer can also learn about structures of communication, of moods and sensitivities, by listening to music. Especially recommended for gaining insight into great music, through fine records and excellent printed commentary—Time-Life's *Story of Great Music*, if you can afford the rather steep ($15) cost per release of records and books.

Marshall McLuhan's *Understanding Media* is provocative for the person involved in print to study.

GLOSSARY

(Some random definitions for selected journalism terms starred (*) in this book)

Anecdote. An incident, a slice of life told in narrative fashion to illustrate an important point, to reveal an important time in the life of a person or an event . . . to serve as an introduction, a conclusion or a transition in a feature story. Example:

> Once when Winston Churchill was a young man and had just grown a moustache, and was talking politics at a dinner party, a young lady insulted him: "I dislike both your politics and your moustache."
> Churchill, most courteously, replied, "Don't distress yourself, madam. You are unlikely to come into contact with either."

Byline. Two lines of type, usually, at the start of a story, crediting authorship, such as:

> By Henry Smythe
> Special Correspondent

It is something beginning reporters survive on, in lieu of paychecks.

Cliché. Something red as a rose, slow as molasses in January, yet at times quick as a wink, old as Methuselah, and decidedly tired as an old boot (or is it comfortable as an old boot?). A cliché is a fresh way of describing something—at first—but through overuse becomes common as dirt. Clichés, in writing and speaking, are signs of the imitator, not the innovator.

Depth reporting. Really, a redundancy, meaning to report in detail an event, which is a goal every reporter should automatically aspire for. Actually, depth reporting has come to mean analyzing and interpreting the facts, as well as reporting them—although purists maintain that that is "interpretative writing." Depth reporting is the product of such thoroughness by the reporter that little is left to the reader's imagination.

Editorializing, editorialization, to editorialize. Anyway you say it, it means to inject too much personal opinion into a news story. To call

205

someone an orn'ry skunk would be, to most people, insulting. To call a journalist an orn'ry skunk would be editorializing. Editorializing is borne along by such simple vehicles as adjectives: Take this sentence, for instance, "The Mets lost in the ninth inning after leading for the rest of the game." Adjectives turn it to: "The hard-fighting Mets lost in the heart-breaking ninth inning after leading commandingly for the rest of the game"; or conversely to, "The lack-lustre Mets lost in the ninth inning, as usual, after leading miraculously for the rest of the game." Nouns and verbs tell stories; adjectives alter them.

Extended leads. See leads.

Focus and followup. The order by which most news stories and features are organized. Basically, the first few words are devoted to introducing the main topic of the story (focus); the rest of the story is devoted, mostly, to expanding the main topic (followup). Some refer to the structure as introduction and body; others, as lead and development. This author, hoping to achieve something memorable, has coined the terms "focus" and "followup." Skeptics refer to this process of terminology as "scientism."

Future book. St. Peter, bettors, and journalists keep them. To the journalist, a future book is a handy little pad in which to list ideas for future stories—as far ahead as a year, perhaps. Every respectable journalist keeps a future book, which is not so much a sign of incipient forgetfulness as a symbol of optimism. A future book has one weakness: it keeps getting misplaced, or left in the suit which went to the cleaners. Editors solve that problem by shackling their future books to the city desk.

Human interest story. A feature story based on the experiences of a person or persons. With several billion persons in the world—and more to come—reporters find no shortage of human interest stories. It is a well-known fact that every man has a story to tell, which he tells first to his bartender, then to his minister, and finally to a reporter.

I-account. A pun, you see. An eye-account is a story based upon first-hand experience, upon eye-witnesses. Generally, the reporter, himself, is on the scene and reports, largely, what he sees and what he hears. Many editors distrust their reporters' eyesight and earsound, but such stories usually are followed with interest by the readers who have much more faith in the authors. Reporters go to great lengths to undergo first-hand experiences, such as going to jail, climbing mountains, hunting for lost explorers and missionaries. It is said that the first man on the moon will be an astronaut, and the second, a journalist trying to get a scoop.

Inverted pattern. News stories come in all kinds of shapes, one of which looks like an upside down pyramid ▽ . That is a graphic way to show how facts should be organized: the important ones at the top of the story, the less important at the bottom. This system is fine, sensible; but the diagram ▽ is misleading, suggesting that the story balances precariously and unnaturally on its weakest section. However, other theorists have come to the rescue to design other graphic ways to construct a news story:

Leads. A confusingly pronounced word (leeds) which refers to the introduction of a news story or a feature story. In the lead, the theme of the story is introduced in a manner interesting (supposedly) to readers. The most venerable lead is the 5-W-and-an-H lead, which stems from the words of poet Rudyard Kipling:

> I have six honest serving men;   5
>   They taught me all I know;
> Their names are Where and What and When
>   And How and Why and Who.

Today, there is reason to forget both Kipling poetry and Kipling advice, especially when 5 W's and one H packed into a lead paragraph can result in a structure like this: "John Smith, chief of police at Owasco, told the city council Friday night that because of the unusually large number of accidents recently caused by drivers going through stop signs, patrolmen have been instructed to ticket all violators on the spot, thus ending a policy of giving only warnings to such violators on first and second offenses, the new orders having been issued in hopes of ending further accidents."

In lieu of the crammed, jammed 5-W's lead, today the extended (not distended) lead is in better repute. The WH factor can be extended throughout the first few paragraphs, resulting in more normal syntax—also encouraging dialogue, anecdotes, narrative style, etc., in the lead.

Legs. A stack of type. If a story is placed across two columns, it would have two legs of type; across the whole page, eight legs. Type is heavily personified, having not only legs, but faces and shoulders.

Mood. The emotional element of a story: happiness, sadness, silliness, fearfulness. Generally speaking, unless the mood is severe, an objective story cannot convey mood—facts are not moody things. Feature stories, for one thing, try to transmit the mood of an event which is often the significant element to the reader who can then experience it vicariously.

Mug shot. An uncomplimentary term for a head-and-shoulders portrait of a person, generally engraved as a one-half column or one-column cut. (In some cases, the term is not uncomplimentary.)

News feature. A feature story developed from on-the-spot coverage of a newsworthy event. Time is the essence here, the event being reported immediately for today's or this week's paper.

Newsmaker story. A biographical sketch of a person who is important in the news. People make news; this type of feature tries to tell about those newsmaking persons. News must be personalized to be interesting. Facts alone are notoriously impersonal.

Packaging the news. Developing several stories and pictures from one news event (straight news story, feature story, newsmaker story, and photograph), which are then placed together on the same page or in successive pages.

Readability. Being attentive to writing a story in a simple, direct style which can be read easily. Readability is a virtue; only political columnists pride themselves in confusing the reader . . . but then that may be because the columnists themselves are confused by the politicians. In recent years, readability has been linked to formulas: using words of so many syllables on the average, sentences containing so many words on the average. Some skeptics say this is the reason why so many newspapermen today are average writers.

Readership. This is the principle of developing a story so that the content is interesting. Dick and Jane stories do exceptionally well when put to readability tests, but they don't do so hot in readership tests. So much concern has been devoted to readability (writing simply) that only simpletons read newspapers. Now, the trend is again to readership—that ancient custom of trying to tell a darn good story.

Sidebar. Simply, a feature story that is written to go along with a straight news story. One provides the facts; the other provides the human interest and the mood of the event.

Straight news story. Telling a story in subjects and verbs mostly, with Facts mainly. There is very little room for creative writing here, although the reporter may have to be ingenious to dig out the Facts.

Subjectivity. The opposite, some think of objectivity. In journalism, objectivity (removing all prejudice, bias, and personal evaluation from reporting and writing the news) is impossible. Subjectivity (injecting personal values into the story) is entirely possible. But reporters, being what they are, are always trying to do the impossible—with editors on the sidelines cheering them on.

Tickler file. Not an instrument of torture, but a filing system in which a reporter keeps clippings, notes, memos, etc., under supposedly easy-to-find headings, all of which can be used for future stories. Most tickler files are fool-proof—they consistently prove that any person trying to find something in them is a fool.